The Politics of Our Selves

NEW DIRECTIONS IN CRITICAL THEORY

Amy Allen, General Editor

New Directions in Critical Theory presents outstanding classic and contemporary texts in the tradition of critical social theory, broadly construed. The series aims to renew and advance the program of critical social theory, with a particular focus on theorizing contemporary struggles around gender, race, sexuality, class, and globalization and their complex interconnections.

María Pía Lara, *Narrating Evil: A Postmetaphysical Theory of Reflective Judgment*

Amy Allen

The Politics of Our Selves

Power, Autonomy, and Gender in
Contemporary Critical Theory

Columbia University Press

New York

Columbia University Press

Publishers Since 1893

New York   Chichester, West Sussex

Copyright © 2008 Columbia University Press

All rights reserved

Library of Congress Cataloging-in-Publication Data

Allen, Amy.

   The politics of our selves : power, autonomy, and gender in contemporary
   critical theory / Amy Allen.

        p.   cm. — (New directions in critical theory)

   Includes bibliographical references and index.

   ISBN 978–0–231–13622–8 (cloth : alk. paper) — ISBN 978–0–231–50984–8
(ebook) 1. Self (Philosophy) 2. Feminist theory. 3. Critical theory. I. Title.
II. Series.

   BD450.A4723 2007

   126—dc22

                           2007024757

Columbia University Press books are printed on permanent and durable
   acid-free paper.

This book is printed on paper with recycled content.

Printed in the United States of America

c 10 9 8 7 6 5 4 3 2 1

For my children
Clark
Oliver
Isabelle
and
Eloise

Contents

Acknowledgments

This book took shape over a number of years—I first conceived of its general framework in the summer of 1998—and, consequently, many individuals and institutions have contributed to its development. I am grateful to all of them and only hope that I can express that gratitude without omitting anyone.

My work on this book was supported by several research fellowships that gave me the greatest gift any academic can ask for: the time to think and reflect. I am grateful to the National Endowment for the Humanities for a grant to attend the summer institute on "The Idea of a Social Science" directed by James Bohman and Paul Roth, where I was first inspired to work out the general structure of the book. I also wish to thank the Marion and Jasper Whiting Foundation for a summer research grant in 2000 that made possible the initial research for chapter 2, and the Centre Michel Foucault at the Institut Mémoires de l'Édition Contemporaine for access to their collection. The American Association of University Women generously awarded me an American fellowship for the calendar year of 2003 that allowed me to work extensively on the first draft of the manuscript. Dartmouth College—in particular, then Associate Dean of the Faculty for the Humanities Lenore Grenoble—supported that fellowship leave and supplemented it with a Junior Faculty Fellowship, which gave me a truly luxurious amount of time off in 2003 and 2004.

I have also benefited enormously from my participation in three vibrant philosophical organizations—the Critical Theory Roundtable, the Colloquium on Philosophy and the Social Sciences in Prague, and the Society for Phenomenology and Existential Philosophy—where early versions of many of the ideas in this book have been presented over the last seven years. These organizations have given me a philosophical home away from home, and I am grateful for the stimulating and challenging environments that they, in their very different ways, provide.

Early versions of individual chapters of this book were also presented in several other venues, including the following: the philosophy department at University College Cork, the department of political science and sociology at the National University of Ireland, the political science department at the University of Florida, the New York Society for Women in Philosophy, the philosophy and gender and women's studies departments at Grinnell College, the Otto Suhr Institut of the Freie Universität of Berlin, the Workshop on Gender and Philosophy at MIT, the philosophy department at Vassar College, and the Humanities Forum at Dartmouth College. I am grateful to the audiences on each of these occasions for their insightful questions and comments.

Many people read and commented on individual chapters, offered me feedback on the ideas worked out in them, or both. In particular, I wish to thank Thomas Biebricher, Susan Brison, Judith Butler, Maeve Cooke, Nancy Fraser, Jürgen Habermas, Amy Hollywood, Axel Honneth, Colin Koopman, Thomas McCarthy, Eduardo Mendieta, Martin Saar, James Schmidt, Sally Sedgwick, James Swindal, Dianna Taylor, Thomas Tresize, and Christopher Zurn. A few brave souls even read and commented on the entire manuscript, and to them I owe an enormous debt of gratitude: Johanna Meehan, María Pía Lara, and Jana Sawicki. All three happen to be wonderful philosophers, constructively critical yet generous readers, and dear friends, and I am extremely grateful for the time they have devoted to helping me refine this book over the years.

I owe a special debt to my Dartmouth presidential scholar, Jared Westheim, who served as my research assistant in the winter and spring of 2007 as I was putting the finishing touches on this manuscript. His careful comments and editorial suggestions on the manuscript helped me to improve it tremendously, and his enthusiasm for the project renewed my own faith in it.

A special thanks also to Wendy Lochner, my editor at Columbia University Press, who believed in this project and its author from the beginning and enthusiastically supported the book through the final stages of development. Her unflagging support and cheerful good sense make working with her a continual joy.

I have also been fortunate enough to have three wonderful colleagues and dear friends at Dartmouth College who have sustained me through the ups and downs of academic life: Denise Anthony, Sam Levey, and Christie Thomas. Without them I would long ago have lost faith in what we do for a living.

Finally, I must thank my husband, Chris Leazier. Although I certainly could have finished this book without him, I am, as ever, infinitely grateful that I did not have to.

Earlier versions of some portions of this book have appeared in print before. An early version of chapter 2 appeared as "Foucault and the Enlightenment: A Critical Reappraisal" in *Constellations* 10:2 (June 2003): 180–98. Most of chapter 4 and a few paragraphs of "Concluding Reflections" were published as "Dependency, Subordination, and Recognition: On Judith Butler's Theory of Subjection" in *Continental Philosophy Review* 38 (2006): 199–222. One section of chapter 5 appeared as "Systematically Distorted Subjectivity? Habermas and the Critique of Power" in *Philosophy and Social Criticism* 33:5 (July 2007): 641–650.

The Politics of Our Selves

Introduction

THE POLITICS OF OUR SELVES

Maybe the problem of the self is not to discover what it is in its positivity, maybe the problem is not to discover a positive self or the positive foundation of the self. Maybe our problem is now to discover that the self is nothing else than the historical correlation of the technology built in our history. Maybe the problem is to change those technologies. And in this case, one of the main political problems would be nowadays, in the strict sense of the word, the politics of ourselves.

—FOUCAULT

IN RETROSPECT, Foucault's claim that the main contemporary political problem is that of the politics of ourselves appears remarkably prescient; it anticipates, even as his own work undoubtedly helped to foster, the heated debates over identity politics and, more recently, the politics of recognition that have been the focus of so much intellectual and political attention over the last twenty-five years.

However, Foucault's call for a politics of ourselves remains a bit ambiguous. It seems to entail two distinct, though related, claims. First, it suggests that the self is not a natural or given entity (which Foucault indicates by saying that we have to give up on discovering the self in its positivity) but a political one, in the sense that it is constituted by power relations. This is why Foucault indicates in his lectures "About the Beginnings of the Hermeneutics of the Self" that technologies of the self have to be studied together with technologies of domination: that is, "if one wants to analyze the genealogy of the subject in Western civilization," one has to "take into account the points where the technologies of domination of individuals over one another have recourse to processes by which the individual acts upon himself. And conversely, he has to take into account the points where the techniques of the self are integrated into structures of coercion or domination."[1] Foucault goes on to call the "contact point" between these two technologies "government."[2] Second, implicit in the idea of technologies of the self is an appeal to some notion of the self's autonomy in the sense of a capacity for self-transformation, as is evident in his definition of "techniques of the self": "techniques which permit individuals to effect, by their own means, a certain number of operations on their own bodies, on their own souls, on their own thoughts, on their own conduct, and this in a manner so as to transform themselves, modify themselves, and to attain a certain state of perfection, of happiness, of purity, of supernatural power, and so on."[3] Implicit here too, though perhaps more so, is a notion of autonomy in the sense of critical reflection: the capacity to reflect critically upon the state of one's self and, on this basis, to chart paths for future transformation. This sense of autonomy comes to the fore more explicitly in some of Foucault's other late writings, for instance, when he refers to the "critical ontology of ourselves ... conceived as an attitude, an ethos, a philosophical life in which the critique of what we are is at one and the same time the historical analysis of the limits that are imposed on us and an experiment with the possibility of going beyond them."[4] These twin notions of autonomy—understood as the capacities for critical reflection and self-transformation—underpin Foucault's notion of the politics of ourselves.

However, this leads us to a difficulty, for these two sides of the politics of the self are often thought to be incompatible with each other. It has been assumed that thinking of the self as political in the first sense, as constituted by power, makes a politics of the self in the second sense impossible, because it reveals agency, autonomy, and critique to be nothing more than illusions, power's clever ruses. This assumption motivates both those who claim that Foucault's late work on practices of the self is contradictory to his archaeological and geneaological writings and those who argue that a Foucaultian account of subjection is incompatible with autonomy understood as critical reflexivity, the capacity to take up a critical perspective on the norms, practices, and institutions that structure our lives. The difficulty in getting past this issue has fueled the Foucault-Habermas debate; its feminist incarnation, the debate between Judith Butler and Seyla Benhabib; and, more generally, debates about the usefulness of postmodernism for feminism.

The central aim of this book is to develop a framework that illuminates both aspects of the politics of the self. My goal is to offer an analysis of power in all its depth and complexity, including an analysis of subjection that explicates how power works at the intrasubjective level to shape and constitute our very subjectivity, *and* an account of autonomy that captures the constituted subject's capacity for critical reflection and self-transformation, its capacity to be self-constituting. Developing this sort of account is crucially important for critical theory. As Benhabib has argued, a critical social theory has two aspects: "explanatory-diagnostic" and "anticipatory-utopian."[5] Under the former aspect, critical theory offers an empirically grounded critical diagnosis of the central crisis tendencies and social pathologies of the present; under the second, it charts paths for future transformation. Without an account of subjection, critical theory cannot fulfill the first task because it cannot fully illuminate the real-world relations of power and subordination along lines of gender, race, and sexuality that it must illuminate if it is to be truly critical. But without a satisfactory account of autonomy, critical theory cannot fulfill the second task; it cannot envision possible paths of social transformation. One of the central arguments of this book is that, to date, Habermasian critical theory has done a much better job with the second task than it has with the first. In order for critical theory to offer a compelling diagnosis of the present, it would do well to take very seriously the analyses of subjection offered by Foucault and Butler.

The account I offer here also has important implications for feminist theory, which has grappled as well with this ambivalent notion of the politics of the self. But in this case the challenge tends to come from the opposite direction. Whereas there has been some controversy over this, many feminist theorists have accepted Foucault's analysis of power and subjection and used it as a framework for their analyses of gender subordination. Although Foucault's analysis of disciplinary and normalizing power has proven extremely fruitful for such explanatory-diagnostic purposes, it has generated a host of problems concerning subjectivity, agency, autonomy, collective social action, and normativity. As I will argue below, there are resources within Foucault's work for responding to some of these challenges, particularly the claim that his analysis of power undermines any possible conception of subjectivity, agency, and autonomy. The remaining issues can be addressed by integrating Foucault's insights into power and subjection with the normative-theoretical insights of Habermas.

This project is situated at the intersection of feminism and critical theory, and it seeks to develop an account of the politics of our selves that would be fruitful for both projects. My account draws on the theoretical resources offered by both Foucault and Habermas and develops these into a framework that is, I hope, useful for theorizing gender, race, and sexual subordination and the possibilities for resisting and transforming such subordination in more emancipatory directions. Given the long-standing debate between Foucault and Habermas and their intellectual progeny and the widespread assumption that these two men offer radically different, even incompatible philosophical and social-theoretical frameworks, this goal might seem quixotic. In order to show why this is not so, I devote a good deal of time in what follows to making the case that there is much more middle ground between Foucault and Habermas than either their critics or their supporters have assumed up to now. In the case of Foucault, this involves arguing that many of the standard Habermasian (and feminist) critiques of his work have been based on a misunderstanding of his oeuvre. In the case of Habermas, it involves offering a weaker, more contextualist, and pragmatic reading of his normative project, in order to make that project compatible with a Foucaultian analysis of power. But the purpose of these interpretive arguments is ultimately a systematic and constructive one: to develop a feminist critical-theoretical account of the politics of our selves that does justice to the ways in which the self is both constituted by power and simultaneously capable of being self-constituting. In the remainder of this chapter, I explore the most difficult challenges that such an account will have to meet.

The Entanglement of Power and Validity

What is at stake for feminist critical theory in this notion of the politics of our selves is revealed in a particularly vivid way in the well-known debate among Judith Butler, Seyla Benhabib, and Nancy Fraser, published as *Feminist Contentions: A Philosophical Exchange*. Inasmuch as this debate also stages a confrontation between Habermasian critical theory and its poststructuralist Foucaultian Other, I think it is worthwhile to start by reviewing this exchange. My focus here is limited to just one strand of this wide-ranging debate, but it is not only the strand that is most relevant to this project, but also, it seems to me, the central point of contention in the debate: the strand that concerns the problem of the subject and the possibility of critique.[6]

Benhabib initiates this thread of the exchange by arguing that an acceptance of what she calls, borrowing Jane Flax's terminology, the postmodern "death of man" thesis is incompatible with feminism. Although Benhabib admits that all parties might agree to a weak version of this thesis, according to which the subject is always situated in various social and linguistic practices, the strong version, which dissolves the subject into just another position in language/discourse, is, in her view, incompatible with the feminist interest in autonomy and emancipation. This interest compels feminists to assume, according to Benhabib, that "the situated and gendered subject is heteronomously determined but still strives toward autonomy. I want to ask how in fact the very project of female emancipation would even be thinkable without such a regulative principle on agency, autonomy, and selfhood?"[7]

Although Butler scoffs at what she sees as Benhabib's overly simplistic characterization of postmodernism, she does defend what she describes as a crucial insight of her (and Foucault's) variant of poststructuralism, which, she insists, does not dissolve, undermine, or dispense with the subject at all. As Butler sees it, "the critique of the subject is not a negation or repudiation of the subject, but rather, a way of interrogating its construction as a pregiven or foundationalist premise."[8] Moreover, she claims that thinking of the subject as constructed by relations of power does not necessitate a denial of agency: "on the contrary, the constituted character of the subject is the very precondition of its agency. For what is it that enables a purposive and significant reconfiguration of cultural and political relations, if not a relation that can be turned against itself, reworked, resisted?"[9]

The closely related issue of how to conceptualize critique first emerges in Benhabib's discussion of another main thesis of postmodernism—the "death of metaphysics" thesis, which asserts the death of grand metanarratives—but it quickly merges into the questions of subjectivity, agency, and critical reflexivity that are raised in her discussion of the death of man thesis. Benhabib argues that the postmodernist commitment to a strong version of the death of metaphysics thesis "would eliminate ... not only metanarratives of legitimation but the practice of legitimation and criticism altogether."[10] Although postmodernists defend a conception of immanent critique, Benhabib contends that such a conception of critique does not in fact exempt such theorists from the task of philosophical and normative justification. Inasmuch as cultures and traditions are made up of, as Benhabib puts it, "competing sets of narratives and incoherent tapestries of meaning," even the practitioner of immanent critique must engage in philosophical and normative justification of her own criteria.[11] In response, Butler appears to sidestep the issue of normative justification, focusing instead on the entanglement of power and validity. As she sees it, "power pervades the very conceptual apparatus that seeks to negotiate its terms, including the subject position of the critic; and, further ... this implication of the terms of criticism in the field of power is *not* the advent of a nihilistic relativism incapable of furnishing norms, but, rather, the very precondition of a politically engaged critique."[12] Here Butler invokes Foucault's (in)famous claim that there is no outside to power; if one starts with this assumption, then all critique is, of necessity, immanent, whether the critic realizes or admits this or not. There is no choice between immanent and transcendent critique. Not only that, but the very positing of a critical perspective that is capable of transcending power relations—even if that perspective is "hypothetical, counterfactual, imaginary"—"is perhaps the most insidious ruse of power."[13] In a footnote to this passage, Butler makes it explicit, although it was already perfectly clear, that she considers Habermasian critical theory to be a prime example of this insidious ruse.[14]

Enter Fraser, who argues that the Butler-Benhabib debate is a false antithesis and, consequently, that feminists do not have to choose between Foucaultian-Butlerian poststructuralism and Habermasian-Benhabibian critical theory. Regarding the disagreement over the death of man thesis, Fraser boldly stakes out a middle ground. Fraser endorses Butler's claim, "pace Benhabib, that it is not sufficient to view the subject as *situated* vis-à-vis a setting or context that is external to it. Instead, we should see the subject as *constituted* in and through power/discourse formations. It follows that there exists no structure of subjectivity that is not always already an effect of a power/discourse matrix; there is no 'ontologically intact reflexivity,' no reflexivity that is not itself culturally constructed."[15] However, given that Butler seems committed to the belief that such constituted subjects have critical capacities, Fraser "take[s] her point here to be that critical capacities are culturally constructed."[16] Although Benhabib is clearly committed to the existence and importance of critical capacities, she does not take a position on the issue of where these capacities come from; moreover, as Fraser sees it, "it is perfectly possible to give an account of the cultural construction of critical capacities. Thus, nothing in principle precludes that subjects are both culturally constructed and capable of critique."[17] However, with Benhabib, Fraser does see a problem with Butler's view, which concerns the way that Butler equates critique with resignification. According to Fraser, this formulation sidesteps the normative dimension of critical theory and thus seems to "valorize change for its own sake and thereby to disempower feminist judgment."[18] So her summation of the debate is that "feminists need to develop an alternative conceptualization of the subject, one that integrates Butler's poststructuralist emphasis on construction with Benhabib's critical-theoretical stress on critique."[19]

In her reply to the initial exchange, Fraser sums up the strengths and weaknesses of each of the two positions, and thus she poses the challenges for the development of such an alternative conceptualization of the subject. Whereas Benhabib's Habermasian framework usefully captures in a nonessentializing, nonfoundationalist, proceduralist way the normative dimension that Fraser takes to be crucial to feminist theorizing, its focus on "justification and validity marginalizes questions about motivation and desire; thus, it cannot help us understand why women sometimes cling to perspectives that disadvantage them, even after the latter have been rationally demystified. More generally ... Benhabib's approach valorizes the active, constituting side of individuals' involvement in communicative practice, to the relative neglect of the passive, constituted side."[20] Butler's Foucaultian account, by contrast, "cogently defends the need for denaturalizing critique, critique that reveals the contingent, performatively constructed character of what passes for necessary and unalterable,"[21] but "its internal normative resources—reification of performativity is bad, dereification is good—are far too meager for feminist purposes,"[22] and it provides no means for theorizing the inter—rather than the intra—subjective dimension of social life. As Fraser sees it, the strengths of Benhabib's approach are precisely complementary to the weaknesses of Butler's, and vice versa.[23]

Now, unlike Amanda Anderson, I do not see Fraser's staking out of a middle ground between Butler and Benhabib here as indicative of a "consumerist approach to the problem, arguing that we should pick and choose elements from each thinker."[24] Nor do I agree with Anderson's assessment that "the paradigmatic divergences between Butler and Benhabib are far too profound to allow for such a mode of reconciliation."[25] Fraser does, I think, have an unfortunate tendency to downplay the significance of the normative and theoretical challenges that Butler's Foucaultian account of subjection poses for core Habermasian notions of autonomy, critique, and validity. In fact, this tendency seems related to her earlier reading of Foucault's account of power as empirically insightful yet normatively confused.[26] Contra Fraser, I think that the significance of Foucault's and Butler's conception of power and subjection goes beyond the "merely" empirical, but this is an issue that will be brought out in the remainder of this book. This downplaying of the conceptual and normative significance of Foucault's and Butler's analyses of power and subjection arguably also leads Fraser to underestimate the degree of difficulty involved in successfully integrating the Benhabibian and Butlerian perspectives. After all, if it is the case that Foucault and Butler offer empirical insights (into how modern power operates, in Foucault's case, or into the intrasubjective dimension of the subject, in Butler's case), but not normative ones, then the task of integrating their perspective with the Habermasian one is relatively easy to accomplish. All one has to do is to incorporate those empirical insights into the broader normative theory proffered by Habermas. Pace Fraser, I do not think that constructing an approach that integrates the critical-theoretical stress on critique with the poststructuralist emphasis on construction will be quite that simple. I agree with her that we would be wise "to avoid metaphysical entanglements. We should adopt the pragmatic view that there are a plurality of different angles from which sociocultural phenomena can be understood. Which is best will depend on one's purposes.... In general, conceptions of discourse, like conceptions of subjectivity, should be treated as tools, not as the property of warring metaphysical sects."[27] But adopting this sort of anti- or a-metaphysical stance by itself is not enough. For once one realizes the full import of the challenge posed by Foucault and Butler to core Habermasian concepts such as autonomy and the context transcendence of validity claims, then the degree of difficulty of the project of integrating these two complementary perspectives greatly increases. Some modifications in each of these perspectives will be necessary: for instance, some room for an account of intersubjectivity will have to be found—or created—in Butler and Foucault; conversely, strong Habermasian claims about the status of his idealizations and the possibility of the context transcendence of validity claims will have to be attenuated.

I want to draw three conclusions from this brief rehearsal of the Butler-Benhabib debate: first, as Fraser argues, Habermasian critical theory has much to offer feminism, specifically its nonfoundationalist, nonessentialist conceptions of justification and normativity and its emphasis on autonomy and intersubjectivity.[28] Second, however, as Fraser also argues, this perspective by itself does not do justice to the complexity of the power relations that are constitutive of subjectivity, and for that reason feminist critical theory must find a way to integrate the Foucaultian account of subjection with the Habermasian account of autonomy. This book attempts to complete the task set but left undone by Fraser, but contra Fraser, and this is the third conclusion, I submit that doing so will require reinterpreting and, to some extent, recasting some of the central insights of Foucault, Butler, Habermas, and Benhabib.

The difficult question of the entanglement of power and validity, which we already saw emerge in Butler's response to Benhabib's critique of postmodern feminism, is one of the most challenging stumbling blocks to an integration of the insights of Foucaultian poststructuralism and Habermasian critical theory and an important theme in this book. My argument will be that a full appreciation of the insights of Foucault's analyses of power and subjection compels us to admit the impurity of autonomy and practical reason. The acknowledgment of this impurity necessitates scaling back the overly ambitious claims that Habermas makes regarding the possibility of untangling validity from power, a possibility that he frames in terms of the context transcendence of validity claims.

In her recent book, Anderson also considers this pivotal issue, attempting to argue for a more straightforwardly Habermasian position. As she announces in her introduction, her aim is to "contest the prevalent skepticism about the possibility or desirability of achieving reflective distance on one's social and cultural positioning."[29] Anderson acknowledges that she is swimming against a rather powerful tide of poststructuralist sensibility that has been predominant in political theory and cultural studies: "Recent scholarly trends have tended to treat ideals of critical detachment as illusory, elitist, and dangerous, invested in unattainable perspectives and disregarding of embodied existence and the experience of differently situated, and differently enfranchised, social groups."[30] Anderson's approach, by contrast, emphasizes the capacity for critical reflexivity, and it does so, in large part, by calling into question the received opposition between rationality and ethos. Rationality, as Anderson sees it, does not have to be understood as an arid, decontexualized, lifeless transcendence of ethos; it embodies an ethos, which Anderson calls "the ethos of reason and argument."[31] Specifically, Anderson argues, Habermasian proceduralism both "requires a specific ethos: the cultivated habit of refusing the comfort of a claimed collective identity (cultural, national, sexual, and so forth)" and "offers one way of refusing the false option between reason and ethos precisely insofar as it affirms the possibility of argument as ethos."[32]

Although I admire Anderson's willingness to buck the pervasive trends in academic theorizing, it seems to me that her formulation of this issue gets it exactly backward. Thus, she misses the real challenge that Foucault's work (her prime example of an ethos-centered view) poses for Habermasian critical theory. The problem is not whether rationality or argument is instantiated in an ethos—Habermas never tires of pointing out that postconventional practices of argumentation and institutions must be anchored in a lifeworld that meets them halfway[33]—the problem is whether they can possibly be thought to *transcend* their ethos in the way that Habermas's account requires. In other words, the real issue is the context transcendence of validity claims, though Anderson doesn't seem to see this.[34] The closest she comes to confronting this issue is when she admits that

> there is a tension in Habermas's conception of sociality. On the one hand, he stresses the value of, and need for, embedded sociality in his emphasis on primary socialization processes and their centrality to moral development, individual autonomy, and the cohesion of cultural groups. On the other hand, Habermas emphasizes the preeminent value of reason's capacity to break free of tradition and custom: reflective distance defines the crowning achievement of modernity.[35]

But Anderson never tells us how she thinks this tension in Habermas's work should be resolved. Habermas, by contrast, is pretty clear about how he thinks it should be resolved: validity claims are raised here and now, in a particular context, but the raising of them breaks through every context.[36] Indeed, Habermas must insist on the context transcendence of validity claims in order to disentangle validity from power, for only such a move can underwrite his strong moral-political universalism. The real problem posed by Foucault's analysis of power is the same one posed by Butler above in response to Benhabib. The challenge is that the disentanglement of power from validity might not be possible, and that the claim that it is possible might itself be an attempt to exercise power. This is an issue that I will explore in more detail in chapter 6. My attempt to resolve it will turn on a more modest, contextualist way of taking up the Habermasian project, one that sees the faith in the context transcendence of validity claims as itself arising out of and rooted in a context, the context of late modernity.

Will the "Truth" Set You Free?

Up to this point, the debate between the Foucaultians and the Habermasians has seemed to turn primarily on the capacity for a reasoned critique of power and the possibility of disentangling the subject's capacity for critique from the power relations that constitute it. To pose the issue in these terms is to assume, as philosophers and feminists have tended to do, not only that the "truth" (about one's subordination, for example) can be known, but also that knowing it will set you free. The debate over the entanglement between power and validity problematizes the possibility of knowing the "truth" about the nature of gender identity or the self more generally or anything at all independent of the power relations that are constitutive of those categories. However, we should also wonder about the second part of this equation, a notion that inspired so much second-wave feminist consciousness raising. What if the "truth" doesn't set you free? What if knowing the "truth" about, for example, the subordinating nature of the gender norms that constitute your identity does little or nothing to loosen their grip on you? What if those who are subordinated remain attached to the terms of their subordination, even after those terms have been, as Fraser put it above, "rationally demystified"? Such a possibility suggests that, in addition to confronting the relationship between power and validity, a feminist critical theory that focuses on the politics of our selves must address difficult questions of motivation, will, and desire.

Here we begin to run up against the limits of both the Foucaultian and the Habermasian frameworks. As Wendy Brown argues, Foucault, despite all his talk about freedom and resistance, exhibits a "distinct lack of attention to what might constitute, negate, or redirect the desire for freedom.... [He] seems to tacitly assume the givenness of the desire for freedom."[37] Brown links this neglect of questions of will and desire both to Foucault's suspicion of psychoanalysis and to his rather truncated reading of Nietzsche: one could say that he takes on board Nietzsche's will to power, minus the will. As a result, Brown suggests, "the problem of freedom for Foucault" is "one of domain and discourse, rather than this problem of the 'will' that it is for Nietzsche."[38] Thus, Brown's brilliant and disturbing critique of the politicization of identity—which centers on the idea that the politicization of identity can be understood as the enactment of a desire for unfreedom, for the reinscription of the pain of subordination and exclusion—cannot be posed from within a strictly Foucaultian framework.

This realization about the limits of Foucault's framework leads Butler, in her recent work, to recast the Foucaultian notion of subjection by integrating it with psychoanalytic insights.[39] In *The Psychic Life of Power*, Butler argues that, as compelling and theoretically fruitful as Foucault's account of subjection is, it fails to explain the psychic mechanisms that make subjection work. That is, and Foucault's resistance to psychoanalysis is probably to blame here, it fails to consider how subjection works at the microlevel, how, through it, power "assumes a psychic form that constitutes the subject's self-identity."[40] This leads Butler to recast her account of subjection such that she can analyze the ways in which those who are subjected to power become passionately attached to, and thus come to desire, their own subordination. The key assumption here is that the subject would rather attach to pain than not attach. The subject is dependent for its survival on social recognition, and it will prefer subordinating modes of recognition over none at all. As I argue in chapter 4, Butler's diagnosis is extremely compelling; she powerfully exposes the ways in which psychic subjection undercuts the will to transformation by compelling the subordinated subject to become attached to and invested in its own subordination. If giving up my investment in subordination means giving up my identity, then I will have strong motivations to hang on to it. However, her account falls short in its articulation of the possibilities for the overcoming of subjection. She tends to understand this either in terms of a reworking of the conditions that subject us (without confronting the issue of the desire for such a reworking) or in terms of a problematic embrace of the incoherence of identity, of a critical desubjectivation. What is missing is the realization that a possible way out of this attachment to subjection lies in collective social experimentation and political transformation, rather than a Nietzschean emphasis on the heroic individual.[41]

The preceding considerations suggest that, even if a rational critique of subjection can be disentangled from power relations enough to give it the necessary critical bite, it will not be enough to envision what it takes for subjected subjects to overcome the power relations that constitute them. Thus, to the extent that a feminist critical theory is interested not only in diagnosing power relations in all their complexity but also in charting possible directions for social transformation, our analysis of power will have to tell us something about how subjection shapes not only our critical capacities but also our will and our desires. Not only that, but our account of autonomy will have to illuminate not just the possibilities for rational, critical reflexivity but also the prospects for reworking will and desire in a direction that motivates emancipatory self-transformation. As Maeve Cooke argues in her recent book, *Re-presenting the Good Society*: It is not enough for critical theory to offer critical diagnoses of the times backed up with good reasons and arguments; critical social theorists must also "motivate their addressees to engage in thought and action aimed at overcoming the social obstacles to human flourishing that they identify."[42]

Interestingly, in his earlier, more psychoanalytically engaged work, Habermas recognized that there is a key motivational component to the achievement of autonomy. For example, in the essay "Moral Development and Ego Identity," Habermas writes:

> Ego identity requires not only cognitive mastery of general levels of communication but also the ability to give one's own needs their due in these communication structures; as long as the ego is cut off from its internal nature and disavows the dependency on needs that still await suitable interpretations, freedom, no matter how much it is guided by principles, remains in truth unfree in relation to existing systems of norms.[43]

However much one might take issue with Habermas's assumption in this essay that one's inner nature can be communicatively rendered transparent and fluid—an issue that I will return to in chapter 5—at least at this point he realizes that engaging with will and desire is necessary for the true realization of freedom with respect to existing norms. However, in his more recent formulations, in which autonomy is understood as what Cooke calls "rational accountability," defined as one's "ability to support what she or he says with reasons," "to enter into argumentation," and to remain open to criticism,[44] the motivational component of autonomy fades into the background. In chapter 5, I trace the consequences of this disappearance, and I consider the implications of reintroducing questions of will and desire into the Habermasian framework.

The Subject of Politics

If Brown's critique of identity politics poses the challenge of how to theorize the relationships between will, desire, and rational critique, Linda Zerilli's recent critique of feminist theory's obsession with the problem of the subject poses a much more fundamental challenge to the project of this book. In her recent book, *Feminism and the Abyss of Freedom*, Zerilli challenges feminist theorists to consider whether questions about subjection and autonomy are even theoretically or politically fruitful for feminism. Zerilli's aim is to displace what she calls the "subject-centered frame," a term that she uses to refer, on the one hand, to discussions of the individual subject, its constitution through subjection, and its possibilities for self-transformation, and, on the other hand, to debates about the "subject of feminism," that is, the meaning of the category of women. According to Zerilli, such debates have led feminists nowhere, and, in Wittgensteinian fashion, she proposes that rather than trying to solve the problems posed within such discussions, we should dissolve them by shifting to a new framework, one centered on the practice of freedom.

What Zerilli calls the subject-centered frame really consists of two quite distinct strands of feminist debate, which are linked by the homonymous use of the word "subject." The first strand focuses on the constitution of the individual subject through practices of subjection, in the Foucaultian sense. Here Butler's work, which has been so influential for so-called third-wave feminism, is Zerilli's main target. In Butler's work, and in work inspired by her (which the vast majority of contemporary feminist scholarship has been in one way or another), "freedom comes to be formulated ... strictly as a subject question, while subject formation comes increasingly to be interpreted in terms of radical subjection to agencies outside the self."[45] According to Zerilli, such a move does nothing to challenge the subject-centered frame of the traditional liberal and existentialist feminism that it aims to move beyond; instead, it simply moves "into [the subject-centered frame's] negative space."[46] As a result, Zerilli finds it difficult to see how this theoretical framework could ever envision or inspire a truly transformative, freedom-enabling politics.[47] If we want to do this, Zerilli argues that feminists should shift our focus away from the Foucaultian drama of individual subjection and self-transformation and toward an Arendtian conception of freedom centered on plurality and action in the public space. Zerilli suggests that we are better off thinking of freedom not as a subject question but as a world question; freedom is, as Hannah Arendt shows us, a collective practice of world building, not, or at least not primarily, an individual practice of or capacity for self-transformation. Though she waffles a bit on this point, Zerilli seems to suggest that subjection and self-transformation are not properly political issues at all.

The second strand of the subject-centered frame concerns the bitter and divisive debates over the category of women and how to theorize the subject of feminism. Such debates have led to a seemingly insurmountable paradox: on the one hand, the category of women is taken to be, like all identity categories, inherently exclusionary;[48] on the other hand, feminism as a political movement seems to require the making of claims in the name of or on behalf of women and so it seems to require the invocation of this exclusionary category. Although many prominent feminists, including Butler, have gestured toward some form of strategic essentialism as the way out of this impasse, Zerilli argues that if we reject the subject-centered frame, the paradox will never arise in the first place. As she puts it:

> The collapse of the category of women need by no means spell the end of feminism, for a freedom-centered feminism never relied on concept-application in the first place. Political claims rely on the ability to exercise imagination, to think from the standpoint of others, and in this way to posit universality and thus community. The universality of such claims depends on their being not epistemologically justified, as most feminists have tended to assume, but taken up by others, in ways that we can neither predict nor control, in a public space.[49]

Here Zerilli tries to shift feminist theory away from a narrow focus on epistemological concerns to a broader conception of imagination, reflective judgment, and the production of what she calls, borrowing from Castoriadis, the "newly thinkable."[50]

Zerilli's argument for this approach to feminist theory proceeds by way of identifying a false opposition between two conceptions of theory. Zerilli maintains that theory is typically understood either as "the critical practice of forming universal concepts that can be applied in rule-like fashion to the particulars of lived experience"[51] or as "the art of description which refuses to say anything beyond the particular case at hand."[52] This opposition generates the further assumption that "political claims are either grounded (and therefore not contestable) or ungrounded (and therefore not persuasive)," but this, according to Zerilli, "occludes a third possibility: rather than knowledge claims that can be redeemed as true or false by means of a cognitive (determinant) judgment, political claims are based on contingently formed public opinions that call for our (reflective) judgment without the mediation of a concept."[53] Thus, Zerilli implies that all existing theories are mired in either foundationalism or relativism; this assumption motivates the acceptance of her alternative proposal, which is grounded in the Kantian/Arendtian notion of reflective judgment. By formulating the existing theoretical landscape in this way, however, Zerilli conveniently overlooks yet another possibility: a theoretical framework that neither seeks to form universal, ideal concepts that can then be applied to the real world nor refuses to generalize about particular cases, but that instead forms its concepts, categories, and analyses through a process of reflecting on social and political realities. Such a framework views political claims neither as truth claims that are to be redeemed through determinant judgment, nor as quasi-aesthetic claims that are to be assessed via reflective judgment, but as normative claims that are to be redeemed through discourse. This path is precisely the one pursued by Habermasian critical theory.

Zerilli's failure to consider this alternative theoretical possibility is rendered even more curious by the fact that her own positive position, grounded in an Arendtian conception of plurality and intersubjective validity, is, in some respects, quite close to Habermas's. Perhaps it is this very proximity that compels her to misread Habermas, insinuating that his account of normative discourse is grounded in a commitment to objective, rather than intersubjective, validity.[54] Zerilli's critique of the overly cognitivist nature of Habermas's account of discourse and of his emphasis on the rational power of argumentation is perfectly legitimate, but the fact that Habermas's account is cognitivist does not mean that it is also objectivist. Likewise, her argument that radical politics involves more than mere rational argumentation over norms and their application, that it often also "expands our sense of what we can communicate,"[55] issues a legitimate challenge to Habermasian discourse ethics and deliberative democracy. Zerilli is no doubt right that Habermas has a difficult time recognizing this sort of aesthetic defamiliarization as a form of political engagement, and that the reasons for this lacuna are conceptually related to his rather strict conceptual separation between the pragmatic, communicative use of language and the aesthetic, world-disclosing use.[56] But this suggestion could just as well be taken up in the direction of the need to develop a more capacious account of discourse or dialogue and what might count as a reason in the context of argumentation; it does not by itself justify the rejection of Habermas's framework.[57]

Moreover, it is not at all clear that Zerilli's attempt to displace the sub-ject-centered frame actually dissolves the problems she aims to dissolve, nor does she avoid generating worrisome problems of her own. In the first place, simply claiming that freedom is a world question rather than a subject question does not obviate the need for thinking about the indi-vidual subject and its capacities for critical reflection and self-transfor-mation, nor does it establish that such matters are not properly political. Indeed, Arendt's definition of "world" cannot make sense without some understanding of the individual subject, for the world is constituted by subjects; it is "related ... to the human artifact, the fabrication of human hands, as well as to affairs which go on among those who inhabit the man-made world together."[58] Similarly, Arendt's definition of "freedom" implicitly refers to a subject with the capacity to act, which Zerilli herself acknowledges in her gloss on this definition: "worldly freedom is political: it requires not only an I-will but an I-can; it requires community. Arendt asserts, 'Only where the I-will and the I-can coincide does freedom come to pass.' "[59] Zerilli frequently repeats this formulation, but seemingly with-out realizing that although it does clearly imply that the individual capac-ity for self-transformation (Arendt's I-will) is not *sufficient* for freedom, it also suggests that such a capacity is nonetheless *necessary*.

The failure to realize this simple point haunts Zerilli's own attempts to formulate a feminist politics of freedom that escapes the subject-centered frame; this conception of politics inevitably presupposes what I have iden-tified as the first strand of that frame, as, for example, when Zerilli claims that "the problem of politics" consists in asking "with whom am I in com-munity?"[60] Similarly, as she admits, Arendt's account of intersubjective va-lidity is grounded in her account of enlarged thinking, which assumes that "the relation to the object is mediated through the subject's relation to the standpoints of other subjects or, more precisely, by taking the viewpoints of others on the same object into account."[61] Even if such formulations do helpfully resituate the individual subject in an intersubjective frame, they obviously do not leave the problem of the subject behind completely; indeed, they cannot even be posed without reference to that very prob-lem. Perhaps it is the recognition of this point that leads Zerilli to pull her punch at the last moment, qualifying her critique of the subject-centered frame in the conclusion to her book, when she writes:

> My point throughout this book has not been to rule out ... the questions
> of subjectivity and identity that have preoccupied feminists. It has been to
> insist that the kind of transformation envisioned by thinkers who focus on
> these questions ... requires the tangible and intangible political relations

that Arendt calls a worldly in-between: that which at once relates and separates us. It is in this space of the common world that differences become meaningful and the newly thinkable, other ways of constituting identities and configuring social relations such as gender, appears.[62]

I could not agree more, but this very way of putting the point suggests that we would do better to strive to develop an *inter*subjective (rather than a *non*subjective, whatever that might mean) frame for feminism.

To some extent, this is precisely what Zerilli does, even though she does not describe her project in these terms. Arendt's notions of freedom, the world, the public, the political, and plurality all refer to the intersubjective, the shared, and the in-between, and to the extent that Zerilli bases her conception of feminist politics on these notions, she cannot help but move the discussion in this direction. However, there are also opposing tendencies in Zerilli's work (as in Arendt's), and it is precisely here that an avowedly intersubjective framework might help her avoid some of the problems generated by her approach. For instance, her appreciation for Arendt's account of political judgment as reflective judgment leads Zerilli to emphasize the role of the spectator—as opposed to the participant—in reflective, political judgment. This leads Zerilli to suggest that we radically recast the debates about the collective subject of feminism. In her view, democratic politics "consists precisely in the making of universal claims (speaking for), hence in closure, and in their acceptance or refusal (speaking back), hence also in openness";[63] as a result, a feminist democratic politics ought to think of "women" "not as a category to be applied like a rule in a determinant judgment but as a claim to speak in someone's name and to be spoken for."[64] This conception curiously fails to consider that democratic politics might involve, first and foremost, speaking *to* and *with* rather than *for* one another. Indeed, one might say that it was precisely the eagerness of white, middle-class, heterosexual feminists to speak *for* others rather than *with* them that generated the heated and fraught debates about identity politics in the first place. Why think that more speaking *for* others—even if that gesture is followed up with a professed willingness to be spoken for, as Zerilli suggests—will get us out of the problems to which those debates have led? This question is especially pressing in light of the unfortunate fact that the voices of the most privileged are those most easily heard, a fact that will tend to foreclose the very openness that Zerilli is trying to preserve.

Zerilli does consider the possibility that democratic politics could be centered on speaking to and with others, that is, on a model of democratic deliberation. But she complains that "the idea that a formal procedure could provide the guarantee of equal access to any debate about who is included in the feminist community, as advocates of Habermas's discourse ethics suggest, does not adequately address the question of what such access can mean if a certain version of the community is more or less invulnerable to question, or if the kind of questioning that can occur must remain within the parameters of what constitutes a certain definition of 'women.'"[65] This is half right. The issues of how power structures the lifeworld and thus the communicative practice of discourse itself are important ones for Habermasian critical theory to grapple with if it is to become truly critical, but the solution to this, as even Zerilli's own argument seems to suggest, can only be more discourse or debate. On what other terms are we to contest or debate (terms that figure prominently in Zerilli's agonistic conception of politics) our definitions of "women"? As Zerilli herself argues in her conclusion, democracy involves two fundamental normative commitments: both a commitment to radical openness to questioning and debate and a commitment to the idea that those who participate in such practices constitute a community of equals.[66] Habermas's discourse ethics is one way of modeling this latter presumption and the norms of reciprocity and equality implicit in it.

To the extent that Zerilli's view fails to appreciate this, it generates another problem: What makes a "newly thinkable" imagined formation normatively acceptable, desirable, even feminist? If freedom is "the capacity to wrest something new from an objective state of affairs without being compelled to do so by a norm or rule" and "a freedom-centered feminism … is concerned not with knowing (that there are women) as such but with doing—with transforming, world-building, beginning anew,"[67] this leaves unanswered the difficult question of which newly thinkables are liberatory and which are not. Zerilli is no doubt right to insist that this issue cannot be decided in advance, but this does not mean that it is inherently undecidable, which her approach comes dangerously close to suggesting. It is here that Habermas's intersubjective, discourse-centered frame might once again prove promising for feminist theory.

Zerilli is right, I think, to wonder "if feminine subjects are constituted as subjected, as feminists of all three waves in their different ways have held, how are they to engage in the free act of founding something new?"[68] This is a key unanswered question for feminists, particularly those who have taken their inspiration from Foucault's and Butler's analyses of subjection, and it is one of the guiding questions of this book. However, contra Zerilli, I do not believe we will arrive at an answer to this difficult question by changing the subject. Rather than attempting, as Zerilli does, to reject the subject-centered frame altogether, we would be better off proceeding by way of determinate negation, shifting from a subjective to an intersubjective frame, a move that is better accomplished through Habermas's normative framework than it is through the agonistic reading of Arendt that Zerilli favors. Such a framework can help us to see both that the transformation of the self is an important political question and that such self-transformation cannot, as Zerilli also understands, be properly understood absent an account of the intersubjective, political conditions that make it possible.

Tasks for a Feminist Critical Theory

To return to the issue of developing a feminist critical-theoretical account of the politics of our selves, it seems to me, based on the foregoing considerations, that such a project has three principal aims: first, to analyze subordination—in particular the subordination of women but also with an eye toward its intersections with other axes of subordination such as race, class, and sexuality—in all its depth, complexity, and specificity; second, to critique such subordination, and in so doing to offer some insight into what shape social transformation might take; and third, to consider how such social transformation might be accomplished, which requires addressing the difficult questions of how power structures desire and will and how these structures might be transformed. The first task focuses on power, the second and third on the twin notions of critique and autonomy, where the latter is understood to ground and legitimate the former. But each of these tasks is implicated in the other: the first implicitly appeals to some conception of critical autonomy inasmuch as presenting a certain social formation as subordinating already requires reflecting critically on those social relations; and the second and third tasks implicitly concern power, inasmuch as the feminist social critic is him- or herself constituted as a subject within and through relations of power and the motivational question cannot avoid confronting the entanglement of power and the desire (or lack thereof) for change.

Foucault's work is enormously helpful for the first task, the task of understanding power and subordination in all its complexity, particularly at the level of subject formation. And although he is less helpful for the second task, I maintain that it is not the case, as many of his feminist and Habermasian critics have alleged, that his work undermines or dispenses with the concepts of subjectivity, agency, autonomy, and critique. As I argue in chapter 2, by way of a reconsideration of Foucault's relationship to Kant, Foucault never dispenses with the subject, but instead he aims to uncover the historically, socially, and culturally specific conditions of possibility for subjectivity. In that sense, his work is a continuation (though admittedly a radically historicized transformation) of the Kantian critical project. In chapter 3, I continue this line of argument by drawing out the conceptions of autonomy and critique in Foucault's late work and arguing that his use of these notions is in fact consistent with his earlier analyses of power and subjection. Moreover, although Foucault's work by itself is not very helpful for the third task, Butler's fusion of Foucault and Freud in her more recent work on subjection is; I discuss this work in chapter 4. However, as Fraser argued in her intervention in the Butler-Benhabib debate, what both Foucault and Butler lack is attention to the inter- (as opposed to the intra-) subjective dimensions of the subject and of autonomy—in Foucault's case this seems to result more from lack of attention than anything else, and in Butler's it stems from her ambivalent use of the term "recognition," but in both cases it leads to problems in their ability to conceptualize adequately the possiblities for transformation.

Thus, in chapter 5 I turn to Habermas's intersubjective account of subjectivation. This account provides a detailed and robust conception of the capacity for autonomy, and his early work, at least, addresses both the cognitive and the motivational aspects of this capacity. However, as I shall argue in chapter 5, this account remains a bit too robust. Habermas, for the most part, overlooks the role that power necessarily plays in the intersubjective formation of subjectivity, and even when he does acknowledge this role, he is overly sanguine about the results. Facing up to the role that power plays in subjectivation problematizes the separation of power and validity on which Habermas's strong notions of autonomy and justification rely. In chapter 6, I argue that the best way to deal with this problem is not to endorse a nihilistic relativism but instead to endorse a weaker, more contextualist, and more pragmatic version of Habermasian critical theory. In chapter 7, I consider Benhabib's attempt to do just this, with her notion of interactive universalism, a notion that she argues is a fruitful basis for both feminist and critical theory. I argue that despite Benhabib's attempt to develop a more concrete and situated version of Habermas's communicative ethics, her own narrative conception of the self falls prey to the same charge of excessive rationalism that she levels against Habermas. Benhabib's account presupposes an ungendered core of the self—a presupposition that is not only incompatible with her own earlier work on the importance of the concrete other for moral and political theory, but that also obscures the role that gendered relations of power play in the constitution of selves. Thus, Benhabib's account, like Habermas's, needs to take more seriously the role that power plays in the constitution of the critical capacities of the autonomous self, and the implications of this for the difficult task of understanding the politics of our selves.

The overall aim of this book is an attempt to accomplish the ambitious task suggested but left undone by Fraser: to envision subjects as both culturally constructed in and through relations of power and yet capable of critique, and to think through the implications of this for how we understand subjectivity, power, critique, and autonomy. But this analysis also goes beyond Fraser to think through the difficult issues of how our cultural construction mires us in modes of subjectivity that attach subjects to their subjection and thus threaten to undermine the motivation for autonomous self-transformation. In my final chapter, I bring these different strands together to construct a framework for understanding the politics of our selves.

In what follows, I take Foucault's formulation of the politics of our selves as my point of departure. However, as will become clear, if it is not already, my position is not that of a doctrinaire Foucaultian, and, although I do attempt to correct some of the more egregious misreadings of Foucault by his feminist and Habermasian critics, my primary aim in doing so is to clear the ground for a more sympathetic and constructive engagement between Foucault and Habermas. In other words, this book is not an exercise in Foucault interpretation. Because, however, the tension between power and autonomy is one that runs not only between Foucault and Habermas but also between Foucault's earlier archaeological and genealogical writings and his late work, my argument here does have some implications for the difficult interpretive issue of how to understand Foucault's oeuvre as a whole.

And yet, there is much more at stake in this discussion than either how best to interpret Foucault or the outcome of the Foucault-Habermas and Butler-Benhabib debates. The general conceptual-philosophical problem that emerges from these debates is the difficulty that we have in thinking through power and autonomy simultaneously. If we start with power in all its complexity, including the role it plays in the formation of subjectivity, we end up seeming to embrace determinism and deny autonomy; conversely, it seems we can only develop a robust enough account of autonomy by denying or ignoring the depth of power's influence on the subject. This book attempts to think through these two concepts—each so crucially important for feminist theory, for critical theory, and for social and political theory more generally—simultaneously and integratively, to figure out how to understand autonomy such that it is compatible with an understanding of power in all its depth and complexity. A critical theory that is truly critical, that is able to illuminate the struggles and wishes of our age and to chart paths of possible emancipatory transformation, can settle for no less.

2

Foucault, Subjectivity, and the Enlightenment

A CRITICAL REAPPRAISAL

A COMMON theme in both feminist and Habermasian criticisms of Foucault is his alleged participation in and celebration of the death of the subject.[1] Since concepts such as agency, autonomy, and self-reflexivity seem to be dependent upon there being a subject in which they are instantiated, the death of the subject threatens to undermine these concepts as well, ultimately threatening, in turn, the project of social critique itself. As Benhabib puts it, "along with this dissolution of the subject ... disappear of course concepts of intentionality, accountability, self-reflexivity and autonomy."[2] Without such concepts, however, social critique is not only pointless—since meaningful social change would seem to require agency—but ultimately impossible. Thus, Benhabib argues that the death of the subject "undermines the possibility of normative criticism at large," including feminist critical theory, which allies itself with this notion "only at the risk of incoherence and self-contradictoriness."[3] Foucault's alleged embrace of the death of the subject has thus been a major stumbling block to an effective dialogue between Foucault's work and the work of both critical social theorists and feminist theorists.

The strongest textual evidence for Foucault's embracing the death of the subject is found in his early, archaeological works. Foucault's substantive critique of humanism in early works such as *The Order of Things*, combined with his methodological bracketing of the concept of subjectivity from archaeological analysis, seems to many critics to entail a rejection not just of the substantive conception of subjectivity presupposed by modern humanism—the transcendental subject—but of the very concept of the subject—the "I think"—itself. As Axel Honneth describes Foucault's archaeological work: "The human is no longer the experiential center of a course of action which he encounters and oversees, but the arbitrary effect of a network of events out of which he can no longer make sense and which is produced by the rules of language."[4] If subjectivity is nothing more than an arbitrary effect of discourse, the argument goes, it is as good as dead.

In several late interviews and essays, however, there are indications that the reports of Foucault's participation in the death of the subject have been greatly exaggerated. Foucault insists that he never argued for a rejection of subjectivity per se.[5] To the contrary, he claims that the goal of his work as a whole is to "create a history of the different modes by which, in our culture, human beings are made subjects"; thus, he maintains, the subject—and not power—is "the general theme of [his] research."[6] Unfortunately, Foucault's critical social theorist and feminist critics have not taken these claims seriously. Instead, they have argued that the "return" of subjectivity in Foucault's late work is both unsatisfactory in itself and contradicts his earlier work.[7] Foucault's claim that the subject is the general theme of his research is thus written off as a post hoc attempt to gloss over serious problems that emerge from his archaeological and genealogical works.

This dispute raises difficult interpretive and theoretical questions. What would it mean to take seriously Foucault's claim that the subject is the general theme of his research? Is there a way of reading his archaeological works that allows us to make sense of this claim? What sort of conception of subjectivity is consistent with his archaeological project? Is this conception consistent with Foucault's late work on the practices and techniques by means of which individuals constitute themselves as subjects? In this chapter, I offer a way of reading Foucault's early works that takes seriously his claim that the subject is the general theme of his research and that shows how his early work on the subject coheres with his later work on the self. To be sure, Foucault argues against a particular conception of the subject—the transcendental (or, as he later comes to call it, transcendental-phenomenological) subject. It is a mistake, however, to assume that this argument is meant to do away with the concept of subjectivity altogether; instead, the point is to clear a space for new conceptions, new forms of subjectivity, such as the one he develops in his late work on the self. My argument for this is based on a reconsideration of Foucault's early work on Kant. Contra Habermas, who reads Foucault's major works as anti-Enlightenment texts, I argue that Foucault's work is best understood as an immanent rather than a total critique of the Kantian Enlightenment project. Specifically, Foucault, in his early work, transforms Kant's notion of the transcendental subject that serves as the condition of possibility for any experience into a subject that is conditioned by its rootedness in specific historical, social, and cultural practices. Moreover, he argues that Kant himself opens the door to this historicophilosophical approach in his writings on pragmatic anthropology. Far from a rejection of the Kantian project, Foucault's inversion of Kant's notion of transcendental subjectivity constitutes a critique of critique itself, a continuation-through-transformation of that project.[8] This suggests that, to the extent that the Foucault-Habermas debate has been understood as compelling us to choose between rejecting the Kantian Enlightenment project and taking it up in a transformative way, it has been misunderstood.[9]

I begin by considering Foucault's complex relationship to Kant. I focus on Habermas's charge that the positive appropriation of Kant in Foucault's late work contradicts his earlier work on Kant, and that this is indicative of deeper, more fundamental contradictions in Foucault's thought as a whole. I argue that this criticism can best be met by reconsidering Foucault's early work, particularly his *thèse complémentaire* on Kant's *Anthropology from a Pragmatic Point of View* and the closely related account of Kant in *The Order of Things*. My argument is that a careful reading of these texts demonstrates that Foucault's early work is best understood not as a rejection of but as a critical engagement with the Kantian critical project, specifically, with the Kantian notion of transcendental subjectivity. When Foucault's work is interpreted in this way, his claim that the question of subjectivity is central to his project from the very beginning becomes plausible. Finally, I defend Foucault's continuation-through-transformation of the Kantian critical project against some of the major criticisms that might be made of it.

Foucault and Kant

In a late discussion of Kant's essay "What is Enlightenment?" Foucault credits Kant with posing "the question of his own present" and positions himself as an inheritor of this Kantian legacy.[10] Foucault has high praise for the critical tradition that emerges from Kant's historical-political reflections on the Enlightenment and the French Revolution; Kant's concern in these writings with "an ontology of the present, an ontology of ourselves" is, he says, characteristic of "a form of philosophy, from Hegel, through Nietzsche and Max Weber, to the Frankfurt school," a form of philosophy with which Foucault, perhaps surprisingly, allies his own work.[11]

In another late essay, Foucault explains in more detail the sense in which he views his work as a continuation of the Kantian critical tradition. Foucault claims that what is central in Kant's discussion of the Enlightenment is not "a theory, a doctrine, nor even a permanent body of knowledge that is accumulating" but instead a distinctively modern attitude, an ethos, one in which "the high value of the present is indissociable from a desperate eagerness to imagine it, to imagine it otherwise than it is, and to transform it not by destroying it but by grasping it in what it is."[12] And although he insists that it is not the case that "one has to be 'for' or 'against' the Enlightenment," he nevertheless once again positions his own work in the Kantian Enlightenment tradition as he understands it, "conceived as an attitude, an ethos, a philosophical life in which the critique of what we are is at one and the same time the historical analysis of the limits that are imposed on us and an experiment with the possibility of going beyond them."[13] From this perspective, Foucault offers a retrospective of his oeuvre, understood as a modified form of Kantian critique. Foucault's critical project no doubt departs significantly from the letter of Kant's philosophy, but not, or so he claims, from its spirit:

> Criticism is no longer going to be practiced in the search for formal structures with universal value but, rather, as a historical investigation into the events that have led us to constitute ourselves and to recognize ourselves as subjects of what we are doing, thinking, saying. In that sense, criticism is not transcendental, and its goal is not that of making a metaphysics possible: it is genealogical in its design and archaeological in its method. Archaeological—and not transcendental—in the sense that it will not seek to identify the universal structures of all knowledge or of all possible moral action, but will seek to treat the instances of discourse that articulate what we think, say, and do as so many historical events. And ... genealogical in the sense that it will not deduce from the form of what we are what it is impossible for us to do and to know; but it will separate out, from the contingency that has made us what we are, the possibility of no longer being, doing, or thinking what we are, do, or think.[14]

Foucault's remarks in these late essays about the Enlightenment tradition in general and about the Kantian version of the Enlightenment project in particular have perplexed his critics and his supporters alike. After all, Kant had seemed to be the great villain of Foucault's account of the rise of the human sciences in *The Order of Things*. In that work, as James Schmidt and Thomas Wartenberg have put the point, "Kant had the dubious honor of awakening philosophy from its 'dogmatic slumber' only to lull it back into what Foucault dubbed 'the anthropological sleep.' ... Kant's legacy ... was viewed as decidedly problematic: a philosophical anthropology caught in the bind of treating 'man' as both an object of empirical inquiry and the transcendental ground of all knowledge."[15] Moreover, although Bentham was perhaps the more obvious target of Foucault's genealogy of disciplinary power in *Discipline and Punish*, Kant's moral philosophy can just as easily be seen to be implicated in one of the central claims of that book, namely, that "the soul is the prison of the body."[16] So what could Foucault possibly have had in mind when, in these late essays, he invoked Kant's critical project and situated his own work within the Kantian Enlightenment tradition?

One possibility, suggested by Habermas, is that Foucault's early, archaeological writings and his late reflections on the Enlightenment offer two different, and ultimately incompatible, readings of Kant. As Habermas puts it:

> In Foucault's lecture ["What Is Enlightenment?"], we do not meet the Kant familiar from *The Order of Things*, the epistemologist who thrust open the door to the age of anthropological thought and the human sciences with his analysis of finiteness. Instead we encounter a *different* Kant—the precursor of the Young Hegelians, the Kant who was the first to make a serious break with the metaphysical heritage, who turned philosophy away from the Eternal Verities and concentrated on what philosophers had until then considered to be without concept and nonexistent, merely contingent and transitory.[17]

Habermas goes on to argue that these two very different readings of Kant map onto a fundamental contradiction in Foucault's own thought. The question, as Habermas presents it, is "how such an affirmative understanding of modern philosophizing ... fits with Foucault's unyielding critique of modernity. How can Foucault's self-understanding as a thinker in the tradition of the Enlightenment be compatible with his unmistakable critique of precisely this form of knowledge, which is that of modernity?"[18] In Habermas's view, Foucault cannot have it both ways; the contradiction between Foucault's critique of modernity and his embrace of (an admittedly idiosyncratic interpretation of) the Enlightenment tradition is inescapable. Thus, Habermas concludes his remembrance, written on the occasion of Foucault's death, by suggesting that perhaps Foucault recognized and, in a characteristically veiled way, admitted as much in his final reflections on Kant. As Habermas puts it, "perhaps it is the force of this contradiction that drew Foucault, in the last of his texts, back into a sphere of influence he had tried to blast open, that of the philosophical discourse of modernity."[19]

In response, Schmidt and Wartenberg have warned against too hasty a dismissal of Foucault's late embrace of Kant and the Enlightenment tradition. They suggest, rightly, I think, that Foucault's "invocation of Kant should neither be written off as simply an ironic gesture nor turned into a deathbed concession of defeat. It is instead a remarkably productive interrogation of a thinker who never ceased to inspire and provoke Foucault."[20] However, despite their insistence that Foucault's embrace of the Kantian version of the Enlightenment project was no passing fancy but was instead a persistent theme in Foucault's writings over his last decade, and despite their serious attention to Foucault's different interpretations of this tradition in these relatively late works, Schmidt and Wartenberg seem to agree with Habermas that the early and late Foucault contain two radically different interpretations of Kant. As they put it, "the Kant we meet in Foucault's essay differs markedly from the thinker Foucault confronted two decades earlier in *The Order of Things....* If the Kant of *The Order of Things* marked the advent of an ultimately empty humanism, the Kant of 'What Is Enlightenment?' was a good deal more interesting and provocative."[21] Thus, although they are, I think, completely right to say that Foucault's "stance toward the enlightenment remained a good deal more nuanced and complex than his critics would lead us to believe," they nonetheless leave Habermas's charge of a fundamental contradiction in Foucault's thought unanswered.[22]

Whereas Schmidt and Wartenberg's defense of Foucault focuses on his proximity to one of his two Kants—Kant the thinker of his own present—David Hoy's defense of Foucault focuses on his distance from the other—Kant the epistemologist. Hoy argues, contra Habermas, that Foucault is not an enemy of reason and Enlightenment, though he is, in the end, a postmodern rather than a modern thinker. Although the jumping-off point for Hoy's argument is an account of Foucault's late essays on Kant and the Enlightenment, much of his argument is devoted to substantiating the claim that the trajectory of Foucault's thought is a process of breaking free from Kant-qua-epistemologist. Whereas Foucault's claims about archaeological methodology in *The Archaeology of Knowledge* look to Hoy, regrettably, "like Kantian transcendental philosophy" inasmuch as Foucault "posits an a priori that can be deduced or at least indirectly inferred by this one particular method," Foucault, by the time he writes *Discipline and Punish*, has seen the error of his ways, and his postmodern "pastiche emulates Nietzsche more than Kant."[23] Both archaeology and genealogy are, according to Hoy, attempts to think the unthought, which Hoy takes to be the task of both modern and postmodern thought. But whereas archaeology, with its "pretensions to epistemology (in the traditional sense of the privileged discourse about the conditions for the possibility of any and every form of knowledge)," remains caught in a modern way of thinking the unthought, genealogy, with its recognition that it is just one among many possible ways of thinking the unthought, an unthought which is itself also multiple, moves beyond Kantian modernism into Nietzschean postmodernism.[24] As Hoy puts it, in the shift from archaeology to genealogy, Foucault "moves from a modernist, quasi-transcendental neo-Kantian stance to a postmodern, neo-Nietzschean stance."[25]

As I see it, the significant drawback of this interpretation of Foucault is that it makes his late embrace of the Kantian critical project even more mystifying than it was before. If Foucault spent his whole life trying to break free of Kant, why would he return to him in the end? If Hoy's reading is correct, how could this return be understood as anything other than the capitulation that Habermas understands it to be? The problem is not just that Hoy does not answer this question. He does not even seem to recognize the need to reconcile the two prima facie incompatible versions of Foucault's relationship to Kant that are present not only in Foucault's work, varied and wide ranging as it was, but also in the pages of Hoy's own essay. Once again, Habermas's charge against Foucault is left unanswered.

Inasmuch as Foucault's admiration for Kant in his late work is quite explicit, it seems to me that Habermas's charge of contradiction can best be met by a reconsideration of Foucault's early work on Kant. Contra Habermas, I do not think that Foucault offers two contradictory readings of Kant; rather, a careful reading of his early work demonstrates that Foucault's reading of Kant was never as rejectionist as has been supposed.[26] Thus, I also dispute Habermas's claim that Foucault's seemingly contradictory readings of Kant are indicative of a deeper, more fundamental contradiction in Foucault's thought.[27] To the contrary, when Foucault's later work is viewed from the perspective of his early work on Kant, a striking continuity emerges, namely, a central and abiding interest in and critical engagement with philosophical anthropology. Foucault's interpretation of Kant treats the *Anthropology* as a central rather than a marginal text and puts the anthropological question—what is man?—at the center of Kant's philosophical work. Whether or not this is the best interpretation of Kant, I shall leave to Kant scholars, who are in a much better position than I am to decide. However, I shall argue that Foucault's early discussions of

Kant demonstrate clearly that the question of subjectivity is central for Foucault's project from the very beginning.

The Empirical and the Transcendental

Foucault's first extended discussion of Kant occurs in his *thèse complémentaire*, which consists of a translation into French of Kant's *Anthropology from a Pragmatic Point of View* and a substantial introduction to the text. In his introduction, Foucault returns again and again to two related themes: the tension between the empirical and the transcendental in the account of man offered in the *Anthropology* itself, and the relationship between the *Anthropology* and Kant's critical philosophy. Both themes ultimately return to the same problematic: the relationship in Kant's thought between the human being as historically constituted, on the one hand, and the structures of the human mind as constitutive of all possible experience, on the other. These themes set the stage both for Foucault's later discussion of Kant in *The Order of Things* and for my reading of Foucault's work.

With respect to the tension between the empirical and the transcendental within the *Anthropology* itself, the first point to notice is that Foucault returns repeatedly to Kant's claim that pragmatic anthropology takes as its object "what man as a free agent makes, or can and should [*kann und soll*] make, of himself."[28] For instance, Foucault notes that, for Kant, "man is not simply 'what he is,' but 'what he makes of himself.' And is this not precisely the field that the *Anthropology* defines for its investigation?"[29] Foucault views the conjunction of the descriptive account of man (what man makes of himself) and the normative account (what man can and should make of himself) in Kant's *Anthropology* as absolutely essential to an understanding of the text, and he draws the following implication from it: "man, in the *Anthropology*, is neither *homo natura*, nor pure subject of liberty; he is caught in the syntheses already brought about by his liaison with the world."[30] In other words, Kant's pragmatic anthropology studies human beings as they are, that is, empirically, but it also makes constant reference to the use and misuse of the various cognitive powers around which Kant organizes his empirical discussion. But even to talk of the use and misuse of those powers is to presuppose a normative notion of humanity (else what sense could be made of the notion of misuse?), and to presuppose a normative ideal for humanity is to assume that human beings are autonomous, that is, free either to live up to that norm or not.[31] On Foucault's reading, then, although pragmatic anthropology is presented as a straightforward empirical study,[32] in reality, its empirical conception of humanity is only articulated with reference to the normative-transcendental conception, with which it stands in an uneasy tension.

A similar tension emerges from Foucault's discussion of the second theme mentioned above, that of the relationship between the *Anthropology* and the critical philosophy. An important argument of Foucault's thesis is that the *Anthropology*, rather than being a marginal text, occupies a central place in Kant's thought. He notes that, even though the text was published only after Kant retired his professorship in 1797, Kant began lecturing on pragmatic anthropology some twenty-five years earlier, in 1772. Thus, all the while that Kant was developing and refining his critical project he was also lecturing every winter on pragmatic anthropology. Foucault suggests that this is more than mere coincidence; rather, he maintains that Kant's thoughts on anthropology are conceptually bound up with his critical philosophy. At the very beginning of his introduction, he asks:

> Was there from 1772, and subsisting perhaps all through the *Critique*, a certain concrete image of man … which is finally formulated, without major modification, in the last of the texts published by Kant? And if this concrete image of man was able to gather together the critical experience … is it not perhaps because it has, until a certain point, if not organized and commanded, at least guided and secretly oriented that experience?[33]

In other words, Foucault maintains that a concrete or empirical conception of humanity haunts the critical philosophy, only to step out of the shadows in Kant's *Anthropology*. Conversely, he suggests that at the heart of Kant's anthropological analysis of man lies the central focus of the critical philosophy, the transcendental subject: "it is also possible that the *Anthropology* had been modified in its major elements to the extent that it developed the critical enterprise: would not the archaeology of the text, if it were possible, permit us to see the birth of a 'homo criticus'?"[34]

Of course, these questions are not meant to suggest an exact equivalence between the *Anthropology* and the critical philosophy. On the contrary, Foucault clearly recognizes the significant differences between these two parts of Kant's system. Unlike the *First Critique*, the *Anthropology* is a strange amalgamation of empirical observations on everything from relations between men and women to dinner table etiquette to physiognomy and its relationship to character. As such, Foucault admits that the *Anthropology* apparently has no "contact" with the main theme of the *First Critique*, namely, the "reflection on the conditions of experience."[35]

However, this lack of contact is only apparent; in fact, Foucault suggests that there is a close relation between the two texts inasmuch as we might view the *Anthropology* as "the negation of the *Critique*."[36] For instance, the conception of man in the *Critique* is that of the transcendental subject; the "I" is presented not as an object, but as the transcendental unity of apperception that serves as the general condition for the possibility of the experience of any object whatsoever. By contrast, the conception of man in the *Anthropology* is empirical; the *Anthropology* is, at first glance anyway, a study of "the region in which observation of the self has access neither to a subject in-itself, nor to an pure 'I' of synthesis, but to a 'me' which is object, and present solely in its phenomenal truth."[37] By viewing the human being as an object rather than a subject, the *Anthropology* negates or inverts the structure of the *First Critique*. However, Foucault insists that the empirical conception of humanity is "not … a stranger to the determining subject."[38] In the *Anthropology*, the "I" "is not given at the start of the game to man, in a sort of a priori of existence, but when it appears, inserting itself into the multiplicity of a sensible chronicle, it offers itself as already-there … : it is in this 'I' that the subject will recognize its past and the synthesis of its identity."[39] The subject of the *Anthropology* is both empirical and transcendental: empirically generated rather than transcendentally given "at the start of the game"; but once generated, it presents itself to itself as always already there.

Foucault also suggests that the interrelationship between the *Anthropology* and the critical philosophy can be seen in Kant's claim that pragmatic anthropology is both popular and systematic. The *Anthropology* is popular in that it is "a knowledge of man that man himself could immediately understand, recognize, and indefinitely prolong."[40] Indeed, the *Anthropology*'s strange combination of anecdotes, advice, and examples renders the text quite accessible to a popular audience. Yet the *Anthropology* is also systematic insofar as it repeats the structure of the critical philosophy; according to Foucault, each of the three books in the first part corresponds to the three *Critiques*, with the second part echoing the texts on history and politics. But this is a repetition with a difference: "The *Anthropology* … repeat[s] the a priori of the Critique in the originary, that is to say, in a truly temporal dimension."[41] By repeating the a priori of the Critique in a temporal dimension, the *Anthropology* balances the a priori forms of possible knowledge, on the one hand, and the principles of an empirically constituted and historically developed knowledge, on the other.[42]

Thus, Foucault suggests, the *Anthropology* (perhaps unwittingly) breaks open the framework of the critical philosophy, revealing the historical specificity of our a priori categories, their rootedness in historically variable social and linguistic practices and institutions.[43] Foucault's reading of Kant's *Anthropology* thus suggests that Kant's system itself contains the seeds of its own radical transformation, a transformation that Foucault will take up in his own work. Specifically, Foucault's work effects a transformation from the conception of the a priori as universal and necessary to the historical a priori, and a related transformation from the transcendental subject that serves as the condition of possibility of all experience to the subject that is conditioned by its rootedness in specific historical, social, and cultural circumstances.

The End of Man

In the tension between the empirical and the transcendental, which Foucault claims is at the core of both Kant's *Anthropology* and his critical philosophy as a whole, Foucault sees "the problematic of contemporary philosophy."[44] He suggests, moreover, that "it will be good one day to envision the whole history of post-Kantian and contemporary philosophy from the point of view of this maintained confusion, that is to say, from this exposed confusion."[45] Viewing the whole of post-Kantian Continental philosophy from the point of view of the tension between the empirical and the transcendental is perhaps as good a way as any of describing the closing chapters of Foucault's archaeological locus classicus, *The Order of Things*. Indeed, Foucault never published his thesis on Kant. What was a 128-page thesis became a 3-page historical preface to Foucault's translation of Kant's *Anthropology* into French, which ends with this final note: "The relationship between critical thought and anthropological reflection will be studied in a later work";[46] that later work is *The Order of Things*. In its closing chapters, Foucault spells out the implications of the tension between the transcendental and empirical sides of the modern subject. Here, this tension, which Foucault had first diagnosed in Kant's *Anthropology*, becomes the defining characteristic of the modern episteme: what is distinctive about the modern age is the concept of man "as the difficult object and sovereign subject of all possible knowledge."[47] The transition to the modern era is marked by the appearance of man "in his ambiguous position as the object of knowledge and as a subject that knows."[48] This tension informs each of the three of man's doublets, most obviously, the empirical/transcendental doublet, in which man "is a being such that knowledge will be attained in him of what renders all knowledge possible," but also the cogito/unthought doublet (in which man tries to think his own unthought and thus get free of it) and the retreat-and-return-of-the-origin doublet (in which man is viewed as both the source of history and an object with a history) as well.[49]

Although Foucault is clearly critical of Kant in these closing pages, he also makes two points that are all-too-often overlooked. First, Foucault credits Kant with opening up the possibility of the modern episteme, which marks a great event in the history of European culture, insofar as it reveals the classical thought that preceded it to be a dogmatic meta- physics. Of course, in the end, Kant's critical philosophy sets up its own metaphysics, a metaphysics of the subject that takes transcendental sub- jectivity to be the unquestioned ground of all possible knowledge, but that does not change the point that Foucault considered the deathblow that Kant dealt to the classical episteme to be of vast importance. Foucault makes this even clearer in the essay "A Preface to Transgression," written at around the same time as *The Order of Things*; there, Foucault clear- ly credits Kant with having "opened the way for the advance of critical thought."[50] Although he goes on to criticize Kant for closing off the very opening that he had created, by substituting a metaphysical notion of the subject for the dogmatic metaphysics that he so effectively demolished, he nonetheless indicates Kant's importance inasmuch as Kant's critical phi- losophy inaugurates the modern episteme and, in so doing, reorders our very ways of thinking about things.

Moreover, in this essay, Foucault also notes that Kant gives expression to "an essential experience for our culture ... the experience of finitude and being, of the limit and transgression," an experience that Foucault was himself very interested in examining.[51] This leads me to the second point about Foucault's analysis in *The Order of Things* that we must take care not to overlook: as Foucault emphasizes again and again throughout that text, inasmuch as we are in the modern episteme, and inasmuch as Foucault takes Kant's thought to be paradigmatic for that episteme, we can't help but think within a Kantian framework.[52] Foucault describes our episteme as "the thought that is contemporaneous with us, and with which, willy-nilly, we think."[53] Our episteme is our historical a priori. As historical, it is contingent; thus, he notes, "there is nothing more tentative, nothing more empirical (superficially at least) than the process of estab- lishing an order among things."[54] But as a priori, the episteme delimits the historically specific conditions of possibility for being a thinking subject, conditions that are necessary in the sense that they are binding upon us whether we want them to be or not (thus, "willy-nilly"). We cannot sim- ply reject these conditions without thereby surrendering our ability to be intelligible. As Foucault puts it in his description of archaeology: "What I am attempting to bring to light is the epistemological field, the episteme in which knowledge, envisaged apart from all criteria having reference to its rational value or to its objective forms, grounds its positivity and thereby manifests a history which is not that of its growing perfection, but rather that of its conditions of possibility."[55] When this sentence is read against the background of Foucault's earlier work on Kant's *Anthropology*, Foucault's claim that the aim of archaeology is to interrogate conditions of possibility for knowledge takes on added significance. Although he still hopes at this point for the coming of a new episteme, and indeed hopes that his work might help to bring it about (hopes that he later views as overly romantic and utopian), Foucault also recognizes that, for now, his only choice is to think with the Kantian tools that he has. His articulation of the historical a priori is perhaps the best example of his early attempt to take up Kantian categories in a transformative way; this attempt must be understood against the background of his own reading of Kant's *Anthropology*, which locates the possibility of just this sort of radical historicizing and contextualizing transformation in Kant's own work. In light of these considerations, however, the interpretation of *The Order of Things* as a straightforward rejection of Kant seems overly simplistic.

This way of interpreting the historical a priori provides a response to Béatrice Han's charge, in her thorough and insightful exploration of the notion of the historical a priori in Foucault's archaeology, that Foucault's project ultimately founders on the irresolvable tension between the historical and the transcendental that he unwittingly inherits from Kant. Indeed, as a result of her reading of Foucault's critique of Kant—a reading that assumes that Foucault's work aims at a rejection of Kant—Han finds his continual adoption of Kantian terminology extremely puzzling. Thus, she wonders, "given the extreme ambivalence of the Kantian heritage and the shadow that it throws over modernity, why borrow from Kant the problematization as well as the necessary concepts to formulate the archaeological analysis?"[56] Han acknowledges that "one might suggest that by virtue of Foucault's very inscription within the modernity that he historically criticizes, he must be defined as a post-Kantian," but she goes on to argue that "the hypothesis of the historical necessity of the Kantian inheritance seems insufficient to explain the fact that Foucault recasts the critical question in the very terms that according to him doomed it to fail."[57] First, I would argue that it is too strong to say that Foucault argues that the Kantian critical project is doomed to failure. The reading I have offered here suggests instead that Foucault maintains that Kant's critical project contains within itself the seeds of its own transformation, that it points beyond itself to historicized conceptions of subjectivity and of critique, conceptions that Foucault spent the rest of his life articulating and defending. Second, if Foucault believes, as I have suggested, that rejecting our historical a priori means surrendering intelligibility, then this would seem to be sufficient to explain why Foucault recasts his critical project in Kantian terms. We have no choice, after all, but to start from where we are.

Reading Foucault's early work on Kant in this way also permits us to rethink the infamous heralding of the end of man with which *The Order of Things* concludes. Although Foucault emphasizes that we cannot know what the next episteme will be like or how the transition will come to pass, he nonetheless hopes that posing questions about it "may well open the way to a future thought," and he hopes that this opening will take us beyond "man"; "man," he calculates, is "an invention of recent date. And one perhaps nearing its end."[58] This statement is well known, even infamous; the question is, how should we understand it? Foucault's Kant thesis sheds some light on this question, since the call for the "end of man" at the end of *The Order of Things* echoes Foucault's call for a "true critique" of the "anthropological illusion" in the closing pages of his *thèse complémentaire*.[59] Foucault characterizes the anthropological illusion as the illusion that anthropology is liberated from the "prejudices and inert weights of the a priori."[60] A "true critique" of this illusion involves the recognition that, as I discussed above, anthropology is from the beginning caught up in the tension between empirical and transcendental. The model for this "true critique" is Nietzschean; thus, the closing line of Foucault's thesis on Kant is as follows: "The trajectory of the question: what is man? in the field of philosophy is achieved in the response which challenges it and disarms it: the Übermensch."[61] However, what I want to emphasize here is Foucault's choice of the word "critique." What Foucault is calling for is a critique of critique, which means not only a criticism of Kant's project for the way in which it closes off the very opening for thought that it had created but also a critique *in the Kantian sense of the term*—that is, an interrogation of the limits and conditions of possibility of that which Kant himself took as his own starting point, namely, the transcendental subject. Such a critique is, in a sense, "transcendental" inasmuch as the historical a priori sets the necessary conditions of possibility that are constitutive for being a thinking subject in a particular episteme and, as such, are indirectly the conditions of possibility for all of that subject's experiences. However, such an account is obviously not transcendental in the same sense in which Kant uses that term, inasmuch as our understanding of those "necessary" conditions is grounded empirically in an analysis of the contingent historical conditions that give rise to them and in which they remain embedded. As Paul Veyne argues, although many commentators have failed to recognize the transcendental element of Foucault's project:

All these practices have in common the fact that they are both empirical and transcendental: empirical and thus always surpassable, transcendental and thus constitutive as long as they are not effaced (and only the devil knows with what force these 'discourses' then impose themselves, since they are the conditions of possibility of all action). Foucault did not object to being made to say that the transcendental was historical.[62]

The end of man thus amounts to the revelation that human subjects are always constituted by and embedded in contingently evolved (and thus transformable) linguistic, historical, and cultural conditions. As Foucault himself put the point in a 1978 interview: "Men are perpetually engaged in a process that, in constituting objects, at the same time displaces man, deforms, transforms, and transfigures him as subject. In speaking of the death of man [in *The Order of Things*], in a confused, simplifying way, that is what I meant to say."[63]

As such, the call for the end of man is not a rejection of the concept of the subject per se, if by that we mean the notion of consciousness or the "I think." Instead, it is a call for a critical interrogation and transformation of the particular notion of transcendental subjectivity first formulated by Kant and later taken up by phenomenology. The paradoxes and instabilities to which the modern age of man gives rise emerge only if man is taken to be both a finite object and a transcendental subject that serves as the condition of possibility of all experience. Thus, the claim that Foucault argues for the death of the subject appears plausible only if we conflate this transcendental conception of subjectivity with the concept of subjectivity itself. Not surprisingly, just such a conflation is evident in many criticisms of Foucault's account of subjectivity. Consider, for example, Linda Alcoff's influential essay on feminism and Foucault. Alcoff cites the following passage from an interview with Foucault conducted in the middle of the 1970s:

One has to dispense with the constituent subject, to get rid of the subject itself, that's to say, to arrive at an analysis which can account for the constitution of the subject within a historical framework. And this is what I would call genealogy, that is, a form of history which can account for the constitution of knowledges, discourses, domains of objects, etc., without having to make reference to a subject which is either transcendental in relation to the field of events or runs in its empty sameness throughout the course of history.[64]

As Alcoff reads this passage, Foucault is arguing that "we need to eliminate and not merely situate the subject"; thus, this passage shows that, for Foucault, "subjectivity is causally inefficacious, historically constructed, even a kind of epiphenomenon of power/knowledge."[65] In short, she interprets this passage as evidence that Foucault rejects the concept of subjectivity.

Alcoff's reading is certainly understandable given Foucault's claim that we have to "get rid of the subject itself." However, if we look more closely at the context for this remark, we can see that her interpretation does not tell the whole story. First, Foucault says that what he wants to get rid of is the "constituent subject," which is to say the transcendental subject, the subject understood as constitutive of the very possibility of its experience. And although he goes on to say that this involves getting rid of "the subject itself," the explicitly stated purpose of doing so is to "arrive at an analysis which can account for the constitution of the subject within a historical framework." In other words, Foucault does not aim to eliminate the concept of subjectivity altogether; instead, he rejects the conception of the subject as constituent in favor of a conception of subjectivity as constituted in and through its historical, cultural, and social particularity. Indeed, one might interpret this passage as making the rather innocuous claim that one does not need to conceive of the subject in terms of strong Kantian notions of transcendental subjectivity in order to be able to conceive of the subject as a thinking being. Moreover, as I argued above, Foucault argues that Kant's own writings on anthropology point beyond this transcendental conception and pave the way for the fully historicized conception of the subject that Foucault later develops.

On this interpretation, Foucault's call for the end of man is perfectly consistent with the project of reconceptualizing subjectivity carried out in Foucault's later work. Foucault's critique of critique, his interrogation of the conditions of possibility of subjectivity itself, leads him to explore first the modes by which the subject is constituted via discourse (archaeology) and social practices (genealogy) and later the subject's modes of self-constitution through practices or technologies of the self (ethics). Although the question of whether Foucault's account of the self is satisfactory remains open, this shift from genealogy to ethics should be seen as a shift in emphasis and perspective, not as a radical break or a contradiction. The subject, as Foucault conceives it, is constituted by forces that can be analyzed empirically in the sense that the discursive and sociocultural conditions of possibility for subjectivity in a given historically specific location can be uncovered through an analysis of power/knowledge regimes. But the subject has always to take up those conditions, and it is in the taking up of them that they can (potentially) be transformed. An episteme, a set of rules for discourse formations, or a power/knowledge regime sets the limits within which I can think, deliberate about ends, and act, but it does not prescribe the specific content of any particular thought or of any particular action (except perhaps in the most extreme cases of domination).[66] The subject takes up these conditions and in and through that taking up constitutes itself as a subject through what Foucault later comes to call "technologies of the self" or "practices of the self." I discuss Foucault's account of these technologies in more detail in chapter 3; for now, my point is that there is no conceptual reason why his archaeological and genealogical insights cannot be integrated with those of his ethics. The charge that these two aspects of Foucault's work contradict each other typically rests on the claim that the notion of practices of the self relies on the very concept of subjectivity eliminated in Foucault's early work.[67] If my interpretation is plausible and Foucault's early work does not eliminate the concept of subjectivity per se, then this claim can only be made good if his notion of practices of the self can be shown to rely upon the particular conception of transcendental subjectivity that he critically interrogates in his earlier work. However, as I will argue in chapter 3, although Foucault does rely in his late work on notions of subjectivity and autonomy, he radically reformulates these concepts; thus, they are not the same as the strictly Kantian and phenomenological notions that are taken up in and transformed by his early work.

This line of interpretation suggests that Foucault's critique of critique is an immanent rather than a total critique of modernity. If this is the case, then Habermas's charge that Foucault "follows Heidegger and Derrida in the abstract negation of the self-referential subject, inasmuch as, put briefly, he declares 'man' to be nonexistent," can be seen to miss the mark.[68] To say that Foucault offers an abstract negation of the self-referential subject is to suggest that he rejects the Kantian subject *tout court* while remaining unwittingly caught in the very same aporias and paradoxes that he himself had diagnosed as endemic to Kantian thought in particular and to the modern era in general. I would argue that instead of abstractly negating the self-referential subject, Foucault interrogates its conditions of possibility. That interrogation is designed to show the historical and cultural specificity and, thus, contingency of this conception of subjectivity, which in turn makes possible new modes of subjectification. In carrying out this interrogation, Foucault does not reject the Kantian critical framework; instead, he takes it up in a radically transformative way. As he puts it in "What Is Enlightenment?":

Criticism indeed consists of analyzing and reflecting upon limits. But if the Kantian question was that of knowing what limits knowledge must renounce exceeding, it seems to me that the critical question today has to be turned back into a positive one: In what is given to us as universal, necessary, obligatory, what place is occupied by whatever is singular, contingent, and the product of arbitrary constraints? The point, in brief, is to transform the critique conducted in the form of necessary limitation into a practical critique that takes the form of a possible crossing-over.[69]

Moreover, as I argued above, Foucault finds inspiration for this transformative project in Kant's own work, specifically, in the *Anthropology*, which, on Foucault's reading, contains the seeds for just such a radical transformation of the Kantian critical project.

Foucault's critical transformation of Kant—a transformation based in the recognition that Kant set the terms of the debate within which philosophy still moves and grounded in Foucault's early reading of Kant's *Anthropology*—informs the whole of Foucault's oeuvre. The following passage from "What Is Enlightenment?" offers an excellent characterization of the guiding impulse of Foucault's work as a whole:

> We must try to proceed with the analysis of ourselves as beings who are historically determined, to a certain extent, by the Enlightenment. Such an analysis implies a series of historical inquiries that are as precise as possible; and these inquires will not be oriented retrospectively toward the "essential kernel of rationality" that can be found in the Enlightenment, which would have to be preserved in any event; they will be oriented toward the "contemporary limits of the necessary," that is, toward what is not or is no longer indispensable for the constitution of ourselves as autonomous subjects.[70]

In other words, Foucault's works offer historically specific analyses of the present—of our experience of madness, health, punishment, sexuality, and so on. These histories of the present are designed to lay out the contingent conditions of possibility of our modern selves; pointing out the contingency of these conditions, moreover, harmonizes with the practical aim of enabling us to transform ourselves. For Kant, the courage to know that was characteristic of the Enlightenment was, as Schmidt and Wartenberg put the point, "ultimately the courage to recognize the limits of our consciousness."[71] For Foucault, the courage to know is ultimately the courage to recognize the contingency of those limits and to begin to think beyond them.

The Impurity of Reason and the Possibility of Critique

The interpretation of Foucault's relationship to Kant that I have defended thus far, if it is convincing, offers a response to Habermas's criticism of Foucault discussed above. Contra Habermas, Foucault does not offer two contradictory readings of Kant; his early work is misunderstood if we interpret it as a straightforward rejection or abstract negation of Kant's Enlightenment project. The early work is better understood as a critique of critique, an interrogation of the conditions of possibility of that which Kant took as his starting point, namely, the transcendental subject. If this is how we interpret Foucault's early work, then Habermas is also wrong to suggest that Foucault's relationship to Kant points to a fundamental contradiction in Foucault's own thought. Instead, I would argue precisely the opposite: Foucault's relationship to Kant suggests a way of viewing Foucault's work as a continuous whole. One might even suggest that Foucault spent his entire career reworking Kant's famous four questions, historicizing and contextualizing them as he went.[72] "What can I know?" becomes, in Foucault's archaeologies, "how have discursive structures positioned me as a speaking and knowing subject?" "What ought I do?" becomes, in Foucault's genealogies, "how have norms functioned insidiously to position me as a normalized, disciplined individual?" "What may I hope?" becomes, in his late work, "how can I attempt to turn myself into an ethical subject and my life into a work of art via practices and techniques of the self?" And, as with Kant, it is the fourth and final question—"what is man?" which we might recast in Foucaultian terms as "what has human subjectivity been and what might it become?"—that sums up the first three and provides the guiding thread that runs throughout Foucault's work as a whole.

However, these general similarities between Foucault's and Kant's projects notwithstanding, one might push Habermas's point by arguing that Foucault's transformation of Kantian critical philosophy is so radical that it might as well be a negation. In other words, what sense can be made of transcendental inquiry that locates the grounds of our subjectivity in historical, social, and cultural contingencies? Why does such a move not void the concept of the transcendental and, in so doing, constitute a negation rather than a continuation of Kantian critical philosophy? In one sense, as I mentioned above, Foucault's move to this historical a priori does void Kant's conception of the transcendental, inasmuch as Kant's use of this term is exclusively tied to nonempirical reflection on the limits and conditions of possibility for experience, whereas Foucault's account of the conditions of possibility for subjectivity is decidedly empirical and historical. However, I have also argued that Foucault arrives at this account by a distinctively Kantian move, namely, by asking after the limits and conditions of possibility of subjectivity itself, which, in turn, serve as the condition of possibility for subjective experience.

By making such a move, Foucault no doubt radicalizes the Kantian approach to critique by presenting the subject as constituted by historical, social, and cultural conditions. As I have argued above, given the development of Foucault's thought, I think that this move is best understood as a transformation of, rather than a negation of, Kantian critical philosophy. Moreover, and this is the important point for my argument, on this point about the embeddedness of the subject in historical, social, and cultural conditions, Habermas and Foucault are actually largely in agreement. I will explore this issue in Habermas's work in more detail in chapter 6. For now, let me simply note that, as Thomas McCarthy has convincingly argued, both Foucault and Habermas accept what McCarthy calls "the impurity of reason": "its embeddedness in culture and society, its entanglement with power and interest, the historical variability of its categories and criteria, the embodied, sensuous and practically engaged character of its bearers."[73] Furthermore, as McCarthy claims, both thinkers "call for a transformation cum radicalization of the Kantian approach to critique."[74] Moreover, as McCarthy points out, for both Foucault and Habermas, this "desublimation of reason goes hand in hand with the decentering of the rational subject."[75] Thus, if historicizing and contextualizing Kant's transcendental subject makes Foucault guilty of negating rather than transforming (or negating by radically transforming) Kant's critical project, then Habermas would seem to be equally guilty. At the end of the day, what I am most concerned with is showing that Foucault and Habermas are both engaged in a radicalization from within of the Kantian critical project; it is this basic similarity that Habermas seems unwilling to recognize when he interprets Foucault's early position on Kant as straightforwardly rejectionist and, on the basis of this reading, claims to uncover a deep contradiction between this reading of Kant and Foucault's late embrace of the Kantian project of Enlightenment.

To be sure, Habermas's attempt to formulate a universal pragmatics that rationally reconstructs the counterfactual idealizations that all competent speakers must presuppose when they engage in discourse—the ideal speech situation—indicates that his willingness to historicize and contextualize the Kantian transcendental subject only goes so far. In the end, though, even more pragmatic and contextualist Habermasians such as McCarthy are unwilling to recognize the depth of the similarity between Habermas's and Foucault's critical projects. McCarthy characterizes the key difference between Foucault and Habermas with respect to their accounts of subjectivity as follows:

> While both approaches seek to get beyond the subject-centeredness of modern Western thought, Foucault understands this as the "end of man"

and of the retinue of humanist conceptions following upon it, whereas [Habermas] attempt[s] to reconstruct notions of subjectivity and autonomy that are consistent with both the social dimensions of individual identity and the situated character of social action.[76]

However, as I argued above, Foucault's talk of the end of man is best understood as the call for a critique of critique and thus as the revelation that human subjects are always embedded in contingently emergent (and thus transformable) linguistic, historical, and cultural conditions. As such, the end of man is not at all incompatible with the project of reconstructing subjectivity and autonomy. As a matter of fact, this is precisely the project with which Foucault concerned himself in his late account of "practices of the self," which are defined as "those intentional and voluntary actions by which men not only set themselves rules of conduct, but also seek to transform themselves, to change themselves in their singular being, and to make their life into an *oeuvre* that carries certain aesthetic values and meets certain stylistic criteria."[77] Now, obviously, there are crucial differences between Habermas's intersubjective and communicative account of subjectivity and autonomy and Foucault's aestheticized account. However, my point is that the differences between Habermas's and Foucault's projects have been seriously overstated, with Habermas cast as the pro-Enlightenment heir to the Kantian critical tradition and Foucault cast as the anti-Enlightenment, antimodern, anti-Kantian. To the extent that the Foucault-Habermas debate has been presented in this way, the possibilities for articulating a middle ground between Foucault's and Habermas's critical projects have been obscured.

Even if we grant this response to the reformulated version of Habermas's charge, it might nonetheless seem that this reading of Foucault has raised more questions than it has answered. Assuming that Foucault's aim is an interrogation of the conditions of possibility of subjectivity, how is such a project even possible? From what perspective can he claim to have access to these conditions? Does not the claim that he can have access to them require Foucault to jump over his own shadow? Ex hypothesi, would not Foucault himself, qua individual who has been conditioned by the current power/knowledge regime, necessarily be influenced (perhaps even determined) by these conditions to such a degree as to make critical reflection upon them impossible? Where exactly does the Foucaultian archaeologist or genealogist stand? If he purports to stand outside of his own episteme, then he seems to contradict his claim that the episteme sets the necessary conditions of possibility for being a subject in a particular time and place. If, on the contrary, he admits to standing inside his episteme, then he no longer seems able to achieve the kind of critical distance that make reflection on one's own episteme possible, thus his claims about it and how it sets conditions of possibility for subjectivity are called into question.

Foucault himself vacillated on this issue over the course of his career. In his early work, he seems to have assumed that it was possible for the archaeologist to stand outside of her own episteme and reflect on it—whence his characterization of himself as a happy positivist. However, by the time he wrote "What Is Enlightenment?" he offered a different response:

> It is true that we have to give up hope of ever acceding to a point of view that could give us access to any complete and definitive knowledge of what may constitute our historical limits. And from this point of view, the theoretical and practical experience we have of our limits, and of the possibility of moving beyond them, is always limited and determined; thus, we are always in the position of beginning again.[78]

In other words, Foucault now recognizes that the genealogist stands within the power/knowledge regime that she analyzes; thus, Foucault himself and, by extension, his thought are conditioned by the very conditions of possibility for subjectivity that he is trying to elucidate. Whereas this way of thinking saves Foucault from the apparent contradiction involved in assuming that it was possible to step outside of one's own episteme, it does so at the risk of undermining the critical force of Foucault's interrogations. However, this difficulty need not be intractable. Perhaps it is the case that epistemes or power/knowledge regimes are more open and supple than Foucault's rhetoric (particularly with respect to the former) tended to suggest. If this is the case, then it is a mistake to think that the only available options are being either wholly inside or wholly outside the episteme in question. Perhaps epistemes or power/knowledge regimes even contain within themselves resources that enable their own critique and transformation, which once again suggests that they are not completely closed inasmuch as they point beyond themselves.[79] Foucault's later work makes this point explicit, but it is already implicit in his early work. Indeed, Foucault's interpretation of Kant rests on precisely this point: the Kantian episteme, though it sets the conditions of possibility for subjectivity in the modern era, provides resources for its own transformation, in the form of the historical and empirical conditions that Foucault finds at the heart of the critical philosophy and its core notion, the transcendental subject. Thus, taking up a critical perspective on this episteme is possible, though that critique is necessarily grounded in that episteme; as a result, critique, for Foucault, is of necessity historically, socially, and culturally specific, and pragmatic rather than universal and ahistorical.

I have endeavored to establish three interrelated points: First, Foucault does not offer two radically different and incompatible interpretations of Kant; his early work is misunderstood if it is interpreted as a straightforward rejection of Kantian thought. Instead, I have argued that Foucault's relationship to Kant is remarkably consistent throughout his life; from his earliest work on Kant up to and including his late essays on the Kantian version of the Enlightenment project, Foucault is engaged in a continuation-through-transformation of Kantian critical thought. Second, clarifying his stance vis-à-vis Kant reveals a fundamental continuity in Foucault's philosophical project as a whole: as Foucault himself claimed, the subject is the general theme of his research. There is no inconsistency between his early call for the end of man—which is indicative not of a rejection of subjectivity *tout court* but of an interrogation of its conditions of possibility—and his late reconceptualization of subjectivity and autonomy in his account of practices of the self. Thus, Foucault's feminist and Habermasian critics have been too quick to dismiss his work on the grounds that it participates in or celebrates the death of the subject. Third, and finally, if the previous two points are convincing, then Foucault can no longer be positioned as the counter-Enlightenment foil to Habermas's Enlightenment hero, or vice versa, depending on your views on "postmodernism." Foucault and Habermas no doubt offer two different ways of completing the project of the Enlightenment, two alternative continuations-through-transformation of the Kantian critical project, but there is much more common ground between their philosophical projects than has been recognized up to now by either side of the Foucault-Habermas debate.[80]

However, in order to move this debate forward, particularly with respect to the relationships between power, autonomy, and the self, it is not enough to establish that Foucault does not argue for the death of the subject, nor is it enough to show that, like Habermas, he is engaged in transforming the Kantian critical project from within. We will also have to examine closely, as I do in the next chapter, how Foucault's work on technologies of the self reformulates the notions of subjectivity and autonomy and how these reformulated notions relate to his extremely important and influential analyses of power and subjection.

3

The Impurity of Practical Reason

POWER AND AUTONOMY IN FOUCAULT

IN A set of lectures delivered at Dartmouth College in 1980, titled "About the Beginning of the Hermeneutics of the Self," Foucault characterizes his research as a "genealogy of the modern subject."[1] Such a genealogy provides a way out of "the philosophy of the subject," a philosophical project that "sets as its task *par excellence* the foundation of all knowledge and the principle of all signification as stemming from the meaningful subject."[2] Foucault's principal targets here are Husserlian phenomenology—which he mentions explicitly in the lecture—and Sartrean existentialism—which, although not mentioned by name, is clearly on Foucault's mind when he notes that the appeal of the philosophy of the subject was enhanced by the political climate of the twentieth century.[3] In the twentieth century, the philosophy of the subject increasingly came under attack from two very different directions: analytic epistemology and structuralism. As Foucault notes with characteristic wit:

> These were not the directions I took. Let me announce once and for all that I am not a structuralist, and I confess with the appropriate chagrin that I am not an analytic philosopher—nobody is perfect. I have tried to explore another direction. I have tried to get out of the philosophy of the subject through a genealogy of the subject, by studying the constitution of

the subject across history which has led us up to the modern concept of the self.[4]

Note that Foucault does not suggest the eradication of the concept of subjectivity, nor does he claim that the subject is a fiction or an illusion. Instead, he proposes a historical investigation of the ways in which the subject has been constituted. Thus, his complaint against the philosophy of the subject is not that it holds on to the concept of subjectivity, but that it gives the subject a foundational and constitutive role vis-à-vis knowledge and meaning. Therefore, as I argued in the previous chapter, his critique is directed not at the concept of subjectivity per se, but at a particular conception of it, namely, the transcendental-phenomenological subject.

Foucault characterizes this genealogy of the subject as "another kind of critical philosophy ... a critical philosophy that seeks the conditions and the indefinite possibility of transforming the subject, of transforming ourselves."[5] Foucault distinguishes two components of this critical-genealogical project: technologies (or techniques) of domination and technologies (or techniques) of the self. The former are "techniques which permit one to determine the conduct of individuals, to impose certain wills on them, and to submit them to certain ends or objectives," whereas the latter are "techniques which permit individuals to effect, by their own means, a certain number of operations on their own bodies, on their own souls, on their own thoughts, on their own conduct, and this in a manner so as to transform themselves, modify themselves, and to attain a certain state of perfection, of happiness, of purity, of supernatural power, and so on."[6] Foucault argues that a critical genealogy of the modern subject must take into account both of these technologies and their interrelation and suggests that "the contact point, where the [way] individuals are driven by others is tied to the way they conduct themselves, is what we can call, I think, government."[7] Whereas he admits that his earlier work focused too narrowly on technologies of domination, he indicates that he intends in his later work to highlight technologies of the self and governmentality.[8]

In this discussion, Foucault seems to presuppose the possibility of autonomy in at least two senses of that term. First, he presupposes that individuals are capable of taking up a critical perspective on the technologies of domination and the self that are currently in use. Second, he presupposes that individuals have the capacity for deliberate transformation of these technologies. In light of Foucault's earlier work on discourse and power, however, this presupposition of autonomy has struck many of Foucault's Habermasian and feminist critics as problematic.[9] These critics maintain that Foucault's archaeological and genealogical works undermine the ideal of autonomy, by showing that, as Fraser has put it, "the conception of freedom as autonomy is a formula for domination *tout court*."[10] McCarthy pushes this point further, arguing that this undermining of the ideal of autonomy poses problems not only at the level of Foucault's description of social practices but also at the metalevel of his genealogical methodology: "If the self-reflecting subject is nothing but the effect of power relations under the pressure of observation, judgment, control, and discipline, how are we to understand the reflection that takes the form of genealogy?" [11] McCarthy acknowledges that Foucault's late work views individuals as capable of reflecting critically on the cultural and institutional systems that organize their practices and, within limits, transforming these systems. As such, his late work "corrects the holistic bias we found in his work of the 1970s"; however, McCarthy continues, "the question now is whether he hasn't gone too far in the opposite direction and replaced it with an individualistic bias."[12] The implication is that Foucault cannot have it both ways: if his analyses of power and subjection are compelling, then autonomy is illusory (and genealogy itself is impossible); if the self is autonomous in the ways Foucault's late work suggests, then his earlier analyses of power and subjection must be wrong.

McCarthy places Foucault in this double bind in part because he misconstrues the relationship between power and subjectivity in Foucault. He assumes that Foucault's middle-period works argue that the subject is *merely* or *nothing more than* an effect of power.[13] If this were true, then the presupposition of an autonomous subject in his late work would indeed be contradictory to that project; a subject that is merely or nothing more than an effect of power would obviously be incapable of reflecting critically on relations of power and acting deliberately so as to transform them. However, as I have argued elsewhere, critics who interpret Foucault's claim that the subject is an effect of power in such strong terms have overreacted to what he actually did say.[14] In what follows, I offer a more faithful and fruitful reading of Foucault's analyses of power and subjection. Although it is no doubt true that some ways of conceiving of autonomy would contradict Foucault's analysis of power and subjection, I argue that the conception of autonomy presented in his late work does not do so. The main reason for this is that Foucault conceives of autonomy—both in the sense of the capacity for critical reflection and in the sense of the capacity for deliberate self-transformation—as always bound up with power. The result may be a somewhat less robust and more ambivalent conception of autonomy than some of Foucault's critics would prefer, but it is compatible with his analyses of power and subjection.

In order to make this case, I begin by reviewing Foucault's analyses of power and subjection. Next, I focus on the concept of governmentality, which serves as a theoretical bridge between Foucault's analysis of power and his later work on the self. When I turn to the later work, my aim is to reconstruct the implicit conception of autonomy in Foucault's late work and argue, contra his feminist and Habermasian critics, that this conception is not only compatible with but also extends in interesting and important ways his analyses of power and subjection. However, this does not mean that Foucault's conception of autonomy and the self is fully satisfactory. In the end, I argue that what is missing from Foucault's account is an appreciation for the role played by nonstrategic relations with others in the constitution of autonomous selves. Although it is common to read Foucault as denying the very possibility of reciprocity, I argue that this is not the case. Nevertheless, this idea is very underdeveloped in Foucault's work; thus, in order to develop a fully satisfactory account of power, autonomy, and the self, we will have to go beyond Foucault.

Technologies of Domination

Fraser, in her influential article on Foucault's conception of power, accuses Foucault of "call[ing] too many different sorts of things power and simply leav[ing] it at that."[15] It is undoubtedly true that Foucault does not distinguish in a careful or consistent manner between power and such related notions as domination, force, and violence. Indeed, he admits as much in a late interview, when he says that "all these concepts have been ill defined, so that one hardly knows what one is talking about. I am not even sure if I made myself clear, or used the right words, when I first became interested in the problem of power."[16] Foucault's tendency to be imprecise with his terminology poses some problems for the commentator. For example, in many of his discussions of power, including the Dartmouth lectures, Foucault uses the terms "power" and "domination" interchangeably.[17] However, in one of his late interviews, he takes care to distinguish between power and domination, using the term "power" to refer to unstable, reversible, microlevel force relations and "domination" to refer to broader, systemic, macrolevel asymmetries of power.[18] When Foucault speaks of "technologies of domination," he seems to be understanding "domination" in the wider sense of the term, the sense in which it is interchangeable with "power." Thus, for now, I will follow Foucault in this usage.[19]

The best way to approach Foucault's notion of technologies of domination, then, is through his conception of power. The first thing to note

about this conception is that Foucault understands power not as a substance, but as a relation. In his 1975–1976 lecture course, *Society Must Be
Defended*, Foucault credits the eighteenth-century French historian Henri
Comte de Boulainvilliers with this insight. He claims that Boulainvilliers
"defined the principle of what might be called the relational character of
power: power is not something that can be possessed, and it is not a form
of might; power is never anything more than a relationship that can, and
must, be studied only by looking at the interplay between the terms of
that relationship."[20] Like Arendt, then, Foucault maintains that "[power] is
something that is exercised and that it exists only in action."[21]

So power is a relation, but what kind of relation is it? Initially, one
might think of power as a relation of repression in which one individual
or group of individuals thwarts or blocks the desires and aims of another
individual or group of individuals. Foucault, by contrast, argues that "the
widespread notion of repression cannot provide an adequate description
of the mechanisms and effects of power, cannot define them."[22] Foucault
makes this case in detail in volume 1 of *The History of Sexuality*, where he
argues that the extraordinary proliferation of discourses concerning sexuality during the nineteenth and twentieth centuries reveals the falsity of
the hypothesis that sexuality in contemporary Western societies is simply
or straightforwardly repressed. And yet it seems obvious that power and
sexuality are intricately intertwined in such societies, so it must be the
case that with respect to sexuality, power cannot be explained solely or
even primarily in terms of repression. Foucault views sexuality as a privileged example, "since power seemed in this instance, more than anywhere
else, to function as prohibition";[23] thus, the debunking of the repressive
hypothesis with respect to sexuality is enough to compel us to search for
new ways of analyzing power that do not understand it as a relation of
repression. Power, for Foucault, is a relation of production; as he puts it,
"we must cease once and for all to describe the effects of power in negative
terms: it 'excludes,' it 'represses,' it 'censors,' it 'abstracts,' it 'masks.' In fact,
power produces; it produces reality; it produces domains of objects and
rituals of truth."[24] Foucault's critique of the repressive hypothesis should
not, however, be taken to mean that he thinks that power never functions
repressively; he acknowledges that it often does so. He insists, however,
that repression is not the sole or even the primary form that relations of
power take.[25]

Rather than analyzing power in terms of repression, Foucault conceives
of it as a strategic relation; hence, his account might most appropriately
be referred to as the strategic model of power.[26] When Foucault defines
power in terms of strategic relations, he seems to have at least two points

in mind: first, that power relations involve a confrontation or struggle be-tween opposing forces; second, that there is an instrumentalist logic to these confrontations or struggles, such that each party to the struggle is concerned with getting the other to do what he/she wants. The strate-gic nature of power is evident in Foucault's definition of "technologies of domination"; as I noted above, technologies of domination "permit one to determine the conduct of individuals, to impose certain wills on them, and to submit them to certain ends or objectives." This emphasis on strat-egy, force, and struggle is also evident in the definition of "power relations" that Foucault offers in volume 1 of *The History of Sexuality*:

> Power must be understood in the first instance as the multiplicity of force relations immanent in the sphere in which they operate and which con-stitute their own organization; as the process which, through ceaseless struggles and confrontations, transforms, strengthens, or reverses them; as the support which these force relations find in one another, thus forming a chain or a system, or on the contrary, the disjunctions or contradictions which isolate them from one another; and lastly, as the strategies in which they take effect, whose general design or institutional crystallization is em-bodied in the state apparatus, in the formulation of the law, in the various social hegemonies.[27]

Despite the other shifts in emphasis and approach between the middle and the late Foucault, the definition of power in terms of strategic rela-tions remains constant. For instance, in an interview conducted in Janu-ary 1984, just a few months before his death, Foucault defines "power" as "the strategies by which individuals try to direct and control the conduct of others."[28]

In *Society Must Be Defended*, Foucault articulates his strategic model of power by contrasting it with the juridical model of power, the pre-dominant conception of power in traditional political philosophy. In this conception, power is understood in terms of law, and the main question is whether an exercise of power by the sovereign is legitimate or illegiti-mate. According to Foucault, the juridical conception presents power "as a right which can be possessed in the way one possesses a commodity, and which can therefore be transferred or alienated, either completely or partly, through a juridical act or an act that founds a right—it does not matter which, for the moment—thanks to the surrender of something or thanks to a contract."[29] Foucault rejects the juridical conception of power on conceptual, normative, and historical grounds. His conceptual point is simply that it is a mistake to conceive of power as something that can be possessed, transferred, or withheld. His normative point is that talk of legitimate and illegitimate uses of power by the sovereign obscures the relations of domination that underwrite and make possible sovereignty. As he puts it,

> I have been trying ... to stress the fact of domination in all its brutality and its secrecy, and then to show not only that right is an instrument of that domination—that is self-evident—but also how, to what extent, and in what form right (and when I say right, I am not thinking just of the law, but of all the apparatuses, institutions, and rules that apply it) serves as a vehicle for and implements relations that are not relations of sovereignty, but relations of domination.[30]

Foucault's point here is not the obvious one that sovereign or juridical power can be used in the service of domination; instead, he is making the more radical claim that sovereignty itself—that is to say, the law and the institutions that apply and enforce it—is a mechanism of domination. Traditional political philosophy, with its discourses of right and sovereignty and its adherence to the juridical model of power, obscures this fact.

Foucault's justification for these conceptual and normative claims is connected to his historical argument, which centers on his contention that although the juridical conception may have been an appropriate way of conceiving of power relations in premodern, feudal societies, it is not appropriate for conceptualizing the power relations that are central to modern societies.[31] Foucault argues that "an important phenomenon occurred in the 17th and 18th centuries: the appearance—one should say the invention—of a new mechanism of power which had very specific procedures, completely new instruments, and very different equipment. It was, I believe, absolutely incompatible with relations of sovereignty."[32] Foucault calls this new mechanism "disciplinary power," and he maintains that it "cannot be described or justified in terms of the theory of sovereignty. It is radically heterogeneous and should logically have led to the complete disappearance of the great juridical edifice of the theory of sovereignty."[33] Curiously, however, the emergence of disciplinary power has not had this result; instead, in the modern era, sovereignty has been superimposed on disciplinary power. According to Foucault, modern "juridical systems, no matter whether they were theories or codes, allowed the democratization of sovereignty, and the establishment of a public right articulated with collective sovereignty, at the very time when, to the extent that, and because the democratization of sovereignty was heavily ballasted by the mechanisms of disciplinary coercion."[34]

Simply put, in the modern era, sovereignty and discipline "necessarily go together."[35]

But what exactly is the relation between sovereignty and disciplinary power? In what way is the democratization of sovereignty stabilized and supported by mechanisms of disciplinary coercion? Why, in other words, does sovereignty need disciplinary power in order to function in the modern era? Foucault's answer is that disciplinary power provides the social cohesion necessary for sovereignty to function. As he puts it, "we have then in modern societies, on the one hand, a legislation, a discourse, and an organization of public right articulated around the principle of sovereignty of the social body and the delegation of individual sovereignty to the State; and we also have a tight grid of disciplinary coercions that actually guarantees the cohesion of that social body."[36] Without disciplinary power, Foucault suggests, there would be no cohesive social body that could either delegate its rights to self-governance to a sovereign, as in Hobbesian social contract theory, or engage in the practice of collective will formation and self-governance, as in Rousseauian theories of popular sovereignty. In both cases, Foucault maintains:

> The general juridical form that guaranteed a system of rights that were egalitarian in principle was supported by these tiny, everyday, physical mechanisms, by all those systems of micro-power that are essentially non-egalitarian and asymmetrical that we call the disciplines.... The disciplines provide, at the base, a guarantee of submission of forces and bodies. The real, corporal disciplines constituted the foundation of the formal, juridical liberties.[37]

Despite this synergy of disciplinary power and sovereign power in the modern era, Foucault insists that the juridical conception of power is useless for illuminating disciplinary power inasmuch as it is "utterly incongruous with the new methods of power whose operation is not ensured by right but by technique, not by law but by normalization, not by punishment but by control, methods that are employed on all levels and in forms that go beyond the state and its apparatus."[38] If we are to understand and critique disciplinary power relations, we must break free of the conception of power as sovereignty; we must, as Foucault famously put it, cut off the head of the king.

Of these three criticisms of the juridical conception of power, the historical point is the most decisive, for both the conceptual and normative arguments rest upon it. Foucault's normative criticism makes sense only in conjunction with his historical claim, since the plausibility of his normative critique of the quasi-ideological function played by the juridical conception of power rests on that of the historical story that he tells about the emergence of disciplinary power in the modern era. Foucault's conceptual claim that power should be thought of as a relation rather than a substance rests on his historical story as well, though in a less obvious way. In the abstract, it is hard to imagine how the conceptual dispute over whether power is a substance or a relation could be settled. One might be tempted to settle it by appealing to metaphysical claims about the nature of power; indeed, Foucault has an unfortunate tendency to succumb to this temptation and to make overly broad claims about the nature of power that leave him vulnerable to this reading. However, such metaphysical claims obviously go against his general postmetaphysical commitments. Moreover, an ahistorical, metaphysical claim about the relational nature of power would be difficult to reconcile with Foucault's acknowledgment that the juridical model of power *is* appropriate for theorizing premodern forms of power. If, however, we connect the conceptual claim to the historical one, then it becomes clear that Foucault's point is not metaphysical but methodological: in light of certain historical developments, power is best understood as a relation rather than as a thing; conceiving of it in this way allows us to understand aspects of the modern world that would otherwise remain obscure. Of course there is a substantive component to this methodology in the sense that it rests on certain assumptions about how power in fact functions in modern Western societies—presumably what makes certain methodologies more appropriate than others is that they do a better job of making sense of the way the social world is—but these assumptions are grounded sociohistorically, not metaphysically. As Foucault puts it, in response to the question of whether we need a "theory" of power: "since a theory assumes a prior objectification, it cannot be asserted as a basis for analytical work. But this analytical work cannot proceed without an ongoing conceptualization. And this conceptualization implies critical thought—a constant checking."[39] An appeal to the nature of power would likewise assume a "prior objectification"; instead, Foucault offers an analysis of power that is informed by the social world that it aims to conceptualize.

The following conceptual and methodological propositions provide a useful summary of Foucault's account of modern power. First, power is not restricted to the sovereign or the state but is instead spread throughout the social body. Thus, when we study power, we ought to look for it at the extremities of the social body, at the points where it becomes "capillary."[40] Second, power comes from below, which is to say that it is generated in the myriad mobile force relations that are spread throughout the social body.[41] Thus, when we study power, we should not view it, at least not initially, as "a phenomenon of mass and homogeneous domination"[42] or as a "binary and all-encompassing opposition between ruler and ruled."[43] Foucault does not deny that wide-ranging, systematic relations of domination exist;[44] indeed, the more restricted use of the term "domination" that I discussed above is an attempt to capture such broad, structural asymmetries of power. However, he does insist that these are best understood not as the *causes* but as the *results* of the power relations that are spread throughout the social body; thus, our analysis of power should be ascending rather than descending.[45] Finally, power relations are "intentional and non-subjective."[46] By "intentional," Foucault means that power relations have a point or an aim, that they are directed toward a certain end, by "non-subjective," that they are neither possessed nor controlled by individual subjects.[47] Thus, rather than attempting to discern the intentions of the one who "has" power, an attempt that would lead us "into a labyrinth from which there is no way out," we should investigate "the multiple peripheral bodies, the bodies that are constituted as subjects by power-effects."[48] In other words, rather than viewing power as subjective—as possessed by a subject—we should view the subject as constituted by power.

This last point brings us to Foucault's account of subjection (*assujettissement*). Whereas the juridical conception of power presupposes "an individual who is naturally endowed ... with rights, capabilities, and so on"[49] and then asks under what circumstances it is legitimate for such a subject to be subjugated by the state, Foucault, by contrast, proposes to "begin with the power relationship itself, with the actual or effective relationship of domination, and see how that relationship itself determines the elements to which it is applied. We should not, therefore, be asking subjects how, why, and by what right they can agree to being subjugated, but showing how actual relations of subjugation manufacture subjects."[50] Foucault's aim is to uncover the "immense labor to which the West has submitted generations in order to produce ... men's subjection: their constitution as subjects in both senses of the word."[51]

As I discussed in the introduction to this chapter, many of Foucault's critics have interpreted the claim that subjects are constituted by or are effects of power as implying that autonomy is a mere illusion. Thus, more than any other, it is this claim that raises the specter of a contradiction between Foucault's analysis of power and his later account of technologies of the self. But consider the following passage, which offers one of the earliest and most nuanced of Foucault's discussions of subjection:

It is … , I think, a mistake to think of the individual as a sort of elementary nucleus, a primitive atom or some multiple, inert matter to which power is applied, or which is struck by a power that subordinates or destroys individuals. In actual fact, one of the first effects of power is that it allows bodies, gestures, discourses, and desires to be identified and constituted as something individual. The individual is not, in other words, power's opposite number; the individual is one of power's first effects. The individual is in fact a power-effect, and at the same time, to the extent that he is a power-effect, the individual is a relay: power passes through the individuals it has constituted.[52]

On the juridical conception of power, the individual itself is unsullied by power relations, an "elementary nucleus" or a "primitive atom" on or against which power is applied. Foucault, by contrast, aims to illuminate how power shapes our very individuality. However, he insists that this does not mean that individuals are merely or nothing more than effects of power; he explicitly rejects this idea when he says that individuals are not "inert." On the contrary, the notion that the individual is always the "relay" of power suggests that individuals play an active role in the maintenance and reproduction of power relations. They convey the power relations that make them who they are; their very individuality is a conduit for power relations. Foucault is not, then, arguing for the obliteration of subjectivity and individuality, as many of his critics have assumed. What he is suggesting is nonetheless potentially disturbing: power is (at least in part) what individuates us; thus, our individuality provides the perfect conduit for power relations. But even this disturbing conclusion does not preclude the existence of a self that is in some sense autonomous, provided that selfhood and autonomy are properly understood. Thus, as I shall discuss in more detail below, it need not contradict his account of technologies of the self.

Unfortunately, however, Foucault did not provide an explicit and detailed account of how his work on the self is to be integrated with his analysis of subjection. The closest he comes to giving such an account is in his work on the notion of government, which he describes as the "contact point" between technologies of domination and technologies of the self. Foucault's account of governmentality is a theoretical bridge between his analyses of power and his work on the self. As a result, it provides important clues as to how his analyses of power and subjection and the conception of autonomy implicit in his work on the self might fit together.

Governmentality and Governmentalization

Up to now, I have discussed only one of the two poles of modern power—disciplinary power. The reason for this is that Foucault initially presents disciplinary power as the unique form of power invented by modern societies.[53] Later, however, Foucault identifies two distinct but interrelated poles of modern power: disciplinary power and biopower.[54] Understanding these two poles and how they are related is crucial for understanding Foucault's analysis of governmentality. Disciplinary power emerges first, in the seventeenth and early eighteenth centuries; it operates at the microphysical level and targets individual bodies. Biopower emerges later, in the latter half of the eighteenth century; it targets not individuals but populations or, in the extreme, the species as a whole. Foucault notes that this new technology of power "does not exclude disciplinary technology, but it does dovetail into it, integrate it, modify it to some extent, and above all, use it by sort of infiltrating it, embedding itself in existing disciplinary techniques."[55] The intertwining of these two technologies results in a mode of power characteristic of modern societies, a mode that is simultaneously individualizing and totalizing.

It is precisely this point—that modern power is simultaneously individualizing and totalizing—that Foucault returns to again and again in his studies of governmentality. According to Foucault, the problematic of government, which he sees as a question of "how to be ruled, how strictly, by whom, to what end, by what methods, and so on," seems "to explode in the sixteenth century."[56] The art of government that emerges in the sixteenth century involves the bottom-up and top-down integration of three levels of government: self-government, the science of which is morality; government of family, the science of which is economics; and government of the state, the science of which is politics. These levels are integrated from the bottom up in the idea that only the individual who governs himself well is fit to govern his family and his state and from the top down in the idea that a well-run state fosters well-governed families and individuals. Since both lines of continuity run through the family, the economic sphere, Foucault suggests that "the essential issue in the establishment of the art of government" is the "introduction of economy into political practice."[57] The result is that the state for the first time takes an interest in "economy" and the economic well-being of its citizens.

Thus, this sixteenth-century development sets the stage for modern biopower, which concerns itself with questions of welfare on a grand scale; eighteenth-century developments, such as the emergence of the new science of demographics, enable biopower to flourish. From that point on, "government has as its purpose not the act of government itself, but the welfare of the population, the improvement of its condition, the increase of its wealth, longevity, health, and so on."[58] Disciplinary power plays a crucial role in this new art of government; with its myriad techniques for disciplining individual bodies, disciplinary power makes possible biopower's management of populations. As Foucault puts it, "discipline was never more important or more valorized than at the moment when it became important to manage a population: the managing of a population not only concerns the collective mass of phenomena, the level of its aggregate effects, but it also implies the management of population in its depths and its details."[59] The modern state both individualizes—through the use of disciplinary techniques—and totalizes—through the management and regulation of populations; Foucault refers to the historical process through which such a state emerges as a process of governmentalization.

Foucault's Tanner Lectures trace the individualizing side of this logic back to its roots in the ancient notion of pastoral power and show how this form of power came to be incorporated into modern centralized states. The paradigm of pastoral power is the shepherd who is responsible for caring for and improving the lives of each and every member of his flock; the task of pastoral power is "to constantly ensure, sustain, and improve the lives of each and every one."[60] Foucault suggests that pastoral power has its roots in ancient Hebraic texts; much later, Christianity picks up and radically transforms the themes laid out in these texts. One of these transformations stands out as particularly significant.[61] The Christian pastoral rests on the shepherd having knowledge of each and every one of his sheep, not only of their material needs and of their sins, but also of their souls. In order to gain this knowledge, Christianity takes over and transforms two Hellenistic practices of the self—self-examination and the guidance of conscience. For the Stoics, Epicureans, and Pythagoreans, self-examination is a practice of taking stock of one's daily activities as a way of measuring one's own progress toward self-mastery, and conscience guiding is a practice of receiving advice in particularly trying circumstances. In the Christian pastoral, by contrast, self-examination becomes a technique designed to open the depths of the sheep's soul to his shepherd, and conscience guiding a permanent rather than an occasional state. The result of this transformation, according to Foucault, is "the organization of a link between total obedience, knowledge of oneself, and confession to someone else."[62]

Although Foucault acknowledges that pastoral power as an ecclesiastical institution has been seriously weakened in the modern era, the function of pastoral power has not. In fact, it has "spread and multiplied outside the ecclesiastical institution" in the modern state, which Foucault characterizes as "a modern matrix of individualization, or a new form of pastoral power."[63] With this change in institutional context, pastoral power has once again been transformed. Whereas the objective of Christian pastoral power is to lead the flock to its salvation in the next world, modern pastoral power has more mundane objectives. Its goal is to ensure "health, well-being (that is, sufficient wealth, standard of living), security, protection against accidents" for the citizens.[64] Pastoral power is also transformed by being incorporated into the globalizing and unified power of the state over its citizens; seventeenth- and eighteenth-century theories of the police (*Polizeiwissenschaft*) provide an example of this process. Whereas we might think of the police as "an institution or mechanism functioning within the state," in this discourse, the police is viewed as "a governmental technology peculiar to the state."[65] Like the shepherd, the police is said to concern itself with the welfare of the citizens of the state; religion, health, roads, public safety, and trade all fall within its purview. The object of the police, then, is life itself. "That people survive, live, and even do better than just that: this is what the police has to ensure."[66] In so doing, the police fosters the happiness of the citizens and, thus, the unity and strength of the state. Despite an apparent tension between the aim of improving the lives of individuals and that of fostering the unity of the state, "the aim of the modern art of government" is "to develop those elements constitutive of individuals' lives in such a way that their development also fosters the strength of the state."[67] According to Foucault, this analysis shows that "right from the start, the state is both individualizing and totalitarian."[68] And the lesson to be learned by anyone who wishes to critique or oppose the modern state is that "opposing the individual and his interests to it is just as hazardous as opposing it with the community and its requirements. . . . Liberation can come only from attacking not just one of these two effects but political rationality's very roots."[69]

If Foucault's diagnosis of the individualizing and totalizing logic of modern state power is compelling, then every demand for state recognition of our individuality only invites the state to extend its reach even further into our lives while simultaneously consolidating its strength and power. But if liberation is not to be won through an appeal to the individual and his interests, (how) is it to be won? What would an attack on the very roots of modern political rationality look like? And, given what Foucault says about the individualizing side of the logic, (how) is such an attack even possible? Foucault provides some answers to the first two questions in the essay "The Subject and Power," where he describes contemporary social movements as "struggles against subjection"[70] and distinguishes them from struggles against religious or ethnic domination and economic exploitation. Although he acknowledges that struggles against domination and exploitation have not disappeared, Foucault maintains that in the contemporary world, struggles against subjection have taken center stage. The reason for this is that the incorporation of pastoral power into the modern Western states has resulted in a "government of individualization," a form of power that "applies itself to immediate everyday life which categorizes the individual, marks him by his own individuality, attaches him to his own identity, imposes a law of truth on him which he must recognize and which others have to recognize in him. It is a form of power which makes individuals subjects."[71] Struggles against subjection "are not exactly for or against the 'individual'"; instead, they are struggles against the logic of subjection and the government of individualization itself.[72]

But how are such struggles against subjection themselves possible, especially in light of Foucault's account of the individualizing side of modern power? In other words, if modern power functions through the very shaping of individuality, then how is resistance to such power possible at all, given that this resistance will of necessity be carried out by individuals who have been constituted by power? In the essay "What Is Critique?" Foucault provides the beginnings of an answer to this question and, at the same time, anticipates the direction of his later work on technologies of the self. Although the modern era is one of progressive governmentalization, it is also the age of the symmetrical but inverse notion of critique; despite—indeed because of—the explosion of discourse concerning the art of government in the modern period, there also emerges a discourse that asks how not to be governed, a discourse of critique. As Foucault puts it:

> If governmentalization is really this movement concerned with subjugating individuals in the very reality of a social practice by mechanisms of power that appeal to a truth, I will say that critique is the movement through which the subject gives itself the right to question truth concerning its power effects and to question power about its discourses of truth. Critique will be the art of voluntary inservitude, or reflective indocility. The essential function of critique would be that of desubjectification in the game of what one could call, in a word, the politics of truth.[73]

If subjection (*assujettissement*) is one of the principal mechanisms through which modern power operates, then to struggle for liberation will require us "to refuse what we are," to refuse to capitulate to the logic of subjection, to engage in a critical desubjectification.[74]

Does Foucault's call for a critical desubjectification imply a wholesale rejection of the concept of subjectivity? Is he then guilty of embracing the death of the subject after all? The answer to both of these questions, I think, is no. "Desubjectification," for Foucault, does not imply a wholesale rejection of the concept of subjectivity. Indeed, the word that is translated "desubjectification" in the passage quoted above is *désassujettissement*, a more consistent translation of which might be "desubjection."[75] With this notion, Foucault calls instead for breaking the link between subjectivity and subjection, disconnecting "the growth of capabilities" from "the intensification of power relations."[76] In other words, he calls for a radical reconceptualization of individuality and subjectivity. As he puts it, "we have to promote new forms of subjectivity through the refusal of this kind of individuality which has been imposed on us for several centuries."[77] Foucault's work on practices or technologies of the self constitutes his attempt to reconceptualize, not eradicate, subjectivity.[78] As Foucault says in response to an interviewer who asks, "But you have always 'forbidden' people to talk to you about the subject in general?":

> No, I have not "forbidden" them. Perhaps I did not explain myself adequately. What I rejected was the idea of starting out with a theory of the subject—as is done, for example, in phenomenology and existentialism— and, on the basis of this theory, asking how a given form of knowledge was possible.... I had to reject a priori theories of the subject in order to analyze the relationships that may exist between the constitution of the subject ... and games of truth, practices of power, and so on. [79]

In the sixteenth-century discourses that inspired Foucault's notion of governmentality, government "did not refer only to political structures or to the management of states; rather it designated the way in which the conduct of individuals might be directed: the government of children, of souls, of communities, of families, of the sick.... To govern, in this sense, is to structure the possible field of action of others."[80] Governmentality in this broad sense thus provides a way of understanding power—which involves determining the conduct of others—while preserving a space for freedom—which is implicit in the idea of technologies of the self. As Foucault puts it, "those who try to control, determine, and limit the freedom of others are themselves free individuals who have at their disposal certain instruments they can use to govern others. Thus, the basis for all this is freedom, the relationship of the self to itself and the relationship to the other."[81]

Technologies of the Self

Foucault's aim in developing his account of technologies of the self, which consists of detailed explorations of the notions of practices and care of the self in ancient Greek and Greco-Roman ethical texts, is to provide some resources for challenging the government of individualization that holds sway in contemporary Western societies. But we must tread lightly here; Foucault is not suggesting that those engaged in contemporary struggles against subjection should live their lives by or organize their social movements around the precepts of ancient Greek ethics. As Foucault emphasizes in a late interview, "I am not looking for an alternative; you can't find the solution of a problem in the solution of another problem raised at another moment by other people."[82] However, as Veyne explains, Foucault "considered one of [Greek ethics'] elements, namely, the idea of a work of the self on the self, to be capable of reacquiring a contemporary meaning, in the manner of one of those pagan temple columns that one occasionally sees reutilized in more recent structures."[83] Greek ethics holds a particular appeal to Foucault because, unlike contemporary morality, it is not bound up with normalization. The emphasis in Greek ethics is on living a beautiful, noble, and memorable life; as a result, Greek ethics does not, indeed cannot, serve a normalizing function.[84] As Foucault puts it, "the idea of the *bios* as a material for an aesthetic piece of art is something that fascinates me. The idea also that ethics can be a very strong structure of existence, without any relation with the juridical per se, with an authoritarian system, with a disciplinary structure. All that is very interesting."[85]

Foucault begins his study of ancient ethics by distinguishing between moral codes, or rules for right action, and ethical forms of subjectivation, which concern "the manner in which one ought to form oneself as an ethical subject acting in reference to the prescriptive elements that make up the code."[86] Foucault maintains that every morality (in the broad sense of that term) consists of these two elements, either one of which might take precedence in a particular culture. Whereas moral experience in contemporary Western societies tends to be more juridified or code oriented, moral experience in ancient Greek and Rome tends to be oriented more toward forms of ethical subjectivation or practices of the self. Although the relative importance of moral codes has increased over time, Foucault claims that there is a striking continuity in the content of those codes. He identifies three moral codes related to sexuality common to Greek and Greco-Roman antiquity, the Christian Middle Ages, and modern Western societies: prohibitions against excessive sexual expenditure, extramarital sexual relations, and homosexual acts. Despite the continuity of these moral codes, however, there are significant shifts from antiquity through Christianity up to the present in the forms of ethical subjectivation. Volumes 2 and 3 of *The History of Sexuality* chart these shifts, focusing on the "rich and complex field of historicity in the way the individual is summoned to recognize himself as an ethical subject of sexual conduct."[87]

Foucault identifies four aspects of these forms of ethical subjectivation. The first is the ethical substance, or "the part of ourselves, or of our behavior, which is relevant for ethical judgment."[88] During Greek and Greco-Roman antiquity, the ethical substance is aphrodisia, "the act linked with pleasure and desire";[89] thus, ethical judgment concerns what one does. This aspect of ethics undergoes a significant shift in the Christian era from aphrodisia to desire; ethical judgment comes to focus not on what one does but on what—or whom—one desires. The second aspect is the mode of subjection, or "the way in which the individual establishes his relation to the [moral] rule and recognizes himself as obliged to put it into practice."[90] For the Greeks, the mode of subjection is both aesthetic and political: one is obliged to follow the moral codes regarding sexuality if one wants to live a beautiful life, where living a beautiful life is necessary for those who want to rule over others. During the Hellenistic period, the mode of subjection shifts as the Stoics, for example, appeal to rationality as the source of moral obligation. And in the Christian period, the mode of subjection shifts again, from rationality to divine law. The third aspect is the ascetic practices, or practices of the self "that one performs on oneself, not only in order to bring one's conduct into compliance with a given rule, but to attempt to transform oneself into the ethical subject of one's behavior."[91] For the Greeks, this ascetic practice is bound up with the general goals of self-control and self-mastery. Greco-Roman antiquity introduces specific techniques such as self-examination and conscience guiding that are later taken up in the Christian era and transformed into self-deciphering techniques that strengthen pastoral power. The final aspect is the telos of ethics, or "the kind of being to which we aspire when we behave in a moral way."[92] For Greek and Greco-Roman antiquity, the telos of ethics is self-mastery, though for the Greeks this is associated with mastery of others, whereas for later antiquity it is associated with reciprocity. For Christianity, the telos of ethics is moral purity and immortality.

What does this account of the transformations of forms of ethical subjectivation in the ancient world and the Middle Ages have to do with Foucault's analysis of contemporary power relations? Foucault notes that the emphasis in ancient ethics on creating the self as a work of art makes the ancients' conception of the self very different from our own.[93] Christianity replaces self-creation with a self-renunciation designed to enable one to attain spiritual purity and immortality. Thus, "the problem of ethics as an aesthetics of existence is covered over by the problem of purification. This new Christian self had to be constantly examined because in this self were lodged concupiscence and desires of the flesh. From that moment on, the self was no longer something to be made but something to be renounced and deciphered."[94] After the Enlightenment, despite the relative decline in the influence of Christianity, these themes of self-renunciation and self-deciphering do not disappear; instead, they are incorporated into the expanding juridical and disciplinary apparatus of the human sciences and the modern secular state. As a result, our own practices of the self remain markedly different from ancient aesthetics of existence.

These practices are different but not unrelated. Indeed, Foucault does not think that "the [classical] culture of the self disappeared or was covered up. You find many elements that have simply been integrated, displaced, reutilized in Christianity."[95] For example, Christianity takes up the notion of care of the self and puts it to work in pastoral power, which centers on the care of others. Similarly, as I discussed above, the Christian pastoral adopts techniques of self-examination and conscience guiding from the Stoics, Epicureans, and Pythagoreans, and it transforms these into techniques for deciphering the souls of its flock and ensuring their obedience. Something akin to these self-examination techniques survives in our own confessional practices, for example, in contemporary psychotherapy.[96] These techniques or practices are neither liberatory nor oppressive in themselves; what matters is how they are used, to what ends, and in what sorts of circumstances. Thus, they can be turned against themselves, taken up in a transformative way. Indeed, if, as Foucault argues, there is no outside to power, then resistance has to take the form of taking up existing relations of power and subjection in a transformative way. As Foucault puts this point, "we cannot jump *outside* the situation, and there is no point where you are free from all power relations. But you can always change it."[97] Thus, resistance to the government of individualization has to take the form of transforming the mechanisms of subjection from within, for example, by turning self-examination from a practice of subjection into a practice of self-mastery and freedom. On Foucault's view, the Greeks provide a model for this sort of practice, and the continuity between their techniques for attaining self-mastery and modern techniques of subjection suggests another reason that he turns to Greek ethics for resources theorizing resistance. It is not just that Greek ethics is nonnormalizing; it is also that our own modes of subjection are related, however distantly, to ancient technologies of the self. It is this continuity that makes it possible for us to recover certain elements of ancient practices of the self. Because of this continuity, modern techniques of subjection contain the resources for their own overcoming.

Now, it would seem that in order for individuals to be capable of deliberately transforming practices of subjectivation in more emancipatory or, if you prefer, less normalizing directions, they have to be autonomous in some sense. Minimally, resistance as Foucault understands it seems to require both the capacity to reflect critically on existing technologies of the self and the capacity to transform deliberately such technologies. Indeed, in his late work, Foucault frequently invokes the capacity for critical reflection, in the context of his understanding of thought. For example, he defines "thought" as "freedom in relation to what one does, the motion by which one detaches oneself from it, establishes it as an object, and reflects on it as a problem."[98] Moreover, Foucault also invokes the concept of autonomy in his late work, though how precisely he understands autonomy and how this notion fits with his analysis of power and subjection is not made explicit. For example, in "What Is Enlightenment?" Foucault characterizes his own work as "oriented toward the 'contemporary limits of the necessary', that is, toward what is not or is no longer indispensable for the constitution of ourselves as autonomous subjects."[99] Here, the constitution of ourselves as autonomous subjects is taken as a desideratum; archaeological and genealogical work aims to identify the arbitrary constraints that we falsely take to be necessary to achieve that goal. Foucault goes on to articulate the principle that is "at the heart of the historical consciousness that the Enlightenment has of itself": "the principle of a critique and a permanent creation of ourselves in our autonomy."[100] Autonomy thus plays a double role in this essay: it is both the precondition for and the goal of critique. The permanent critique of ourselves that is characteristic of what Foucault calls the "attitude of modernity" presupposes autonomy in the sense that, following Kant, one must be mature enough to use one's own reason in order to engage in such a critique; but critique also aims toward autonomy in the sense that critique opens up the space for what Foucault calls the "permanent creation of ourselves in our autonomy." It is this latter point that connects Foucault's reflections on autonomy, critique, and the Enlightenment with his ethics. The practices of the self that Foucault uncovered in ancient Greece and Rome were practices of freedom, and this is precisely why Foucault was interested in them.

It is worth noting that many of Foucault's references to autonomy occur in the context of his discussions of Kant, which suggests that Foucault is deliberately invoking the Kantian conception of autonomy while simultaneously transforming it. Indeed, just as it was for Kant's, autonomy is central to Foucault's conception of critique and to his ethics.[101] Of course there are obvious differences between Foucault's and Kant's uses of the notion of autonomy, the most obvious being that, for Kant, autonomy is equivalent to conformity to the categorical imperative, whereas, for Foucault, "the search for a form of morality acceptable to everybody in the sense that everybody should submit to it" is "catastrophic."[102] However, placing too much emphasis on this and other obvious differences might lead us to overlook the peculiarly Kantian flavor of autonomy in Foucault's work and thus to misunderstand Foucault's ethics. Indeed, I contend that Foucault's conception of autonomy should be understood—in much the same way as I interpreted his conception of subjectivity in the previous chapter—as a transformation from within, an inversion of the Kantian conception. Kant defines "autonomy" as "the property the will has of being a law to itself."[103] Central to Kant's understanding of autonomy is the interplay of necessity and freedom. This is evident both in the *First Critique*, in which Kant argues that the idea of freedom is compatible with the causal necessity that governs the phenomenal world, and in the *Groundwork* and the *Second Critique*, in which autonomy is defined in terms of the will's freely binding itself to universal laws. The interplay of necessity and freedom is likewise central to Foucault's conception of autonomy, but Foucault turns this relationship on its head. For Foucault, autonomy does not consist in freely binding oneself to a necessity in the form of the moral law; instead, it consists in freely calling into question that which is presented to us as necessary, thus opening up the space for a possible transgression of those limits that turn out to be both contingent and linked to objectionable forms of constraint. This critique is practical in the sense that it is oriented toward possible action, action that goes beyond the limits of the arbitrary constraints imposed upon us by the power/knowledge regimes that structure our social world.

But there is another, more radical, sense in which this reconceptualization of autonomy is tied to the idea of a practical critique, as it contains an implicit critique of Kant's very notion of pure practical reason. Once autonomy is understood as the calling into question of those limits and constraints that we have previously taken to be necessary, the impurity of practical reason, its embeddedness in contingent, historically specific practices, and its rootedness in relations of power, come to the fore. The question then becomes: "For what excesses of power ... is this reason itself historically responsible?"[104] Foucault, echoing his earlier argument about Kant's pragmatic anthropology, hints that Kant himself opens the door for this move in his own reflections on the Enlightenment, for these reflections are located "at the crossroads of critical reflection and reflection on history."[105] Foucault even goes so far as to suggest that Kant's text represents the first time a philosopher has articulated the connections between his philosophical work and what is going on in his contemporary historical moment. In so doing, Foucault suggests, Kant made possible the kind of historicophilosophical method of inquiry into the historically emergent, contingent conditions of possibility for knowledge and action that Foucault later perfected.[106]

What are the implications of the impurity of practical reason, its embeddedness in contingent, historically and culturally specific relations of power? Does this impurity mean that we should reject reason, even supposing that to be possible? Foucault's Habermasian critics have accused him of drawing precisely this conclusion. For example, although McCarthy acknowledges that Habermas is also committed to the intrinsic impurity of reason, he argues that Foucault and Habermas draw crucially different inferences from this fact:

> While both approaches seek to transform the critique of reason through shifting the level of analysis to social practice, Foucault, like Nietzsche, sees this as leading to a critique that is radical in the etymological sense of that term, one that attacks rationalism at its very roots, whereas critical social theorists, following Hegel and Marx, understand critique rather in the sense of a determinate negation that aims at a more adequate conception of reason.[107]

Foucault, by contrast, denies that his critique of reason is radical in this sense. He considers three possible reactions to the entanglement of reason with power. The first response is to reject reason, but Foucault rejects this possibility out of hand, saying that "nothing would be more sterile."[108] The second option is to investigate the link between rationalization and the growth of domination in modernity; this, according to Foucault, is the approach taken by the Frankfurt School. Foucault expresses sympathy with this approach, but worries that "the word rationalization is dangerous. What we have to do is analyze specific rationalities rather than always invoking the progress of rationalization in general."[109] Foucault favors the third response, which involves examining the specific modes of rationalization and forms of resistance that have taken shape in specific experiences, for example, madness, death, crime, or sexuality. Recognizing the impurity of practical reason, then, does not commit us to rejecting reason altogether; instead, it commits us to an interrogation of specific forms of rationality and the ways in which they are connected to relations of power and modes of subjection.

Accordingly, Foucault casts the difference between himself and Habermas in somewhat different terms. Since Kant and perhaps because of him, the question of Enlightenment has typically been posed as one of knowledge; the crucial question is, "what false idea did knowledge make of itself, and to what excessive use was it found exposed, to what domination consequently was it found tied?"[110] Foucault understands Habermas's conception of Enlightenment in this way. Foucault, by contrast, wants to "envision a different procedure. It could take as an entry into the question of Aufklärung, not the problem of knowledge, but that of power."[111] This does not entail reducing all forms of knowledge or rationality to relations of domination, though it does entail being attentive to the complex relationships between knowledge and power. If we follow this shift, the critical question is no longer that of how to determine, through either a transcendental or a quasi-transcendental argument, the legitimate limits of reason. Instead, the critical question is this:

> How can the inseparability of knowledge and power in the game of multiple interactions and strategies induce at once singularities that fix themselves on the basis of their conditions of acceptability and a field of possibilities, of openings, of indecisions, of reversals, and of eventual dislocations that make them fragile, that make them impermanent, that make of these effects events—nothing more, nothing less than events?[112]

How, in other words, do relations of knowledge and power both structure our experience of ourselves and of the world while providing resources for their own overcoming? Asking this question involves taking what Foucault calls an "inverse path" to the one taken by Kant and post-Kantian critical theorists, though it preserves what Foucault calls the "critical attitude": "if it is necessary to pose the question of knowledge in its relation to domination, it would be first and foremost on the basis of a certain decisive will not to be governed, this decisive will, an attitude at once individual and collective of emerging, as Kant said, from one's immaturity. A question of attitude."[113]

If practical reason is impure, then it follows that autonomy in both of the senses that I delineated above—the capacity for critical reflection or what Foucault calls simply "thought" and the capacity for deliberate self-transformation—is necessarily linked to power relations. Critical reflection, as a function of practical reason itself, is always inflected with power. Thus, we have to give up hope of acceding to a point of view outside of power from which we can critique power. But from this it does not follow that critique is futile, even though it is "always limited and determined; thus, we are always in the position of beginning again."[114] Similarly, deliberate self-transformation is guided by the faculty of practical reason and informed by critique; as such, although Foucault understands this as a practice of freedom, such practices are always connected to relations of power in at least two ways. First of all, power presupposes freedom. As Foucault puts it, "power is exercised only over free subjects, and only insofar as they are free."[115] Moreover, since there is no outside to power, freedom always involves strategically reworking the power relations to which we are subjected. Thus, Foucault speaks of an "agonism" between power and freedom, "of a relationship which is at the same time reciprocal incitation and struggle; less of a face-to-face confrontation which paralyzes both sides than a permanent provocation."[116]

Foucault's reconceptualization of autonomy, in light of its emphasis on the relationships between critique, freedom, and power, does not contradict his analysis of power; instead, it complements and extends it. As a result, however, his conception of autonomy is admittedly less robust and more ambivalent than Kant's and, as we shall see, Habermas's. Foucault understands critique as always internal to power relations, but it is not for this reason doomed to failure, especially if we emphasize the openness and suppleness of power/knowledge regimes, the ways in which they contain the resources for their own transformation. As for freedom, it always operates within the horizon of power relationships. As a result, deliberate self-transformation in Foucault's sense necessarily involves taking up in a transformative way the relations of subjection that have made us who we are.[117]

Resistance, Strategy, and Reciprocity

Although the preceding discussion does show that Foucault's account of autonomy is compatible with his analyses of power and subjection, it nevertheless leaves unanswered the question of what it is that enables us to take up relations of subjection in a transformative way. How can selves who have been constituted by relations of power and subjection take up a self-constituting relation to themselves that is empowering and transformative? How can resistance to prevailing modes of subjection be accomplished in a context of subjection? In other words, as Jean Grimshaw put this point, the crucial question is "when forms of self-discipline or self-surveillance can with any justification be seen as exercises of autonomy or self-creation, or when they should be seen, rather, as forms of discipline to which the self is subjected, and by which autonomy is constrained."[118] For example, Grimshaw wonders, "when should we see a concern for one's body, a programme of monitoring of one's fitness or concern for one's appearance, as an exercise of creative self-mastery rather than as a result of the internalisation of norms of bodily appearance which serve to undermine other norms of autonomy?"[119] Does Foucault offer us the resources for distinguishing disciplinary practices or technologies of the self that reproduce and reinforce existing relations of power from those that resist and transform such relations?

Here we run up against the limits of Foucault's account of the politics of our selves. As I discussed above, Foucault consistently defines power in terms of strategic relations, and he suggests that the exercise of freedom always involves engaging with power in this sense. As a result, he seems committed to a rather narrow and impoverished conception of social interaction, according to which all such interaction is strategic. If this is the case, then, his conception of the self will necessarily overlook the role played by nonstrategic social relations, relations based on communication, reciprocity, and mutual recognition, in the development of autonomy and the self. Indeed, many of Foucault's Habermasian and feminist critics have criticized his account of the self on just this point. For example, McCarthy argues that Foucault's "one-dimensional view of social interaction as strategic interaction displaces autonomy outside of the social network.... Foucault's aesthetic individualism is no more adequate to [the] social dimension of autonomy than was the possessive individualism of early modern political theory."[120] Lois McNay identifies a similar problem with Foucault's account of the self and argues that Foucault's account of resistance to the government of individualization is unsatisfactory for this reason. As she puts it, "without an interactional notion of the self ... the individual cannot distinguish between what constitutes a radical exploration of identity and what is simply an arbitrary stylization of life."[121] Absent some understanding of social interaction in nonstrategic terms, Foucault cannot make sense of how individuals cooperate with one another in collective social and political action to agitate for progressive change, nor can he make sense of how the resulting collective social and political movements generate the conceptual and normative resources on which individuals draw in their own efforts to transform subjection into liberation.

In other words, a broader view of social relations than that offered by Foucault—one that envisions social relations as not just strategic but also as (potentially) communicative and reciprocal—is needed if we are to be able to distinguish capitulation to the logic of subjection from subversive self-transformation.[122] This limitation of Foucault's work provides a motivation for turning to Habermas, whose intersubjective account of subjectivity and autonomy is grounded in his conception of communicative interaction. However, such a turn will only make sense if it is the case that Foucault's work does not preclude the possibility of nonstrategic interaction. After all, if Foucault's conception of power undermines any possible account of nonstrategic social interaction, then the project of integrating his insights into power, autonomy, and the self with those of Habermas will be difficult, if not impossible, to achieve. There is certainly a plausible strong reading of some of Foucault's remarks about power according to which any talk of nonstrategic, reciprocal interactions is strictly ruled out. Undergraduates who are in the grip of this interpretation are particularly adept at rede-scribing any candidate for a nonstrategic interaction in strategic terms (for example, the baby's smile is actually her way of manipulating her mother into giving her more juice). Fortunately, Foucault himself did not seem to hold such a reductive view of social relations. In fact, in several late inter-views and essays, he gestures, albeit tentatively, toward what seems like a normative conception of reciprocity. For example, he distinguishes be-tween friendship and sexual relations by pointing out that "friendship is reciprocal, and sexual relations are not reciprocal: in sexual relations, you can penetrate or you are penetrated."[123] His criticisms of Greek sexual eth-ics appeal implicitly to a normative conception of reciprocity: "The Greek ethics of pleasure is linked to a virile society, to dissymmetry, exclusion of the other, an obsession with penetration, and a kind of threat of being dispossessed of your own energy, and so on. All that is quite disgusting!"[124] And he wonders out loud whether it is possible to develop an ethics of sexual pleasure that is governed by this implicit norm of reciprocity: "Are we able to have an ethics of acts and their pleasures which would be able to take into account the pleasure of the other? Is the pleasure of the other something that can be integrated in our pleasure, without reference to law, to marriage, to I don't know what?"[125]

To be sure, Foucault remains hesitant about embracing such a norma-tive ideal of reciprocity. In a late interview, for example, in response to a question about whether he is willing to endorse the normative notion of consensus offered in the work of Habermas and Arendt, Foucault says: "The farthest I would go is to say that perhaps one must not be for con-sensuality, but one must be against nonconsensuality."[126] Still, comments such as this one indicate that although the ideal of reciprocity is far from sufficiently developed in Foucault's work, his strategic analysis of power is not meant to preclude such a notion. Perhaps this is why Foucault is will-ing to say, "I am interested in what Habermas is doing. I know that he does not agree with what I say—I am a little more in agreement with him."[127]

My overall aim has been to reconstruct the implicit conception of au-tonomy in Foucault's work on technologies of the self and to argue that this conception is not only compatible with but also extends in interesting and important ways his analyses of power and subjection. As I argued with respect to subjectivity in the previous chapter, Kant provides the inspiration for Foucault's reconceptualization of autonomy. Not only does Foucault argue that Kant's writings on the Enlightenment open the door for the historicized version of critique that Foucault practices, his conception of autonomy also inverts the relationship between freedom and necessity that is at the heart of the Kantian conception. Given Foucault's commitment to the impurity of practical reason, his analysis focuses on the connections between autonomy—both in the sense of the capacity for thought or critical reflection and in the sense of the capacity for deliberate self-transformation—and power. However, in order to distinguish between the reinscription of modes of subjection and their transformation, Foucault needs some nonstrategic account of social interaction. Although there are gestures toward such a notion in some of Foucault's late interviews, they are tentative and undeveloped. For a fully developed account of reciprocal, communicative interaction and the role that it plays in the constitution of autonomous selves, we will have to look beyond Foucault to Habermas. Before turning to a consideration of Habermas, however, I will first consider Butler's recent analysis of subjection; as we shall see in the next chapter, although this analysis extends Foucault's account in important and productive ways, it ultimately suffers from a similar lack of an account of the intersubjective dimension of subjectivity.

Dependency, Subordination, and Recognition

BUTLER ON SUBJECTION

"AS A form of power," Judith Butler writes in the opening of her book *The Psychic Life of Power*, "subjection is paradoxical."[1] "Subjection" refers to the ambivalent process whereby one is constituted as a subject in and through the process of being subjected to disciplinary norms. It is one thing to think of power as an external force that dominates us; as painful as it can be to be subjected to power in this sense, there is nothing particularly paradoxical about it. "But if, following Foucault," Butler continues, "we understand power as *forming* the subject as well, as providing the very condition of its existence…. then power is not simply what we oppose but also, in a strong sense, what we depend on for our existence and what we harbor and preserve in the beings that we are."[2] Foucault's analysis of subjection brilliantly captures the ways in which power constitutes forms of identity that both constrain subordinated subjects by compelling them to take up subordinating norms, practices, and so on while simultaneously enabling them to be subjects with the capacity to act. This analysis has proved enormously useful for feminist theorists analyzing the ways in which gender subordination is maintained and reproduced via compelling adherence to disciplinary norms of femininity.[3]

And yet, as Butler argues, Foucault's analysis of subjection is incomplete. Although he says many times that power constitutes the subject, "he does not elaborate on the specific mechanisms of how the subject is formed in submission."[4] Specifically, and here his complicated relationship to psychoanalysis is no doubt to blame, he does not address the issue of the "psychic form that power takes."[5] As Butler shows clearly in her earlier work, the notion of subjection does not deny agency; to the contrary, it presupposes agency, for the disciplinary norms to which we are subject cannot reproduce themselves, they must be cited or performed by individuals.[6] However, this raises the question of why individuals subject themselves to those norms, what motivates them to take up disciplinary norms in the first place. As I suggested in chapter 1, following Brown, Foucault might be thought to gives us Nietzsche's will to power minus the will; Butler's analysis of subjection, by contrast, explores the complicated relationships between will, desire, and power. Drawing on both Foucault and psychoanalysis, Butler's account in *The Psychic Life of Power* expands the notion of subjection by analyzing the ways in which subordinated individuals become passionately attached to, and thus come to desire, their own subordination.

The resulting account of the passionate and stubborn attachment to subjection offers a compelling diagnosis of an otherwise quite puzzling phenomenon, one that has been particularly puzzling to feminist theorists. It is not at all uncommon for those who are subordinated to remain attached to pernicious and oppressive norms, practices, or institutions even after they have been "rationally demystified," to repeat the phrase from Fraser that I quoted in chapter 1.[7] For example, Sandra Bartky, in her recent book, tells the story of a student who complimented her for teaching a controversial class on the moral and political implications of sex roles "without sacrificing [her] femininity."[8] Bartky, who has written incisive and influential feminist critiques of normative femininity,[9] was dismayed, not because the student had misinterpreted her, but because she realized that this student was right. She writes:

So why am I writing polemics against femininity, yet comporting myself in ways that fall more into the "feminine" than the "masculine" slot? Now, on the face of it, my little inconsistencies or even my vanities, are hardly of general interest. But is there perhaps an interesting theoretical problem lurking here somewhere? The feminist critique of many aspects of "normative femininity" is one of the glories of Second Wave feminist theory and I am happy to have made some small contribution to it. The question that may well be lurking behind the contradictions in my own life is this: have feminists produced a theory (here a critique of normative femininity) for which (for reasons not yet articulated) there is no effective practice?[10]

In other words, Bartky wonders, how and why does an attachment to pernicious and subordinating norms—of femininity, for example—persist alongside a rational critique of those very norms in one and the same self? And does this persistence mean, as Bartky suggests, that feminist theorists have produced a theory for which there is no effective practice? What can such persistence tell us about what a feminist practice of resistance (individual and collective) to and transformation of subjection of this sort should look like? What sorts of social and political conditions would make such resistance and transformation possible, let alone effective?

In what follows, I argue that Butler's theory of subjection provides a useful starting point for thinking through these questions. Butler's psychoanalytic extension of Foucault's account of subjection offers a compelling diagnosis of the sort of phenomenon that Bartky describes and thus helps to illuminate the peculiar recalcitrance of certain modes of gender subordination to feminist critique. With respect to the task of clarifying the necessary conditions for an effective feminist practice of individual and collective resistance to subjection, however, Butler's account is more limited in its usefulness. Her account of resistance in *The Psychic Life of Power* is plagued both by familiar problems concerning normative criteria and the motivation for resistance that emerge in new and arguably more intractable forms and by new concerns about her conceptions of dependency, subordination, and recognition. Butler fails to distinguish adequately between dependency and subordination, and she remains ambivalent about the possibility of mutual recognition, at some times implicitly invoking this possibility, at other times, disavowing it. Her account of resistance—specifically, her ability to differentiate critical and subversive reinscriptions of subordinating norms from faithful ones—suffers as a result of this ambivalence.

My overall aim, then, is to assess the strengths and weaknesses of Butler's account of subjection both for diagnosing subjection to normative femininity and for thinking about how it can be effectively resisted and transformed at the individual and collective levels. My first task will be to reconstruct Butler's account of the psychic grounds for subjection. Although her account provides a provocative set of answers to the question of why and how subjects become psychically attached to their own subordination, it also generates some problems. I focus on two such problems: first, the conceptual and normative difficulties that result from her conflation of dependency and subordination, and second, her lack of an account of the role that mutual recognition plays in subjectivation. In several recent essays, Butler has begun to expand her account of the relationship between power and recognition. I argue that Butler's recent work is marked by a fundamental ambivalence about recognition; her critique of subjection implicitly depends on the possibility of mutual recognition, a possibility that she has explicitly denied and disavowed. I conclude that an account of mutual recognition, along the lines of the account offered by Jessica Benjamin, is needed if Butler is to bridge the gap between her theoretical critique of subjection and the political practices of resistance to and transformation of subjection.

Subjection

The general question that motivates Butler's account of subjection is this: How does a "power that at first appears external, pressed upon the subject, pressing the subject into subordination, assume[] a psychic form that constitutes the subject's self-identity"?[11] The initial answer to this question is that the subordinated subject is formed by power turning back on itself; as Butler puts it, "the subject is the effect of power in recoil."[12] This means that the very identity of the subordinated subject is dependent upon the relations of power that shape it. The dismantling of those relations of power, then, threatens the subject's identity and sense of self. Because these relations of power both sustain the subject's identity and subordinate her—and sustain her identity by subordinating her—she develops an attachment to them, despite the damage done by subordination. Faced with a choice between an identity based on subordination and no identity at all, the subordinated subject chooses the former.

This way of understanding subjection brings Butler back to a problem that she has grappled with throughout her work: namely, if subordination is understood as the condition of possibility for the subject, then how are agency and resistance to subordination possible? In an attempt to address this problem, Butler makes a distinction between two uses or modalities of power: on the one hand, power as the condition of possibility for the very existence of the subject; on the other hand, power as it is wielded through the subject's own actions.[13] "As a subject *of* power (where 'of' connotes both 'belonging to' and 'wielding'), the subject eclipses the conditions of its own emergence; it eclipses power with power."[14] This eclipsing of power with power is the site of agency and, thus, resistance to power. However, since this agency is made possible by subjection to power in the first place, it is a "radically conditioned" and inherently ambivalent form of agency.[15] Thus, Butler understands the subject as "*neither* fully determined by power *nor* fully determining of power (but significantly and partially both)."[16]

Whereas Butler's earlier work tended to focus exclusively on the social norms, practices, and discourses that individuals are compelled to cite or reiterate through their own performative utterances, in *The Psychic Life of Power*, she draws on Hegel, Nietzsche, Freud, Althusser, and Foucault to trace "the peculiar turning of a subject against itself that takes place in acts of self-reproach, conscience, and melancholia that work in tandem with" such "processes of social regulation."[17] On Butler's account, a prohibition turns the subject back on itself, creating the very interiority of the subject. This turning back on itself is the condition for the reflexivity of the subject; moreover, inasmuch as the capacity for reflexivity or self-consciousness is taken to be one of the hallmarks of subjectivity, it becomes the condition of possibility for subjectivity itself.[18] Following Foucault, Butler understands this turning of a subject against itself that generates reflexivity as a "self-incarcerating movement."[19] The subject is founded when it turns (what will come to be seen as) an "external" prohibition back against itself, when it imprisons itself in its own gestures of self-reproach or self-beratement, that is to say, in its own conscience.

Butler traces the roots of this idea back to the section on "The Unhappy Consciousness" in Hegel's *Phenomenology*.[20] In this discussion, which immediately follows the famous "Lordship and Bondage" section that has been so influential for the French reception of Hegel,[21] the ethical sphere emerges as a defensive reaction to consciousness's fear of death, thus, by extension, fear of the body, which is finite in character. Without going into the details of Butler's inventive reading of Hegel, the central insight that emerges from it is this: "If wretchedness, agony, and pain are sites or modes of stubbornness, ways of attaching to oneself, negatively articulated modes of reflexivity, then that is because they are given by regulatory regimes as the sites available for attachment, and a subject will attach to pain rather than not attach at all."[22] According to Butler, this insight reemerges in Freud's claims that the infant can form an attachment to any excitation, even a painful or traumatic one, and in Nietzsche's famous one-liner: the will "will rather will *nothingness* than *not* will."[23] Hegel, Nietzsche, and Freud, as Butler reads them, all point to the rootedness of reflexivity in the subject's repetitive self-beratement, a structure that comes to be called "conscience"; for all three thinkers, "there is no formation of the subject without a passionate attachment to subjection."[24]

According to Butler, regulatory regimes exploit the subject's willingness to attach to pain rather than not attach by compelling subjects to attach to structures of subordination. The resulting "disciplinary cultivation of *an attachment to subjection*" is possible because regulatory regimes are constructed in such a way that "the terms by which we gain social recognition for ourselves are those by which we are regulated *and* gain social existence."[25] Thus, "to affirm one's existence is to capitulate to one's subordination."[26] If the subject would rather attach to pain and subordination than not attach, then even if the terms of our social existence involve incorporating into our sense of ourselves norms or social categories that subordinate us, we will still prefer this to lacking any social existence whatsoever. The structures by which social recognition are conferred thus exploit our narcissistic attachment to our own continued existence.

Although this might seem to paint a rather dark picture of the possibilities for agency and resistance, Butler maintains that "the attachment that a regulatory regime requires prove[s] to be both its constitutive failure and the potential site of resistance."[27] Regulatory regimes cannot maintain and reproduce themselves; instead, they must be maintained and upheld by the individuals whom they regulate. The cultivation of an attachment to those regimes is an extremely effective and economical tool for getting individuals to maintain and uphold such regimes; in that sense, the regime needs the attachment of the individuals it regulates in order to persist. It is this inability of the regulatory regime to determine completely the behavior of its subjects, its dependence on the continued allegiance of those who adhere to it, that accounts for the constitutive failure of such regimes. Because regulatory regimes rely upon not only the compliance of the individuals whom they regulate but also their desire to comply, that desire itself becomes the site of possible resistance to and subversion of such regimes. As Butler puts it, "if desire has as its final aim the continuation of itself ... then the capacity of desire to be withdrawn and to reattach will constitute something like the vulnerability of every strategy of subjection."[28]

In contrast with some interpretations of psychoanalysis that would locate resistance in an extradiscursive psychic domain, Butler, following Foucault, understands resistance as internal to the very power that it opposes.[29] Subjects are the kinds of creatures who actively take up and enact their own position as subjects, who rearticulate and reiterate the norms to which they are subjected; thus, when disciplinary regimes produce subjects, they thereby also produce the possibility of their own subversion. The key to successful resistance, then, is figuring out how to "work the power relations by which we are worked, and in what direction."[30] As was the case for Foucault, however, the crucial question for Butler is this: "If we reject theoretically the source of resistance in a psychic domain that is said to precede or exceed the social, as we must, can we reformulate psychic resistance *in terms of the social* without that reformulation becoming a domestication or normalization?"[31] In other words, if resistance always comes from within the relations of power to which it is opposed, then how can we differentiate subversive reiterations or reenactments of the law from those that reinforce and uphold it?

Butler attempts to distinguish faithful from subversive reenactments of the law through her reconsideration of Althusser's account of interpellation. Her discussion of the famous Althusserian scene in which the subject of the law is hailed into existence by the call of the policeman who shouts "Hey, you there!" focuses on the question of what motivates the subject to turn and thus to capitulate to the interpellating power. In other words, the crucial questions are: "Who is speaking? Why should I turn around? Why should I accept the terms by which I am hailed?"[32] The answer turns out to be deceptively simple: I am compelled to turn toward the law because it promises me my identity and thus my social existence. In other words, my desire for my own existence, my desire to desire, provides the motivation for my acceptance of the term by which I am hailed. As before, Butler suggests that this very attachment, this very desire that makes interpellation possible also accounts for its constitutive failure. If this is true, however, then it is a mistake to view the law as a monolithic force that completely determines the possibilities for human existence; indeed, Butler suggests that this way of thinking of the law represents a "theological fantasy of the law."[33] Once we realize that this is a fantasy, we might discover "a possibility of being elsewhere or otherwise.... Such a possibility would require a different kind of turn, one that, enabled by the law, turns away from the law, resisting its lure of identity.... Such a turn demands a willingness *not* to be—a critical desubjectivation—in order to expose the law as less powerful than it seems."[34] Butler does not say much about what this desubjectivation entails, though it clearly has something to do with escaping the constraints of self-identity: "Such a failure of interpellation may well undermine the capacity of the subject to 'be' in a self-identical sense, but it may also mark the path toward a more open, even more ethical, kind of being, one of or for the future."[35] I shall return to this point below.

Having developed this conception of the psychic attachment to subjection, Butler turns to a rethinking of gender identity, now understood through the framework of Freud's notion of melancholia. Following Freud, Butler understands melancholia as the unfinished process of grieving a lost object. Because this process is unfinished, the attachment to the lost object is never fully broken; instead, the object is installed within the psyche through a process of identification, preserving the object as part of the psyche itself. By the time he wrote *The Ego and the Id*, Freud had come to realize that this process of regressive identification is actually quite common; as he put it in a well-known passage, "we have come to understand that this kind of substitution has a great share in determining the form taken by the ego and that it makes an essential contribution towards building up what is called its 'character.'"[36] Butler maintains that Freud's account of melancholia leads to an understanding of the ego as "the sedimentation of objects loved and lost, the archaeological remainder, as it were, of unresolved grief."[37] More important, Freud also came to realize that the process of regressive identification that he identified in his analysis of melancholia is responsible for the formation of the superego; the superego emerges as a result of the process of identification that takes place after the resolution of the Oedipus complex. Whereas Freud readily admits the similarity between the processes of identification involved in melancholia and in the formation of the superego, Butler inventively reads the latter in terms of the former, interpreting the superego as itself a site of the unresolved grief felt by the child for the loss of the Oedipal attachments prohibited by the incest taboo. As Butler describes this process:

> The ego splits into the critical agency and the ego as object of criticism and judgment. Thus the relation to the object reappears "in" the ego, not merely as a mental event or singular representation, but as a scene of self-beratement that reconfigures the topography of the ego, a fantasy of internal partition and judgment that comes to structure the representation of psychic life *tout court*. The ego now stands for the object, and the critical agency comes to represent the ego's disowned rage, reified as a psychic agency separate from the ego itself.[38]

The superego vents its ambivalence and rage over the loss of the object by cruelly attacking and berating the ego, which has become a substitute, but always an inferior one, for the lost object.

Butler reads gender identification in terms of melancholic identification, which means that "masculine" and "feminine" identity are established by means of "prohibitions which *demand the loss* of certain sexual attachments, and demand as well that those losses *not* be avowed, and *not* be grieved."[39] Because the accomplishment of masculinity and femininity is linked culturally with the attainment of a heterosexual orientation, gender identification demands "the abandonment of homosexual attachments or, perhaps more trenchantly, *preempt[s]* the possibility of homosexual attachment, a foreclosure of possibility which produces a domain of homosexuality understood as unlivable passion and ungrievable loss."[40] The result is that heterosexist societies are marked by a constitutive melancholy.[41] Having a coherent gender identity is, in a society such as ours, necessary for social recognition and thus for having a social existence at all. In this sense, given that the attainment of a coherent gender identity is predicated upon the disavowal of homosexual attachment, the subject's very identity is constituted by the disavowal of homosexual attachment. Thus, the avowal of homosexual attachment threatens to undermine the identity of the subject. As Stephen White notes, "this pervasive threat of dissolution of self, when combined with the aggressiveness spawned by the melancholic reaction, creates a potent mix in terms of social power. For the aggressiveness that is initially self-directed in the symptoms of heightened self-beratement of conscience can be turned outward as well."[42] The image of an enraged superego turning its self-beratement outward against those whose avowal of homosexual love it finds threatening provides a powerful lens for analyzing the extreme violence and aggression exhibited toward gays and lesbians in our culture, the continuing panic caused by the prospect of state recognition of gay marriages, and the unwillingness to acknowledge and grieve the loss of life caused by AIDS.

Although this not Butler's explicit aim, her analysis of the psychic roots of subjection also provides clues to a plausible diagnosis of the recalcitrance of women's subordination in the wake of decades of feminist critique and political activism. Simone de Beauvoir inaugurated second-wave feminism by arguing in *The Second Sex* that gender is not a natural but a social kind and that it is socially constructed in such a way that gender is never merely difference but always also implies a relationship of dominance and subordination. In the 1990s, feminists turned this social constructionist argument on biological sex as well.[43] As a result of these social constructionist critiques of gender and sex, feminists have tended to adopt what Zerilli has called a "gender-troublerian" view, which assumes that once we have recognized that our beliefs about gender and sex have been exposed as contingent, it will be easy to dismantle these belief systems, thus undermining the systems of dominance and subordination with which they are intertwined.[44] But doing so has proved to be much more difficult than the social constructionist view of gender and sex would suggest. Drawing on Butler's analysis of subjection in *The Psychic Life of Power*, we might venture a possible reason for this difficulty: as useful as it can be to see gender and sex categories as social rather than natural kinds, doing so leaves unexplained the ambivalent attachments that we all form to our sex and gender identity (which Beauvoir analyzed in terms of bad faith). As a result of these attachments, the mere realization that sex and gender are contingent, historically emergent social categories that serve to subordinate some people to others is not enough to unseat the sexed and gendered expectations, norms, and ideals that structure our lives. If we can remain stubbornly attached to the fantasies of sex and gender identity even as we accept the validity of feminist critiques of these very concepts, then genuine transformation of the sex/gender system will require still more radical changes than feminists have tended to envision up to this point.[45] It will not be enough to change how we *think* about gender and sex. Critical reflection on gender subordination may be necessary for engaging in practices of resistance and self-transformation, but, if Butler's account of subjection is plausible, clearly it is not sufficient.

Dependency, Subordination, and Recognition

Consider the following passage from Butler's introduction to *The Psychic Life of Power*:

> No subject emerges without a passionate attachment to those on whom he or she is fundamentally dependent (even if that passion is "negative" in the psychoanalytic sense). Although the dependency of the child is not *political* subordination in any usual sense, the formation of primary passion in dependency renders the child vulnerable to subordination and exploitation.... Moreover, this situation of primary dependency conditions the political formation and regulation of subjects and becomes the means of their subjection. If there is no formation of the subject without a passionate attachment to those by whom she or he is subordinated, then subordination proves central to the becoming of the subject.[46]

What is troublesome about this passage is Butler's subtle slide from the vulnerability to subordination that results from the situation of primary dependency to subordination itself. Her claim that subjectivation requires a passionate attachment to those on whom we are fundamentally dependent, even if this attachment is a subordinating one, is both plausible and compelling. She notes that "the infant as well as the child must attach in order to persist in and as itself," that is, that emotional attachment to a caregiver is a necessary condition for the infant's and the child's physical survival and psychological and cognitive development.[47] But the child does not and indeed cannot discriminate between healthy and unhealthy (subordinating) attachments. The fact of primary dependency thus renders all human beings *vulnerable to* subordination by compelling us to settle for whatever form of attachment is available to us, whether subordinating or not. However, from this it does not follow, as Butler concludes, that subjectivation is always subordinating. Butler makes this move, I think, because she equates dependency with power, and power with subordination; thus, she is led to conflate dependency with subordination. The fact of primary dependency shows, according to Butler, that "one is dependent on power for one's very formation, that that formation is impossible without dependency."[48] To be sure, it makes sense to think of dependency as a power relation; those on whom we are dependent are in a position of power over us because they can either foster or thwart our aims, desires, and overall well-being. But is dependence necessarily a relation of subordination? Butler seems to suggest that it is; as she puts it, "to desire the conditions of one's own subordination is thus required to persist as oneself."[49] It would make perfect sense if Butler had concluded this discussion by claiming that "to desire the conditions of one's *dependency* is required to persist as oneself." Or, to put it more precisely, she might have said: "to desire the conditions of one's dependency *even though this dependency makes one vulnerable to subordination*" or even "to desire the conditions of one's dependency *even when that dependency takes the form of subordination*." But to say that desiring the conditions of one's own *subordination* is required to persist as oneself is something else altogether.

Perhaps one could just say that Butler defines dependency as a form of subordination and leave it at that. But this would still not solve the problem, because the conflation of dependency and subordination points, I think, to a fundamental ambiguity in Butler's account of subjection. Is this account offered as an explanation of the formation of the subject simpliciter? Is she suggesting that subjection is always subordinating? Or is it an account of what can go wrong in the formation of subjectivity, of the ways in which the process of subjection necessarily leaves us vulnerable to particular pathological modes of subordination? Sometimes it seems as if Butler understands her view in the former way, for example, when she says things like "subordination proves central to the becoming of the subject," "subordination provides the subject's continuing condition of possibility," and "to desire the conditions of one's own subordination is ... required to persist as oneself."[50] At other times, however, such as in her discussion of gender melancholia, it seems as if Butler understands her view in the latter sort of way; gender melancholia is presented as a pathological form of subject formation, one that results from the processes of social regulation that uphold compulsory heterosexuality and from the familial and kinship structures that reinforce heterosexism taking on a psychic form.[51]

Granted, these two ways of understanding Butler's project are not incompatible. Perhaps her view is both that becoming a subject always involves submitting to subordination (and the concomitant psychic attachment to such subordination) and that the formation of gender identity through the process of melancholic identification is one of the particular forms that this process can take. There would be no inconsistency in holding such a position, as far as I can see. However, the problem is that whereas we might have good reasons for accepting the view that gender identity under current social and cultural conditions requires some individuals to become attached to their own subordination, there do not seem to be good reasons for accepting the view that becoming a subject necessarily involves such an attachment to subordination. Although in *The Psychic Life of Power* Butler seems unwilling to admit or perhaps unable to imagine the possibility of nonsubordinating modes of dependency or of relations of power that do not involve subordination, this does not mean that such relations to others are impossible. I will return to this issue below. If it establishes anything about subject formation in general, then, Butler's view establishes the somewhat weaker claim that desiring the conditions of one's dependency even when that dependency takes the form of subordination is required in order to persist as oneself.

To put the point another way, even the central insight that Butler gleans from Hegel that proves to be a recurring motif in the book—that the subject would rather attach to pain than not attach—leaves open the possibility of an attachment to painless or nonsubordinating (or, at least, less painful and less subordinating) modes of subjectivity. The question is, does Butler's view really provide for this possibility? The account of resistance that Butler offers in *The Psychic Life of Power* suggests that it does not. As in her earlier work, here Butler understands resistance primarily in terms of resignification; resistance is a matter of reworking "the power relations by which we are worked," a process that involves "occupying—being occupied by—that injurious term [by which I am called] ... , recasting the power that constitutes me as the power I oppose."[52] In addition to this familiar notion of resistance, however, there is another account of resistance at work in this text, an account that figures resistance as "a critical desubjectivation" or an embrace of the "*incoherence* of identity."[53] If we follow the strict logic of Butler's argument, then it makes perfect sense that she would be drawn toward such a conception of resistance. After all, if becoming a subject necessarily involves capitulating to subordination, then resistance to subordination would ultimately require the refusal to be a subject, the refusal to capitulate to the logic of subjection.[54] However, if, as Butler has argued, our only alternatives are either submitting to the logic of subjection or having no social existence whatsoever, then such refusal threatens a form of social suicide that is both undesirable in itself and incompatible with Butler's own claims about our primary narcissism, our desire for recognition, whatever the price.[55] Following the logic of Butler's analysis of subjection to its natural conclusion thus seems to lead us to a theoretical and political dead end. To avoid this dead end, we must resist Butler's conflation of dependence and subordination. If we resist the idea that subjection is per se subordinating, then this opens up the possibility of conceptualizing forms of dependency, attachment, and recognition that are nonsubordinating, or at the very least less subordinating; only relationships such as these can support the development of forms of subjectivity that are not mired in subordination.

Such a move would also allow us to make sense of the motivation to resist the particular forms of psychic attachment to subordination (such as gender melancholia) in which Butler is interested. After all, if becoming a subject always already involves becoming attached to subordination, then why resist any particular form that such subordinating subjection takes; why seek out different forms of attachment, if they all lead to subordination? This point echoes a familiar criticism of Butler's earlier work and of the Foucaultian account of power that inspired it.[56] But, in light of Butler's emphasis on the psychic attachment to subordination, this familiar problem appears here in a new, and arguably more intractable, form. In order to recast the power that constitutes me as the power I oppose, I must be motivated to do so. If I am psychically invested in and attached to my own subordination, if my very sense of myself as a coherent individual is a function of my subordination, then I will need to have a fairly strong motivation to give that investment up. But we can only make sense of such a motivation against the backdrop of a normative distinction between "better and worse subjectivating practices," to borrow Fraser's phrase.[57] In this context, what is required is a distinction between subordination as a normatively problematic relationship and dependency as a normatively neutral one, albeit a relationship that is fraught with danger insofar as it renders us vulnerable to subordination. Such a distinction would enable us to envision alternative modes of attachment that are painless and nonsubordinating, or at least less painful and less subordinating.

This alternative vision must be filled out with a more detailed account of nonsubordinating modes of dependency and attachment; such an account could be provided by an analysis of the concept of mutual recognition. Butler's *Psychic Life of Power*, however, not only lacks an account of mutual recognition, it seems to deny that such a form of recognition is possible. Following Hegel's account of the master/slave dialectic in *The Phenomenology of Spirit*, Butler presents recognition at the individual level as a weapon in the subject's struggle to the death with the Other. At the social level, recognition is figured as a mechanism of subordination and condemnation wielded by disciplinary regimes, withheld unless and until individuals comply with their normative demands. In this text,

Butler seems implicitly to deny the possibility of nonsubordinating forms of mutual recognition and, thus, of nonsubordinating forms of social relations.[58] All social relations implicate us in the struggle for recognition, and thus all social relations are ultimately relations of power.[59] With this move, Butler denies herself the theoretical resources—specifically, an account of nonsubordinating modes of dependency and attachment grounded in the notion of mutual recognition—that she needs to make her analysis of resistance to subjection work.

Butler is no doubt right to assume that human beings so crave recognition that we will take whatever kind of recognition we can get, even when that recognition is predicated upon capitulating to our own subordination. But from this it does not follow that subordinating modes of recognition are the best we can hope for. In order to give some shape and direction to that hope, however, we will have to move beyond Butler's *Psychic Life of Power*.

Ambivalent Recognition

In the recent essay "Bodies and Power Revisited," Butler speculates that "the moment of resistance, of opposition, emerges precisely when we find ourselves attached to our constraint, and so constrained in our very attachment. To the extent that we question the promise of those norms that constrain our recognizability, we open the way for attachment itself to live in some less constrained way."[60] Here, Butler explicitly invokes the distinction between better and worse subjectivating practices and envisions the possibility of less constraining modes of subjectivity. She goes on in the next sentence to link this vision to the problematic of recognition, claiming that "for attachment to live in a less constrained way is for it to risk unrecognizability."[61] As in *The Psychic Life of Power*, she locates less constraining modes of subjectivity outside of the logic of recognition. The implication is that recognition itself is a form of subordination. However, Butler also maintains in this essay that Foucault's ethical work opens up the crucial question of "how desire might become produced beyond the norms of recognition, even as it makes a new demand for recognition. And here he seems to find the seeds of transformation in the life of a passion that lives and thrives at the borders of recognizability."[62] In this passage, even as Butler posits recognition as an ethical ideal (by articulating a new demand for it), her reference to living beyond or at the borders of recognizability simultaneously suggests a rejection of recognition as an ideal on the grounds that it is intrinsically bound up with subjection (understood as a subordinating mode of subjectivation).

The conflicting tendencies evident in this essay are symptomatic of a broader ambivalence in Butler's recent work toward the notion of recognition. Such ambivalence should perhaps not be surprising. After all, one might argue that Butler's work necessarily presupposes the possibility of unantagonistic, positive social relations, relations structured by reciprocity and mutual recognition. Absent such a presupposition, why would Butler think, as she clearly does, that the denial or withholding of recognition to those socially abjected others who fail to conform to regulatory power is objectionable?[63] It would seem that Butler needs a positive account of recognition in order to give her account of subjection its critical force. As I will argue here, at times, her recent work acknowledges this need, more or less explicitly. And yet she is thoroughly convinced by her reading of Hegel's *Phenomenology* that such a positive account of recognition is impossible. As a result, in her most recent discussion of recognition, she disavows her own gestures toward recognition as an ideal. In the end, I will argue, she rejects precisely the sort of notion of mutual or nonsubordinating recognition that her account of subjection and resistance requires.

Butler's most explicit gestures toward the possibility of nonsubordinating modes of relationship and recognition are to be found in the essay "Violence, Mourning, Politics" and the book *Giving an Account of Oneself.* In these two texts, Butler begins to develop a conception of the human—if not a new basis for humanism—predicated upon our primary vulnerability to and dependence upon others. This vulnerability and dependency means that we are from the very start "given over to the other."[64] Indeed, she writes, "if, at the beginning ... *I am only in the address to you,* then the 'I' that I am is nothing without this 'you,' and cannot even begin to refer to itself outside the relation to the other by which its capacity for self-reference emerges. I am mired, given over, and even the word *dependency* cannot do the job here."[65] Butler notes that "this conception means that we are vulnerable to those we are too young to know and to judge and, hence, vulnerable to violence; but also vulnerable to another range of touch, a range that includes the eradication of our being at the one end, and the physical support for our lives at the other."[66] Unlike in *The Psychic Life of Power*, Butler is now careful to distinguish subordination from dependency as a feature of our humanity that renders us vulnerable to subordination. Indeed, she now admits that in that book she "perhaps too quickly accepted [Nietzsche's] punitive scene of inauguration for the subject," the scene that led her to understand subjectivation in terms of subordination.[67] Indeed, she now goes so far as to claim that the Nietzschean postulation of the self as a "cause" has a genealogy that must be understood as part of the reduction of ethical philosophy to the inward mutilations of conscience. Such a move not only severs the task of ethics from the matter of social life and the historically revisable grids of intelligibility within which any of us emerge, if we do, but it fails to understand the resource of primary and irreducible relations to others as a precondition of ethical responsiveness.[68]

In other words, Butler now wishes to identify a range of vulnerability and dependency that has, at one end, the destructive withholding of recognition and, at the other end, a fundamental relationality that supports and nurtures us as physical (not to mention psychic) beings.

Thus, these recent texts also suggest a new understanding of the range of what is possible in social relationships. Whereas earlier Butler seemed to understand social relations in antagonistic and oppositional terms, in this essay she articulates a conception of attachments to others as sustaining forms of connection. "It is not as if an 'I' exists independently over here and then simply loses a 'you' over there," she writes, "especially if the attachment to 'you' is part of what composes who 'I' am. If I lose you, under these conditions, then I not only mourn the loss, but I become inscrutable to myself. Who 'am' I, without you?"[69] Although Butler claims that we are marked by a "fundamental" or "primary sociality,"[70] she also cautions that such a claim should not be understood as a straightforward endorsement of a relational view of the self. "We may need other language to approach the issue that concerns us, a way of thinking about how we are not only constituted by our relations but also dispossessed by them as well."[71] Other language seems necessary because our primary vulnerability reveals two social dimensions of the self: on the one hand, "at the most intimate levels, we are social; we are comported toward a 'you'"; on the other hand, we are outside ourselves in another sense, "constituted in cultural norms that precede and exceed us, given over to a set of cultural norms and a field of power that condition us fundamentally."[72]

The more nuanced account of sociality offered in these texts also leads Butler to gesture toward a broader notion of recognition. As she writes in "Violence, Mourning, Politics," "we are not separate identities in the struggle for recognition but are already involved in a reciprocal exchange, an exchange that dislocates us from our positions, our subject-positions, and allows us to see that community itself requires the recognition that we are all, in different ways, striving for recognition."[73] In this passage, Butler invokes a recognition of our common humanity, grounded in our common corporeal vulnerability, that structures the individual pursuit of recognition. Furthermore, Butler suggests that our common human vulnerability is the basis for both political community and collective resistance. The fact of our primary sociality thus calls attention to the "ongoing normative dimension of our social and political lives, one in which we are compelled to take stock of our interdependence."[74] This leads Butler to pose the following question: "Can this insight lead to a normative reorientation for politics?"[75] Later on in the essay, Butler discusses the need to expand and render more inclusive our cultural assumptions about whose physical vulnerability matters and ought to be ameliorated and about whose lives are livable and whose deaths grievable. This suggests that the normative reorientation that Butler has in mind consists in an ethical obligation to foster and promote nonsubordinating forms of recognition, to try, to the extent that this is possible, to disentangle recognition from subordination. Such a vision clearly implies that nonsubordinating or, at least, less subordinating, forms of recognition are possible, at least in principle, at least as a regulative ideal.[76]

However, it is precisely this ideal that Butler seems to disavow in her recent critique of Benjamin's intersubjective psychoanalytic theory. Butler claims that "although Benjamin clearly makes the point that recognition risks falling into destruction, it seems to me that she still holds out for an ideal of recognition in which destruction is an occasional and lamentable occurrence, one that is reversed and overcome in the therapeutic situation, and which does not turn out to constitute recognition essentially."[77] The implication is that Butler believes that destruction does constitute recognition essentially. Similarly, she complains that, when reading Benjamin, one gets the sense "that recognition is something other than aggression or that, minimally, recognition can do without aggression."[78] On Benjamin's view, "misrecognition is occasional, but not a constitutive or unsurpassable feature of psychic reality, as Lacan has argued, and that recognition, conceived as free of misrecognition, not only ought to triumph, but can."[79] Although "Violence, Mourning, Politics" and *Giving an Account of Oneself* seem to hold out the possibility of nondestructive, nonaggressive forms of recognition, here Butler is highly skeptical about such hope. As she puts it, "what I hope to do in what follows is less to counter this exemplar of happiness than to offer a few rejoinders from the ranks of ambivalence where some of us continue to dwell."[80]

Ambivalence strikes me as an appropriate word choice. On the one hand, Butler writes: "I do not have a problem with the norm of recognition as it functions in Benjamin's work, and I think, in fact, that it is an appropriate norm for psychoanalysis. But I do wonder whether an untenable hopefulness has entered into her descriptions of what is possible under the rubric of recognition."[81] On the other hand, what Butler seems to find untenable is not so much the description of what is possible under the rubric of recognition, but the idea of recognition as a norm or ideal itself. On Butler's reading, Benjamin presupposes the possibility of an intersubjective space that is free of destruction. "My question is whether intersubjective space, in its 'authentic' mode, is really ever free of destruction? And if it is free of destruction, utterly, is it also beyond the psyche in a way that is no longer of use for psychoanalysis?"[82] As Butler understands it, Benjamin's work implies that destruction can be overcome, but she wonders "is this ever really possible—for humans, that is? And would we trust those who claimed to have overcome destructiveness for the harmonious dyad once and for all? I, for one, would be wary."[83] On Butler's view of the psyche, "destructiveness poses itself continually as a risk. That risk is a perennial and irresolvable aspect of human psychic life. As a result, any therapeutic norm that seeks to overcome destructiveness seems to be basing itself on an impossible premise."[84]

Unfortunately, however, this critique misconstrues Benjamin's work; moreover, it does so in ways that reveal inadequacies in Butler's own account of recognition. First, Benjamin agrees with Butler that destructiveness is a continual risk. Indeed, she argues throughout her recent work that "destruction is recognition's other side,"[85] that "destruction is the Other of recognition."[86] Following Winnicott, Benjamin maintains that recognition depends upon the psyche's ability to symbolically process destruction, understood as "the mental refusal to recognize the other, the negation of the external."[87] It is in this sense that destruction or negation is—necessarily and ineradicably—the other side of recognition. But there is another sense in which Benjamin acknowledges the destructive capabilities of the human psyche. In her view, the ideal toward which we should strive—both psychically and socially—is not the overcoming of negation or destructiveness, but the maintaining of a tension between recognition and destruction. Benjamin acknowledges, however, that breakdowns of this tension are inevitable. As she puts it, "alienated forms of complementarity, based on the idealization and repudiation created by splitting, are inevitable. In the best of circumstances, these alternate with recognition."[88]

In other words, Benjamin does not suggest that recognition can triumph once and for all, nor does she posit an intersubjective space that is free of destruction.[89] Instead, she argues that the negative, destructive aspect of human relationships does not undermine or eliminate the possibility of recognition. The key is that Benjamin theorizes intersubjectivity as a temporally dynamic process, not as a static state of affairs. For Benjamin, recognition is possible only as a moment within ongoing, temporally unfolding, dynamic human relationships. Recognition continually leads to breakdown, which, on Benjamin's view, is what leads to domination.[90] But breakdown, in turn, can lead to repair. Butler's critique completely overlooks the way in which Benjamin understands human intersubjectivity to be fundamentally dynamic. Butler's view, by contrast, seems curiously static. For Butler, relations with others, however they may appear on the surface, always take the same form: a struggle to the death in which the veneer of recognition covers over the fundamental psychic destructiveness of human beings. The other continually threatens the self with misrecognition, if not outright annihilation. Even in one of her most hopeful moments, in "Violence, Mourning, Politics," the primary lesson that Butler draws from the fundamental sociality of the self is how vulnerable this makes us to the apparently dangerous, threatening Other.

What Butler seems to be missing in the context of her critique of Benjamin is the insight that she acknowledges elsewhere: that if we are undone by others, this is only because we are "done" by them as well. Whereas Butler's view tends to emphasize one side of this tension—the ways in which we are vulnerable to the negativity, destructiveness, and aggression of the other—Benjamin's view captures both sides. As Benjamin puts it:

> If the clash of two wills is an inherent part of intersubjective relations, then no perfect environment can take the sting from the encounter with otherness. The question becomes how the inevitable elements of negation are processed. It is "good enough" that the inward movement of negating reality and creating fantasy should eventually be counterbalanced by an outward movement of recognizing the outside.... A relational psychoanalysis should leave room for the messy, intrapsychic side of creativity and aggression; it is the contribution of the intersubjective view that may give these elements a more hopeful cast, showing destruction to be the Other of recognition.[91]

Benjamin, already in her first book, *The Bonds of Love*, argued for the necessity of both intrapsychic and intersubjective perspectives in psychoanalysis. Butler's work, by contrast, focuses primarily on the intrapsychic—on incorporation, fantasy, splitting, abjection, melancholia, and so forth.[92] As a result, Butler risks conflating the fantasied and the concrete other. Benjamin diagnoses this tendency in Butler's early critiques of identity,[93] but it is arguably even more pronounced in her work on subjection. For instance, as Butler notes in her discussion of gender melancholia, "the effect of melancholia ... appears to be the loss of the social world, the substitution of psychic parts and antagonisms for external relations among social actors."[94] Instead of having relationships with actual, concrete others, the melancholic has relationships with the internal, fantasied others that she has installed in her own psyche. In effect, the melancholic subject is a monad. Benjamin, by contrast, proposes that the intrapsychic account be complemented with her intersubjective account. The intersubjective view emphasizes "that the individual grows in and through the relationship to other subjects.... The idea of intersubjectivity reorients the conception of the psychic world from a subject's relation to its object toward a subject meeting another subject."[95] Although our relationships with actual others are no doubt complicated by our fantasied projections of them, these relationships are nonetheless possible and constitute a sustaining source of connection.

I do not doubt Butler's claim that recognition is bound up with power in many ways, as her recent work has brilliantly exposed, nor do I question her claim that the achievement of a state of human intersubjectivity that is completely free of power relations and is structured entirely by mutual recognition is an illusion, and a pernicious one at that. As I will argue in chapters 5 and 6, Habermas has an unfortunate tendency to be seduced by this illusion. And yet, it is possible to articulate a more pragmatic and contextualist version of Habermasian critical theory that is not vulnerable to this criticism. If we take more seriously than Butler does the temporal and dynamic aspects of social relationships, we can theorize mutual recognition as a permanent, though temporally fleeting, possibility within social life. Doing so does not require us to posit a possible social world that is completely free of power; Butler is right, I think, to insist that even if it were possible to envision such a world, such a world would not be recognizably human. I raise this point against Habermas's theory of communicative action in chapter 6. But claiming that power is a permanent and ineradicable feature of human social life does not commit one to the idea that all human social relationships are at all times nothing more than the expression of power. We could agree with Foucault and Butler that there is no outside to power, in the sense that there is no possible human social world from which power has been completely eliminated, without denying that *moments* of mutual recognition remain possible within ongoing, dynamically unfolding, social relationships.

Thinking of the relationship between power and recognition in this way allows us to theorize—in a more coherent and less ambivalent way than Butler does—the forms of intersubjectivity that provide the kind of sustaining connection with others that, as Benjamin argues, allows us to form a sense of self and to navigate our social world. Understanding the politics of our selves requires understanding not only the inscription of disciplinary norms but also this positive moment of recognition as well. As Benjamin emphasizes, understanding intersubjectivity in this way does not entail denying aggression, destruction, and negativity and the important role that they play in both the individual psyche and relationships with others. Whereas Benjamin seeks to do justice to the ambivalent nature of intersubjectivity, Butler just seems ambivalent about it: on the one hand, her critique of subjection seems to depend upon a positive conception of recognition, and at times in her recent work she acknowledges this dependency; on the other hand, in her critique of Benjamin, she explicitly denies and disavows recognition as a normative ideal. Although she claims that our common human vulnerability provides the basis for political community and collective resistance, she denies the possibility of a mutual recognition of such commonality. Although she claims that human relationships are fundamentally ambivalent,[96] in fact, she has the tendency to collapse this ambivalence into a one-sided negativity. As I argued above, in doing so, she disavows precisely that normative notion of recognition on which her critique of subjection implicitly depends.

Perhaps Butler's ambivalence can be explained as a failure to reconcile her progressive political agenda with her theoretical commitments. If this is the right explanation, then this brings us back to Bartky's worry about the split between theory and practice. What good, we might wonder, is a theory that fails to line up with our practice? What good is a theory for which, indeed, there may be no possible practice? And, conversely, what good is a political practice that cannot be adequately explained and justified by our best theories?

Concluding Political Postscript

Butler, in one of her contributions to *Contingency, Hegemony, Universality: Contemporary Dialogues on the Left*, broaches this question of theory and practice. "It seems important," she writes, "to be able to move as intellectuals between the kinds of questions that predominate these pages, in which the conditions of possibility for the political are debated, and the struggles that constitute the present life of hegemonic struggle: the development and universalization of various new social movements, the concrete workings of coalitional efforts, and especially, those alliances that tend to cross-cut identitarian politics."[97] The question is, what enables us to bridge this gap? I would argue that in order for Butler to link up her political-theoretical reflections with a critical account of contemporary social movements, she needs a theoretical understanding of solidarity or collective resistance, and for that she requires some notion of what binds individuals together in social and political movements, namely, nonsubordinating, mutual recognition. As Benjamin argues, such recognition does not entail the denial or the obliteration of difference; recognizing the other does not entail seeing her as just like me. Instead, it entails recognizing her as like me inasmuch as we are both totally unique, irreplaceable subjects.[98] As Benjamin puts it, "real recognition of the other entails being able to perceive commonality through difference."[99] With this idea, Benjamin evokes Arendt's notion of plurality, according to which "we are all the same, that is, human, in such a way that nobody is ever the same as anyone else who ever lived, lives, or will live."[100] Plurality, for Arendt, is the condition of possibility of action and, thus, of politics. Without a more fully developed and less ambivalent notion of recognition, Butler is left unable to explain the possibility of collective or, ultimately, individual resistance. Instead, she writes, "it is not simply that the psyche invests in its oppression, but that the very terms that bring the subject into political viability orchestrate the trajectory of identification and become, with luck, the site for a disidentificatory resistance."[101] Without an account of how the recognition of our commonality provides the basis for political community and collective resistance, Butler is left suggesting that the transformation from identification to disidentification, from signification to resignification, from subjectivation to a critical desubjectivation, is nothing more than a matter of luck.

Surely good luck and good timing are a part of any act of individual or collective resistance, but I think theory can and should give us more to go on than this. If we accept, as I think we should, Butler's diagnosis of the psychic attachment to subordination, the pressing practical question is this: How can members of subordinated groups form nonsubordinating or at least less oppressive attachments? This is a deep and difficult question, and I suspect that there is more than one way of answering it, but I want to at least suggest one possible answer. One of the ways in which members of oppressed groups form less oppressive attachments is by drawing on the resources of social and political movements that create alternative modes of attachment and structures of social recognition. Collective social movements, such as the feminist and the queer movements, generate conceptual and normative resources, create networks of psychological and emotional support, and foster counterpublic spaces, all of which aid individuals in their efforts to resist regulatory regimes by providing new modes of recognition, new possibilities for attachment, and thus new ways of becoming subjects. The existence of these alternative sources of recognition, in turn, makes it possible for individuals to risk becoming unrecognizable in the terms set by regulatory regimes. Understood in this way, resistance does not require the overly demanding suspension of our primary narcissism, our fundamental desire for recognition; instead, it entails the creation, within the context of social movements, of alternative sources of recognition that sustain us in our struggle. Butler's view fails to account fully for this fact, and her disavowal of recognition as a normative ideal in the context of her critique of Benjamin makes it difficult to see how she could acknowledge it.

The crucial question is: What kinds of social conditions foster resistance to the modes of psychic subjection that Butler's work so helpfully diagnoses? Conceiving of resistance in terms of a refusal to be a subject, or of an embrace of unrecognizability, does not seem particularly promising, both because it is unclear what this would mean and because such a refusal denies the subordinated the recognition that, ex hypothesi, we all crave. Butler's conception of resistance in terms of reworking subjection from within via a subversive performance is much more promising. However, that conception of resistance is plagued by the difficulty of seeing how we might distinguish resistance from reinscription without making some distinction between subordinating and nonsubordinating forms of attachment, which would seem to require a more developed, less ambivalent conception of recognition than Butler has to offer.

To be sure, even if we were armed with such a distinction, this task would remain a difficult, perhaps impossible, one. However, even if we assume that, for example, what appears at first glance to be faithfulness to gender norms can also be understood as a way of reworking, for example, feminine subjection from within, the important question is, what sorts of social conditions foster such a reworking? Answering this question will involve articulating the social conditions of recognition that allow subordinated individuals to overcome their internalized self-hatred. One such social condition might be the kind of consciousness raising that early second-wave feminist groups practiced and that still goes on, to some extent, in women's and gender studies classrooms. Another might be the formation and preservation of public and private spaces in which girls and women are granted recognition for their intelligence, wit, humor, talent, ambition, athletic prowess, accomplishments, and so forth rather than for how closely they adhere to normative femininity, and/or in which everyone is encouraged to critically examine and experiment with their gender performance, to explore and enact the full range of gendered experience. Another might be the existence of a vibrant community of feminist and queer activists and scholars who are engaged in a project of challenging and questioning existing gender norms and reworking social patterns of recognition. Thinking through these possibilities and their implications requires, in turn, acknowledging recognition as an ethical ideal and understanding it as a permanent—though temporally fleeting—possibility in human relationships.

5

Empowering the Lifeworld?

AUTONOMY AND POWER IN HABERMAS

AUTONOMY HAS long held a central place in Habermas's critical social theory. As he argues in his inaugural Frankfurt lecture in 1965, "the human interest in autonomy and responsibility is not mere fancy, for it can be apprehended a priori. What raises us out of nature is the only thing whose nature we can know: *language*. Through its structure, autonomy and responsibility are posited for us."[1] Although Habermas later rejected many aspects of his account of knowledge and human interests, about which more in the next chapter, the ideas of the rootedness of autonomy in the communicative use of language and of its definitive role in the development of the human person remain central to his mature social theory. Indeed, in a lecture given on the occasion of the fiftieth anniversary of the Institute for Social Research, in July 1974, Habermas argues that the notion of the autonomous ego is a crucial one for critical social theory, despite the gloomy and, in Habermas's view, overly pessimistic pronouncements of the end of the individual that were popular at the time.[2]

Despite the importance of the notion of autonomy to Habermas's thought,[3] his account of autonomy is complex and the various conceptions of autonomy that he employs are not always clearly differentiated. In his early work, for example, he seems to use autonomy more or less interchangeably with freedom from unjust social constraint; thus, the human interest in autonomy is connected to the interest in emancipation. In his mature social theory, however, the focus shifts to a notion of *moral* autonomy that is both derived from and importantly distinct from the Kantian notion of autonomy. As he puts it: "Discourse ethics reformulates the concept of autonomy. In Kant, autonomy was conceived as freedom under self-given laws, which involves an element of coercive subordination of subjective nature. In discourse ethics, the idea of autonomy is intersubjective. It takes into account that the free actualization of the personality of one individual depends on the actualization of freedom for all."[4] As Cooke has argued, Habermas's morally autonomous self gives herself the moral law, judges and acts morally, but does so with the expectation that her actions would be approved of by an unlimited communication community.[5] Thus, like Kant, Habermas holds that the "autonomous self is the self who chooses freely not what she or he wants to do but what it is right for her or him to do."[6] However, two important differences result from Habermas's intersubjective reading of Kant: first, Habermas disagrees with Kant's claim that autonomy requires the denial or suppression of inclination, though it does presuppose the capacity to distance oneself temporarily from one's needs and desires; second, claims to the rightness of one's actions are not settled monologically, by the internal deliberations of the autonomous individual, but only dialogically, in actual moral discourses.[7]

The difficulty with this account of moral autonomy, as Cooke argues, is that, in pluralistic societies, agreement on the rightness of moral norms is likely to be exceedingly rare and the domain of properly moral issues highly circumscribed; thus, "if autonomy is tied to such a rationally motivated consensus, then autonomy will be, at the very least, increasingly difficult."[8] Given that Habermas sees the achievement of autonomy as a crucial constitutive feature of ego identity in postconventional societies, the difficulty of rational consensus poses a serious problem for his account. Cooke suggests, therefore, that rather than seeing Habermas's overly stringent conception of moral autonomy as the centerpiece of his theory, we should focus instead on the notion of *personal* autonomy that she sees implicit in his work. Autonomy in this sense is defined as rational accountability; on this conception, "the autonomy of a person would be measured against her or his ability to support what she or he says with reasons, as well as against her or his willingness to enter into argumentation and against his or her openness to criticism."[9] Although Cooke maintains that this account of autonomy remains largely implicit in Habermas's work, in a subsequent essay, Habermas refers explicitly to a notion of rational accountability that "presupposes a reflected self-relation on the part of the person to what she believes, says, and does."[10] The key is the capacity for reflexivity, the capacity to take up reflective distance on one's beliefs, activities, norm-governed actions, and existential life projects (both individual and collective). Although Habermas does not discuss this capacity under the heading of personal autonomy, he does maintain that "a person's ability to distance himself in this way in these various dimensions from himself and his expressions is a necessary condition of his *freedom*."[11]

In what follows, my focus will be primarily on this notion of personal autonomy, understood as the capacity for rational accountability or critical reflexivity with respect to existing norms, beliefs, practices, institutions, cultural forms, and so on. My aim is to sort out the complicated but largely undertheorized relationship between autonomy in this sense and power in Habermas's account of the intersubjective constitution of the self, and to begin to think through the implications of this relationship for developing a critical-theoretical analysis of gender subordination.[12]

On the face of it, it might seem as though there is not much interesting to say about the relationship between power and autonomy in Habermas's work. His central distinction between system integration (contexts in which agents' actions are functionally integrated, for example, in the economic and administrative/political domains by the steering media of money and power, respectively) and social integration (contexts in which agents coordinate their interactions on the basis of either implicit or explicit consensus about shared norms, values, or goals and reproduce their lifeworld in the dimensions of culture, society, and personality) has seemed to many critics to entail the problematic conclusion that there is no power in the lifeworld and thus no power involved in the socialization of autonomous individuals (since such socialization takes place within the lifeworld).[13] For example, Fraser has criticized Habermas along precisely these lines, arguing that by confining his discussion of power to system contexts, Habermas effectively screens power out of the lifeworld, the social domain that is structured by symbolically mediated forms of social integration. Fraser argues that this move threatens to make Habermasian critical theory blind to forms of dominance and subordination that are rooted in the lifeworld, including masculine domination, which is to a large extent reproduced and maintained in lifeworld contexts such as the family, cultural traditions and understandings of gender, and social norms. This leads Fraser to suggest that, when it comes to gender, Habermasian critical theory may not be nearly critical enough. Although Habermas does distinguish between normatively secured consensus—merely de facto consensus that may or may not be legitimate—and communicatively achieved consensus—consensus that is secured through fair and rational deliberation—as Fraser points out, "what is insufficiently stressed ... is that actions coordinated by normatively secured consensus in the male-headed nuclear family are actions regulated by power. It seems to me a grave mistake to restrict the use of the term 'power' to bureaucratic contexts."[14] As McNay puts it, summarizing Fraser's critique, "Habermas regards the family solely as an institution of the lifeworld and thereby misses its 'dual aspect', that is, that the family perpetuates systemic relations of oppression as much as it reproduces values and cultural norms."[15] Fraser insists that, in order to be truly critical, critical theory must provide "a framework capable of foregrounding the evil of dominance and subordination,"[16] which Habermas's dualistic social-theoretic framework seems incapable of doing.

In a sense, Fraser's criticism is the inverse of one of the more incisive criticisms of Foucault that Habermas was developing at about the same time. In *The Philosophical Discourse of Modernity*, Habermas complains that Foucault's "genealogical historiography deals with an object domain from which the theory of power has erased all traces of communicative action entangled in lifeworld contexts."[17] According to Habermas, this makes it difficult if not impossible for Foucault to explain how social order is possible at all, and yet Foucault's own work is premised on the assumption that power is institutionalized in more or less stable social orders. Moreover, Habermas argues that "if one admits only the model of empowerment, the socialization of succeeding generations can also be presented only in the image of wily confrontation. Then, however, the socialization of subjects capable of speech and action cannot be simultaneously conceived as individuation, but only as the progressive subsumption of bodies and of all vital substrata under technologies of power."[18] Fraser's contention that Habermas screens power out of the lifeworld can be interpreted as suggesting that Habermas's conception of the lifeworld presents an object domain from which all traces of power have been erased. If Habermas is guilty of this erasure, then his theory will have a difficult time conceiving of the socialization of subjects simultaneously as subjection, as a mechanism for the maintenance and reproduction of social structures of dominance and subordination.

In response to charges that he erases power from the lifeworld, Habermas maintains categorically that he never intended to claim that the lifeworld is free of power relations. "The lifeworld," he insists, "by no means offers an innocent image of 'power-free spheres of communication.'"[19] To the contrary, Habermas specifies two ways in which his social theory acknowledges and analyzes the potential influence of power on the lifeworld. The first is a result of his colonization of the lifeworld thesis, which highlights the ways in which increasingly complex systems-theoretical forms of power intrude upon lifeworld contexts, producing pathologies that "de-world" the lifeworld.[20] The second is his analysis of the ways in which power is capable of penetrating the structures of communicative action themselves; in such cases, "macrosociological power relations are mirrored in that microphysics of power which is built into the structures of distorted communication."[21] Habermas's analysis of systematically distorted communication explores this process and its implications. Beyond these two ways in which Habermas explicitly situates power in the lifeworld, I maintain that there is a third, and potentially more interesting, account of power in the lifeworld that is implicit yet undertheorized in Habermas's work. This account is rooted in his discussion of individuation through socialization, a lifeworld process that Habermas acknowledges is necessarily structured by asymmetrical relations of power, even as he remains utterly sanguine about the consequences of this necessity.

In this chapter, I propose to reconsider the role that power plays in the Habermasian lifeworld, particularly in the socialization processes that give rise to autonomous individuals.[22] This somewhat narrow focus is justified by the key role that socialization plays in Habermas's mature social theory. It is, after all, the account of individuation through socialization that explains the possibility of autonomy, which Habermas regards to be the normative core of his philosophical project. Habermas's robust account of autonomy as rational accountability, if convincing, would prove extremely useful for thinking through how subordinated individuals can achieve critical and reflective distance on the power relations to which they are subject. However, one might worry that Habermas purchases this robust account of autonomy at the price of his ability to do justice to the depth and complexity of power relations, particularly to the complicated and ambivalent phenomenon of subjection that our discussion of Foucault and Butler has focused upon. My overall aim in what follows is to consider whether this is the case.

I begin by considering the two ways in which Habermas explicitly lets power into the lifeworld—via the colonization of the lifeworld thesis and the analysis of systematically distorted communication—and asking whether either of these moves enables him to make sense of subjection. Even though Habermas is right to insist that he doesn't totally screen power out of the lifeworld, he appears to admit it only in very circumscribed ways; as a result, neither of these analyses gives Habermas a way of analyzing subjection as a form of power. However, implicit in Habermas's account of individuation through socialization is an acknowledgment of the role that power necessarily plays in socialization processes, an acknowledgment that brings him closer to Foucault's and Butler's accounts of subjection than he might care to admit.

Systematically Distorted Subjectivity?

As I mentioned above, Habermas maintains that his social-theory illuminates the role that power plays in the lifeworld in two main ways. First, via the colonization of the lifeworld thesis, Habermas explores the ways in which the system-steering medium of power can encroach upon the lifeworld, producing pathological side effects. As Habermas explains: "The thesis of internal colonization states that the subsystems of the economy and state [steered by the media of money and power, respectively] become more and more complex as a consequence of capitalist growth, and penetrate ever deeper into the symbolic reproduction of the lifeworld."[23] The critical aim of *The Theory of Communicative Action*, particularly volume 2 of this work, is precisely a diagnosis of this encroachment and an insistence on the need "to protect areas of life that are functionally dependent on social integration through values, norms, and consensus formation, to preserve them from falling prey to the systemic imperatives of economic and administrative subsystems growing with dynamics of their own, and to defend them from becoming converted over, through the steering medium of law, to a principle of sociation that is, for them, dysfunctional."[24] The pathologies that emerge when money- and power-laden systemic imperatives colonize the lifeworld are explained in terms of the de-worlding effects of such colonization. "Normally, the strategic actor retains his/her lifeworld at least as a fallback even if this has lost its coordinating efficacy; switching over to media-steered interactions, however, is accompanied by a specific 'de-worlding' effect which is experienced in the form of an objectification of social relations."[25]

Although it is true that this is a way of acknowledging that there is power in the lifeworld, it does not seem to meet the full force of the original objection. After all, as Fraser had originally put the point, the problem had to do with Habermas's reserving the use of the word "power" to refer to administrative or bureaucratic contexts, a usage that the colonization thesis clearly preserves. Although with this thesis Habermas admits that systems of power and the lifeworld can and do interpenetrate, this does not amount to a recognition of the ways in which core domains of the lifeworld are *themselves* structured by power relations—the family, which serves as the crucible for socialization processes, being just one example. As McCarthy points out, such a recognition is crucial for developing a critical-theoretical analysis of gender and racial oppression, both of which must be understood "not only in terms of economic inequalities and political dependencies, but also in terms of cultural patterns of interpretation and evaluation, social roles and normative expectations, socialization processes and ascriptive identities—and, of course, in terms of their myriad interconnections.... For these purposes the 'colonization of the lifeworld' perspective will not suffice."[26] In order to make sense of these phenomena and, thus, to make sense of the complexities of racial and gender subordination, power will have to be admitted into the lifeworld in a much less circumscribed fashion.

Habermas's most developed attempt to think through the relationship between power and the communicative fabric of the lifeworld can be found in his analysis of systematically distorted communication. As he suggests at the end of the second volume of *The Theory of Communicative Action*, it is this concept that serves as the reference point for diagnosing pathologies of individual development.[27] Although he has mental illness in mind here, commentators have shown that his account of systematically distorted communication can serve as the reference point for a critique of ideology and ideological forms of consciousness and reflection.[28] Thus, this account seems like the natural place to turn to investigate the theoretical resources that Habermas makes available for analyzing subordinating modes of subjectivation. So the question becomes, does Habermas's account of systematically distorted communication offer us a way of understanding what I will call systematically distorted subjectivity? By this I mean not that all forms of subjectivity are systematically distorted; my main criticism of Butler in the preceding chapter turned on the idea that her view of subjection seems to imply that all forms of subjectivity are subordinating, and that this implication is problematic. Instead, I use this phrase to highlight the ways in which subordinated or oppressed subjectivities are not just distorted, but systematically distorted, in that they are constituted in and through social relations of power that have been systematically distorted into relations of dominance and subordination.

In his 1974 essay "Reflections on Communicative Pathology," Habermas defines systematically distorted communication with reference to a distinction between the external organization of speech—roughly, its social context—and the internal organization—the universal and necessary presuppositions of communication. Communication becomes systematically distorted when the external organization of speech is overburdened, and this burden is shifted onto the internal organization of speech.[29] Thus, systematically distorted communication does not simply disrupt the social context in which speech acts take place; it disrupts the very "validity basis of speech" itself.[30] The disruption arises because in cases such as this,

> the validity basis of linguistic communication is curtailed *surreptitiously*; that is, without leading to a break in communication or to the transition to openly declared and permissible strategic action. The validity basis of speech is curtailed surreptitiously if at least one of the three universal validity claims to intelligibility (of the expression), sincerity (of the intention expressed by the speaker), and normative rightness (of the expression relative to a normative background) is violated and communication nonetheless continues on the presumption of communicative (not strategic) action oriented toward reaching mutual understanding.[31]

Thus, there is a sense in which systematically distorted communication is not really communicative at all, because it is defined as latent strategic action. However, because the strategic element is latent, there is no break in communication, giving distorted communication the contradictory sense of being communicative after all. Although Habermas insists that "even a flawed communication is a communication," he also notes that systematic distortions are "confounding" in that "the same validity claims that are being violated ... at the same time serve to keep up the appearance of consensual action."[32]

When Habermas relates the concept of systematically distorted communication to the formation of identity, this tension deepens into a paradox. Because identity can only be secured through intersubjective recognition, Habermas explains, "if an identity is threatened by the withholding of recognition, it is often defended in a paradoxical manner. On the one hand, every defense is a strategic action; it can be optimized only under the maxims of purposive action. On the other hand, the goal of the defense cannot be attained strategically, that is, by winning a fight or a game by defeating one's opponent—recognition ultimately cannot be won by force."[33] In such cases, the individual is oriented strategically toward the aim of defending her identity, and yet she must at the same time suppress the conflictual nature of this relationship, else the communicative foundation necessary for true recognition will be undermined. Habermas suggests that the family, as the site of identity formation (for children) and management (for adults), is frequently (though not exclusively) the locus of such systematically distorted identity conflicts. Families that are marked by "an asymmetrical distribution of power, with dominance relations and coalition formations, as well as by corresponding tensions, discrepant expectations, reciprocal deprecation, and so on" tend to generate symptoms of systematically distorted communication.[34] In such families, the asymmetrical distribution of power among family members means that the external organization of speech within the family is overburdened; it is "too rigid to produce the flexible relation between proximity and distance, between equality and difference, between action initiatives and behavioral responses, between inside and outside, which ... are required for the development and maintenance of the ego identity of family members."[35] As a result, the burden shifts to the internal structure of speech, which becomes systematically distorted. Identity conflicts within such families are "stabilized but remain[] unresolved"; they smolder.[36]

Now, it seems to me that the elephant in the room here is the traditional, heterosexual, nuclear family's role in the reproduction and maintenance of gender and sexual identity and relations of dominance and subordination. After all, one might wonder, what heterosexual family is not structured by asymmetrical relations of power? As many second-wave feminists have shown, the gender division of paid and unpaid labor, the second shift, the gender gap in wages, and the sex-segmented labor market all serve to systematically disadvantage women in heterosexual families. These structural economic forces combined with ideological norms of masculinity, femininity, motherhood, fatherhood, and heterosexuality itself serve to encourage individuals to enter into such asymmetrical family relationships in the first place. Moreover, although Habermas says that his interest in this essay is on individual rather than collective identity, the family is the locus not only of the formation of individual ego identity, but also of each individual's gender identity. Arguably, then, the smoldering conflicts that arise from gendered power asymmetries will serve to systematically distort communication between men and women in most families; such distortions will in turn suppress those conflicts so that they continue to smolder beneath the surface of apparently communicative interaction. If this admittedly broad sketch is at all accurate, then it becomes apparent that the scope of systematically distorted communication in identity conflicts is much broader than Habermas seems to assume; indeed, it appears pervasive.

But the problem is not just the gender blindness of Habermas's account, though that is no doubt a problem for a theory that purports to be critical, as Fraser convincingly argues in her critique of Habermas. Given the way that he defines systematically distorted communication, there is a further, and potentially more serious, problem for Habermas. As I discussed above, the concept of systematically distorted communication appears to trouble the distinction between communicative and strategic interaction; systematically distorted communications, because they are latently strategic, are neither fully strategic nor fully communicative. This raises a diffi-culty for Habermas, who needs to rely on this very distinction to diagnose and critique systematic distortions of communication. Since Habermas argues that linguistic intersubjectivity is the source of the capacity for self-reflection, which is in turn the source of the capacity to reflect critically on relations of power (thus, the source of autonomy in the sense relevant for this discussion), he must appeal to the notion of communicative action—that is, to the validity basis of speech—in order to distinguish between interactions that are genuinely communicative and those that are merely apparently so (when in fact latently strategic). Although this is not neces-sarily a vicious circle, it does raise the difficult question of how confident we can ever hope to be in our judgments that communications are or are not systematically distorted.

With respect to the possibility of systematically distorted subjectiv-ity/identity—a possibility that Habermas needs to consider if he is to do justice to the complexity of subordination—the problem is even deeper. For if individual identity is always constituted and sustained through in-tersubjective recognition, then we will have an interest in sticking with those modes of communication and recognition that serve to stabilize and confirm our identities, whether they are systematically distorted by asym-metrical relations of power or not. As Butler argues in *The Psychic Life of Power*, the subject's psychic attachment to and investment in subjection makes it difficult to gain critical traction on that subjection at the same time that it renders critical reflection by itself powerless to transform such subordinated identities.

Indeed, gender identity provides an excellent example of this. It is not just that traditionally or stereotypically feminine modes of subjectivity and identity serve to reinforce and reproduce women's subordination;[37] beyond this, having a coherent gender identity, either masculine or femi-nine, is a requirement for social and cultural intelligibility, thus, for being a subject at all.[38] As a result, taking up a critical perspective not only on normative femininity but also on gender dimorphism itself threatens our very identities and self-understandings. This might help to explain the cu-rious recalcitrance of gender identity and subordination to critique, but it also calls into question a critical-theoretical view that identifies freedom with the capacity for rational accountability and reflexivity, as Habermas's notion of autonomy tends to do. Moreover, because systematically dis-torted communication troubles the all-important distinction between strategic and communicative action and raises difficult questions about how one could ever know if communication or the identity shaped by it is systematically distorted, this discussion raises questions about whether

Habermas's early account of systematically distorted communication is even compatible with the notion of rational autonomy that forms the core of Habermas's normative project. Once Habermas lets power into the life-world in this way, it becomes difficult to see how one can achieve the kind of reflexive distance from one's beliefs, practices, norms, and life projects that is requisite for genuine autonomy and that supplies that notion critical bite. Indeed, it becomes difficult to make sense of systematically distorted communication at all, inasmuch as this notion relies implicitly on the possibility of *un*distorted communication and subjectivity while simultaneously calling into question the very distinction between communicative and strategic interaction that would make it possible to identify a communication or form of subjectivity as such.

If power is capable of systematically distorting our subjectivity, won't this affect us at not only a rational but also a psychic-affective level? In that sense, might we have not only a rational self-interest in allowing identity conflicts to smolder—namely, in that getting the recognition we need depends on suppressing them—but also a psychic investment in and attachment to them? How are we to gain reflexive distance on such attachments and investments? (How) can autonomy be both theoretically and practically disentangled from systematically distorted subjectivity? Not only does Habermas not answer these questions, after the middle of the 1970s, he more or less abandons his discussions of systematically distorted communication altogether, focusing instead on the formal-pragmatic analysis of communication and its ramifications for social theory, moral philosophy, and legal and political theory. As a result, he never really develops an account of the systematic distortions of subjectivity that arise in contexts of subordination. Instead, he turns his attention to a formal-pragmatic account of individuation through socialization. As we shall see, however, implicit in this account is a third and potentially more radical vision of the role that power plays in the lifeworld.

Individuation Through Socialization

The closely related notions of communicative rationality and intersubjectivity form the conceptual core of Habermas's philosophical project. As Habermas argues in *The Philosophical Discourse of Modernity*, he shares with his French post-structuralist counterparts a desire to move beyond the paradigm of the philosophy of consciousness or the philosophy of the subject, a paradigm that reached its apex in the first half of the twentieth century with the flowering of phenomenology and existentialism.

However, unlike his French counterparts, at least as he interprets them, Habermas proposes a determinate rather than an abstract negation of the paradigm of the philosophy of the subject;[39] as he puts it, "a paradigm only loses its force when it is negated in a *determinate* manner by a *different* paradigm, that is, when it is devalued in an *insightful* way; it is certainly resistant to any simple invocation of the extinction of the subject."[40] Habermas suggests that we replace the paradigm of philosophy of the subject with "the paradigm of mutual understanding, that is, of the intersubjective relationship between individuals who are socialized through communication and reciprocally recognize one another."[41]

Habermas's proposed paradigm shift is thus conceptually dependent upon his account of socialization into a communicatively structured lifeworld. By communicative interaction, Habermas means a form of social interaction in which "the participants coordinate their plans of action consensually, with the agreement reached at any point being evaluated in terms of the intersubjective recognition of validity claims."[42] He contrasts this mode of interaction with strategic action, in which "one actor seeks to *influence* the behavior of another by means of the threat of sanctions or the prospect of gratification in order to *cause* the interaction to continue as the first actor desires."[43] In communicative action, "one actor seeks *rationally* to *motivate* another by relying on the illocutionary binding/bonding effect (*Bindungseffekt*) of the offer contained in the speech act";[44] this binding/bonding effect is the result of the speaker's willingness to redeem the validity claim that she has implicitly raised if it is called into question. The concepts of communicative action and the lifeworld are closely related, though not, Habermas insists, equivalent.[45] As Habermas puts it: "Subjects acting communicatively always come to an understanding in the horizon of a lifeworld. Their lifeworld is formed from more or less diffuse, always unproblematic, background convictions. This lifeworld background serves as a source of situation definitions that are presupposed by participants as unproblematic."[46]

Habermas delineates three dimensions of the lifeworld—culture, society, and personality—to which correspond three distinct processes—cultural reproduction of commonly accepted beliefs, meanings, and interpretations; social integration via shared norms and behavioral expectations; and the production of shared competencies through socialization processes. As Habermas puts it, "participants draw from this *lifeworld* not just consensual patterns of interpretation (the background knowledge from which propositional contents are fed), but also normatively reliable patterns of social relations (the tacitly presupposed solidarities on which illocutionary acts are based) and the competences acquired in socialization processes (the background of the speaker's intentions)."[47] However, Habermas acknowledges that the communicatively structured lifeworld and functionally, strategically integrated systems can and do interpenetrate; as I discussed above, it is precisely this acknowledgment that underpins his colonization of the lifeworld thesis, which tracks the pathological side effects that emerge when economic and power-laden system imperatives encroach upon lifeworld processes.[48]

The shift away from the paradigm of the philosophy of the subject to the paradigm of mutual understanding and intersubjectivity is central to Habermas's account of subjectivation as well, which he lays out through his reading of G. H. Mead in the essay "Individuation Through Socialization: On George Herbert Mead's Theory of Subjectivity."[49] Habermas claims that Mead's central insight is to conceive of individuation "not as the self-realization of an independently acting subject carried out in isolation and freedom but as a linguistically mediated process of socialization and the simultaneous constitution of a life-history that is conscious of itself."[50] Whereas the philosophy of consciousness grounds its account of subjectivity in the abstract self-reflection of the knowing subject, Habermas insists that it is the "self-understanding of a subject who is capable of speech and action, one who in the face of other dialogue participants presents and, if necessary, justifies himself as an irreplaceable and distinctive person" that "ground[s] the identity of the ego."[51] In other words, the identity of the ego is grounded not in abstract reflective knowledge (as the philosophical tradition from Leibniz through Kant to Fichte had understood it) but in a practical ethical self-relation; moreover, this self-relation implicitly refers to the self's relation to an other, on whom one is dependent for recognition and to whom one is accountable. What the philosophy of consciousness fails to see is that the abstract knowing subject that it takes as its starting point is actually the *result* of a complex intersubjective process: "The self of an ethical self-understanding is dependent upon recognition by addressees because it generates itself as a response to the demands of the other in the first place."[52] The self has an intersubjective core because it is generated communicatively, "on the path from without to within, through the symbolically mediated relationship to a partner in interaction."[53]

The key to understanding the intersubjective core of the self is Mead's distinction between the "I" and the "me," although Habermas ultimately departs in crucial ways from Mead's account of this distinction. For Mead, the "I" is the spontaneous, creative subject that cannot be accessed through direct reflection, for as soon as I reflect on the "I," it is transformed from a subject to the object of my reflection.[54] The "me," by contrast, is, as Peter Dews has put it, "the socially constructed self, which is established through processes of identification with the reactions of others, and—at the limit—through an identification with the social process as a whole, in the form which he describes as the 'generalized Other.'"[55] As Habermas interprets Mead, both the epistemic and the practical relations to self are generated intersubjectively. With respect to the epistemic self-relation, Habermas notes that "the self of self-consciousness is not the spontaneously acting 'I'; the latter is given only in the refraction of the symbolically captured meaning that it took on for its interaction partner 'a second ago' in the role of alter ego."[56] In other words, the "me," which is generated through an interaction with an alter ego, solidifies the "I" in memory. With respect to the practical self-relation, the process has the same intersubjective structure, but the emphasis is on taking over alter's normative (rather than cognitive) expectations. In the practical relation to self, the "me" is the generalized other, whose perspective is internalized as a mechanism for placing limits on the impulses and creativity of the "I." In this sense, for Mead, as Habermas notes, "the 'me' of the practical relation-to-self proves to be a conservative force. This agency is closely united with what already exists. It mirrors the forms of life and the institutions that are practiced and recognized in a particular society. It functions in the consciousness of the socialized individual as society's agent and drives everything that spontaneously deviates out of the individual's consciousness."[57]

Thus, for Mead, the "me" is associated with inauthenticity and repression of the authentic "I." As Habermas puts it, Mead's "'me' characterizes an identity formation that makes responsible action possible only at the price of blind subjugation to external social controls, which remain external in spite of the internalizing effect of role-taking."[58] As a metaphysical account of the self, this is obviously quite problematic for Habermas, who prefers to envision the socially and intersubjectivity constituted self as the locus not of internalized subjugation but of genuine autonomy in the sense of rational accountability. Thus, Habermas decides to reinterpret Mead's metaphysical claim about the nature of the self as a historical one by arguing that the "me" is only oppressive and inauthentic in the context of conventional, traditional societies.[59] In postconventional, modern societies, by contrast, socialization processes make it possible for individuals to reconcile the "I" with the "me" precisely because the postconventional subject, through the internalization of external social controls, "takes what the reference person expects of him and first *makes it his own.*"[60] Postconventional identity is predicated on the anticipation of reciprocal recognition in the context of an unlimited communication community, and the norms of the postconventional self are tested through an actual discursive process of taking up the position of others who are potentially affected by such norms. As Habermas argues elsewhere, the progression from preconventional to conventional to post-conventional modes of ego identity is marked by increasing degrees of abstraction, generalization, and reflexivity: "the simple behavioral expectation of the first level becomes reflexive at the next level—expectations can be reciprocally expected; and the reflexive behavioral expectation of the second level again becomes reflexive at the third level—norms can be normed."[61] It is this greater degree of reflexivity that explains how Habermas can view postconventional individuals as *produced through* but not *determined by* socialization. As he puts it, "Identity is produced through *socialization*, that is, through the fact that the growing child first of all integrates into a specific social system by appropriating symbolic generalities; it is later secured and developed through *individuation*, that is, precisely through a growing independence in relation to social systems."[62]

Habermas argues that there are two dimensions of this intersubjective formation of the self: ethical self-realization and moral self-determination (or moral autonomy). The postconventional self thus anticipates itself as a "free will in moral self-reflection" and a "fully individuated being in existential self reflection."[63] Both of these dimensions of the self are dependent upon the anticipation of relationships of mutual, reciprocal recognition: self-realization is dependent upon others' "recognition of my claim to uniqueness and irreplaceability,"[64] and self-determination upon their recognition of the moral rightness of my actions and judgments. Both of these modes of recognition refer ultimately to the counterfactual ideal of an unlimited communication community. "In communicative action, the suppositions of self-determination and self-realization retain a rigorously intersubjective sense: whoever judges and acts morally must be capable of anticipating the agreement of an unlimited communication community, and whoever realizes himself in a responsibly accepted life history must be capable of anticipating recognition from this unlimited community."[65] As a result, neither can be captured adequately by a view that understands social interaction in solely strategic terms:

> Under conditions of strategic interaction, the self of self-determination and of self-realization slips out of intersubjective relations. The strategic actor no longer draws from an intersubjectively shared lifeworld; having himself become worldless, as it were, he stands over and against the objective world and makes decisions solely according to standards of subjective preference. He does not rely therein upon recognition by others. Autonomy is then transformed into freedom of choice, and the individuation of the socialized subject is transformed into the isolation of a liberated subject who possesses himself.[66]

There is an interesting convergence between Habermas's critique of the philosophy of consciousness and Foucault's critique of the transcendental-phenomenological subject. As I argued in chapter 2, Foucault too was critical of the philosophy of the subject for assuming the knowing, self-reflective subject as given, and he too interrogated the social conditions of possibility for the formation of that subject. However, whereas Habermas turns to Mead for inspiration for rethinking this isolated knowing subject as an intersubjective self-in-relation, Foucault turns to Kant's anthropological writings, read through a Nietzschean lens. This leads to a crucial difference between their two accounts: although both could agree that the subject is formed on the path from without to within, they have very different conceptions of the without—that is, of the realm of the social—and thus different understandings of the within. For Foucault, the social is infused with power relations, whereas for Habermas it is structured in terms of mutual, reciprocal recognition. This basic disagreement brings us back to Habermas's distinction between system and lifeworld and his tendency, at least in *The Theory of Communicative Action*, to reserve the term "power" to refer to the former.

It is precisely his tendency to connect power with the systemic level of analysis—despite his account of systematically distorted communication—that leads Habermas to mischaracterize Foucault as a systems theorist.[67] Although there are some superficial resemblances between Foucaultian genealogy and systems theory, this is a serious mistake. Habermas associates both strategic action and the adoption of a third person, observer perspective with systems theory;[68] because Foucault understands power strategically and because genealogy makes methodological use of a distantiated third person perspective, Habermas infers that Foucault must be a systems theorist. However, Foucault is not actually concerned with what Habermas refers to as systems or the systems-theoretical perspective at all. As he repeatedly makes clear in his discussions of power, Foucault is not interested in studying the way power functions in the state or the official economy (the two domains highlighted by systems theory).[69] Rather, Foucault's analysis of power is concerned precisely with uncovering how power functions in the lifeworld, how it informs our everyday social practices and our taken-for-granted background beliefs, norms, self-understandings, and so on. Moreover, Foucault's account of power focuses on precisely the three core domains of the lifeworld that Habermas identifies: on cultural patterns of knowledge and their imbrication with relations of power, on social patterns of normative expectations and their normalizing effects, and on the socialization processes by means of which individuals are subjected, that is, transformed into subjects. Perhaps in part because Habermas fails to pay sufficient attention to the role that power plays in the lifeworld, he has difficulty recognizing that this is precisely where Foucault situates power. Although it is true that Foucaultian genealogy makes use of a third person, observer perspective, this is a methodological tool that enables him to reveal the contingency and power-ladenness of our lifeworld; not unlike Garfinkel's ethnomethodology, genealogy is a way of making lifeworld contexts strange, as a first step toward critically assessing them.[70]

To put this point another way: Habermas criticizes Foucault for having an "unsociological" conception of the social and of power.[71] By this he seems to mean that because Foucault understands social interaction in terms of power and power, in turn, in terms of strategic interaction, he cannot explain the possibility of social order, for such an explanation depends upon the realization that "it is not the use of propositions per se, but only the *communicative* use of propositionally differentiated language that is proper to our sociocultural form of life and is constitutive for the level of a genuinely social reproduction of life."[72] However, Habermas, we might say, has an *unpolitical* or *depoliticized* conception of the lifeworld. He pays insufficient attention to the way that power operates in the lifeworld contexts of cultural meanings, social practices, and socialization of individual and group identities. His most developed attempt to analyze power in the lifeworld through the concept of systematically distorted communication is unsatisfactory and, perhaps for that reason, ends up being sidelined in his later work. Indeed, in a reply to his critics, Habermas rather feebly insists that "the theory of communicative action is not a completely unpolitical project."[73] Habermas complains that Foucault's analysis of power is "not up to the ambiguous phenomena of modernity"[74] and that Foucault, like Adorno, Heidegger, and Derrida, is "insensitive to the highly *ambivalent* content of cultural and social modernity."[75] However, reflecting on the depoliticized nature of his account of the lifeworld, one wonders whether Habermas's account is up to the task either. Specifically, can Habermas's account make sense of the role that power plays in socialization processes through the mechanism of subjection, which in turn serves to help maintain and reproduce existing structures of social subordination?

The Morally Disciplined Personality

A closer reading of Habermas's account of individuation through socialization reveals that he does acknowledge a more substantial and integral role for power in the lifeworld, and that this acknowledgment comes precisely in the context of his discussions of socialization, particularly in his account of the intersubjective process of the formation of moral autonomy. Interestingly enough, particularly in light of his debate with Foucault, he refers to this as the development of a "morally disciplined personality."[76] However, even as he acknowledges this link, he is utterly sanguine about it both because he views the relevant power relations as legitimate and because he sees them as necessary for the formation of autonomy, the attainment of which enables individuals to break free of whatever relations of power and dependency have structured their early development. Thus, even this account of the role that power plays in the socialization of autonomous individuals seems strangely unpolitical.

Following Freud and Mead, Habermas argues that the internalization of structures of authority is a necessary feature of the process of individuation through socialization. In general, Habermas regards "the transposition of external structures into internal structures" as "an important learning mechanism."[77] With respect to the development of moral autonomy in particular, Habermas argues that

> the task of passing to the conventional stage of interaction consists in reworking the imperative arbitrary will of a dominant figure of this kind [that is, a parent] into the authority of a suprapersonal will detached from this specific person. As we know, Freud and Mead alike assumed that particular behavior patterns become detached from the context-bound intentions and speech acts of specific individuals and take on the external form of social norms to the extent that the sanctions associated with them are *internalized* …, that is, to the extent that they are assimilated into the personality of the growing child and thus made independent of the sanctioning power of concrete reference persons.[78]

As Habermas sees it, the internalization of parental power and authority is a necessary step on the developmental trajectory that leads to full autonomy. The growing child undergoes a transformation from an initial dependence on a wholly external authority (usually a parent) for judgments of right and wrong (the preconventional stage) through an internalization of that authority relation that results in feelings of guilt and shame (the conventional stage) to an ability to reflect autonomously on social norms and consider whether such norms are genuinely valid (the achievement of postconventional autonomy).

However, Habermas's account of internalization is based more on Mead, who concentrates on the socially generated cognitive processes that make such internalization possible, than on Freud, who focuses on the psychodynamics and the psychic costs of this process.[79] The key developmental advance toward the conventional stage consists not only in the ego's ability to take up the position of an alter, but also in the ability to adopt "an objectivating attitude toward his own actions," to view them from the point of view of not some particular other but a generalized other.[80] "Only when A in his interaction with B adopts the attitude of an impartial member of their social group toward them both can he become aware of the *interchangeability* of his and B's positions."[81] This gives him the idea of a social behavior pattern or expectation that expresses the collective will of the group:

> The group's power to punish and reward, which stands behind social roles, loses the character of a higher-stage imperative only when the growing child once again internalizes the power of institutions (which at first confronts him as a fact of life) and anchors it internally as a system of behavioral controls. Only when A has learned to conceive of group sanctions as his own sanctions, which he *himself* has set up against *himself*, does he have to *presuppose* his consent to a norm whose violation he punishes in this way.[82]

Once again, however, Habermas parts company with Mead by arguing that Mead's account only gets you as far as the conventional stage of development. At this stage of development, the child's affirmations of social norms or imperatives "do *not yet* have the character of affirmative responses to criticizable validity claims. If it were otherwise, one would have to assume that the mere acceptance of norms of action is always and everywhere based on some rationally motivated agreement by all concerned."[83] But to remain at this level is to collapse the distinction between mere de facto and rational, or legitimate, consensus. Only at the postconventional stage do "the actors rely, in the act of consenting, on the complete reversibility of their relations with other participants in argumentation and *at the same time* attribute the position they take to the persuasive force of the better argument, no matter how their consensus was reached in actual fact."[84] The transition to the postconventional stage of development "undermines the normative power of the factual"; institutions, norms, and practices lose their "quasi-natural" character, and their validity and worthiness of being recognized is thrown open to discursive questioning.[85] Only at the postconventional level is genuinely moral action—understood as "normatively regulated action in which the actor is oriented toward reflectively tested claims to validity"[86]—possible.

However, for our purposes, the interesting point is that Habermas seems perfectly willing to admit that power plays a crucial role in the formation and development of the autonomous postconventional self, that it is in fact *necessary* for the development of this self. This comes out in Habermas's account of the ontogenetic development of a decentered understanding of the world, a development that requires the achievement of an interrelated set of speaker perspectives—including the ability to take up the first, second, and third person perspectives, not just grammatically but also in terms of action orientations—and world perspectives—including the ability to differentiate between things in the objective world, the intersubjective (social) world, and the subject's own internal world. Habermas argues that "*the ontogenesis of speaker and world perspectives* that leads to a decentered understanding of the world can be explained only in connection with the development of … corresponding structures of interaction."[87] In his account of these interaction structures, Habermas focuses on the difficult transition from the preconventional to the conventional level. At the preconventional level, the child has mastered the "I-thou perspectives learned through experience in the roles of speaker and hearer."[88] At this level, interactions are structured either in terms of what Habermas calls "authority-governed complementarity" or "interest-governed symmetry." Authority-governed complementarity is "a nonsymmetrical form of reciprocity" that obtains whenever authority is unequal, as in the parent-child relationship.[89] A relationship structured by interest-governed symmetry, by contrast, is an egalitarian one grounded in shared behavioral expectations, as in, for example, friendship. At this stage of the child's development, neither strategic nor communicative or normatively regulated interaction is possible; Habermas claims that these action orientations only become possible at the conventional level of development, once the child has learned to integrate the observer perspective into his system of interaction structures.[90] Competitive behavior is possible at the preconventional level, but only in the context of relationships between peers. When conflicts arise between parents and children, in the context of unequal power relationships, the child "will try to resolve the conflict between his own needs and alter's demands by avoiding threatened sanctions."[91] At the conventional level, the possibility of strategic action is secured simply by the addition of the observer perspective to the competitive behavior of the previous level, but in order for normatively regulated communicative action to be possible, a further development is needed, namely, the detachment of authority relations from particular individuals (usually the parents) and the emergence of the notion of a suprapersonal will or generalized other.[92]

The intricate details of this account need not concern us here. What is of interest is the apparent tension between the admission that power plays a crucial role in the formation of autonomy and Habermas's contention that the idea of morality—in both philosophy and everyday life—is grounded in relationships of reciprocity and mutual recognition. The moral point of view, according to Habermas, "originates in a fundamental reciprocity that is built into action oriented toward reaching understanding."[93] However, it would seem that, on Habermas's own view, the capacity for engaging in communicative action is itself rooted in an asymmetrical power relation, namely, the relation between parent and child, in which the child's physical and psychic survival and flourishing are radically dependent on parental protection, care, and love.[94] Habermas glosses over this aspect of the origin of the moral point of view by calling the authority-governed complementarity of the parent-child relationship a form of *reciprocity*. Though he admits that it is a "nonsymmetrical form of reciprocity," he nonetheless characterizes it as a form of reciprocity in the sense that the interaction entails "the reciprocity of action perspectives" in which speaker and hearer assume "I-thou perspectives ... vis-à-vis one another."[95] However, the crucial difference between the two forms of "reciprocity" at this early stage of interaction is that in authority-governed relationships of complementarity "one person [namely, the parent] controls the other's contribution to the interaction," whereas in interest-governed relationships of symmetry, "the participants exercise mutual control over their contributions to the interaction."[96]

The trouble is that Habermas seems to conflate two distinct uses of the term "reciprocity" here. Relationships of authority-governed complementarity are reciprocal only in the thin sense that both parties to such a relationship contribute something to it and are capable of imaginatively taking up the perspective of the other. In this sense, virtually all social relationships, including all but the most extreme forms of domination, are reciprocal as well. But this is not the same thing as the thicker notion of normative reciprocity, grounded in mutual respect and recognition, that is characteristic of a relationship between peers or equals. Habermas trades on the ambiguity here, using the undeniable fact that the parent-child relationship is reciprocal in the thin sense to motivate the conclusion that this relationship is one of reciprocity in the thick sense, thus, that it is capable of grounding the moral point of view. This conflation is evident in his claim that "at the preconventional level the child views authority ... relations as relations of exchange (e.g., exchange of obedience for security and guidance ...)."[97] This makes it sound as if the parent-child relationship is some sort of social contract between free and equal parties to the exchange, a characterization that completely obscures the fact that children depend on their parents not only for security and guidance but also, as Butler argued, for the love and recognition that enables them to stabilize their identities. Habermas glosses over this aspect of the parent-child relationship and thus obscures the rootedness of communicative action and, hence, of the moral point of view, in an asymmetrical relationship of power.

Of course, Habermas's use of the term "authority" is crucial here because it implies that the power relation that the growing child must internalize in order to achieve the conventional stage of development is a legitimate one. However, even if we agree with Habermas that this is the case, the child, as Butler has argued, is not capable of assessing its legitimacy. Indeed, she *cannot* be in that position because she is only capable of taking up the moral point of view once she has already internalized that power relation. Habermas acknowledges this point when he says that "for the growing child this question [of whether a norm is valid] has already been given an affirmative answer before it can pose itself to him *as* a question. The de facto power of a generalized imperative still attaches to the moment of generality in the generalized other, for the concept is constructed by way of internalizing a concrete group's power to sanction."[98] However, once again it is his account of the possibility for postconventional identity that allows him to avoid the pessimistic conclusions of Butler and Mead: "And yet, that same moment of generality *also* already contains the claim—aiming at insight—that a norm deserves to be valid only insofar as, in connection with some matter requiring regulation, it takes into account the interests of everyone involved, and only insofar as it embodies the will that all could form in common, each in his own interest, as the will of the generalized other."[99] Thus, Habermas insists that "the social control exercised via norms that are valid for specific groups is not based on repression *alone*."[100] This suggests that Habermas is willing to admit that the social control that is made possible by the internalization of structures of authority is at least in part based on repression; the key point for Habermas is that norms cannot be based solely on repression, else "they could not obligate the actors to obey but only force them into submissiveness."[101] However, the question remains, how does the internalization of structures of power/authority make them legitimate, especially given that the child has *first* to internalize them in order to be able to in a second step decide whether or not they are legitimate?

Habermas might respond here by appealing to the distinction between the internal motivating force of reasons and the force of external sanctions. As William Rehg puts this point, the force of moral norms

does not derive from extrinsic considerations ... Rather, we experience this force of the "ought," feel bound to respect its command, even when—

perhaps especially when—it is not in our own interests, when no punitive consequences will result from breaking the norm.... Moral "oughts,"
in contrast to simple imperatives, carry an internal force or motivating
power within the command itself, a force that seems neither to depend
on external threats and gratifications nor to express merely the speaker's
contingent will.[102]

Similarly, Habermas himself puts it this way: "We do not adhere to recognized norms from a sense of duty because they are *imposed* upon us by
the threat of sanctions but because we *give* them to ourselves."[103] However, this way of putting it overlooks the fact that, as Habermas himself has
argued, we are only able to become the sort of beings who feel obligated in
the first place because of the internalization of structures of authority that
is accomplished largely through the mechanism of parental discipline.

In his recent book, *The Future of Human Nature*, Habermas acknowledges this difficulty, but he insists that it is neutralized by the development
of the capacity for autonomy itself, by means of which "adolescents ... can
retrospectively compensate for the asymmetry of filial dependency by lib-
erating themselves through a critical reappraisal of the genesis of such re-
strictive socialization processes. Even neurotic fixations may be resolved
analytically, through an elaboration of self-reflexive insights."[104]

At this point, it is instructive to consider Butler's alternative, Nietzschean account of the emergence of conscience in *The Psychic Life of Power*.
As Butler argues, Nietzsche too understands conscience as formed as "the
consequence of a distinctive kind of internalization,"[105] namely, the internalization of structures of social regulation that turn the subject against
itself, that lead it to engage in repeated self-beratement. However, as she
goes on to argue, the term "internalization" is potentially misleading, for
"although one is tempted to claim that social regulation is simply internalized, taken from the outside and brought into the psyche, the problem
is more complicated and, indeed, more insidious. For the boundary that
divides the outside from the inside is in the process of being installed,
precisely through the regulation of the subject."[106] As Butler herself acknowledges, this leads to a thorny if not intractable problem. If the subject is formed through what Butler interprets as a violent turning back
on itself, then this means that "the subject who would oppose violence,
even violence to itself, is itself the effect of a prior violence without which
the subject could not have emerged. Can that particular circle be broken?
How and when does that breakage occur?"[107]

As I argued in the previous chapter, Butler's assumption that subjection is per se subordinating is, in my view, too strong.[108] Nevertheless,

she does raise the very important point that the role that power necessarily plays in subjection makes us *vulnerable* to becoming psychically attached to subordinating modes of identity. It is precisely this dimension of subjectivation and the psychic cost of the subjugation necessary for socialization that Habermas glosses over. To take one of his standard formulations: "Individuation is merely the reverse side of socialization. Only in relations of reciprocal recognition can a person constitute and reproduce his identity."[109] In this statement, Habermas makes it clear that reciprocal recognition is a *necessary* condition for the formation of the individual self; however, Habermas's own account of the ontogenesis of the subject makes it clear that reciprocal recognition—in the thick, normative sense—is not in fact *sufficient* for the self's formation. The internalization of an asymmetrical power relationship between parent and child is also necessary. The question thus becomes: What are the psychic and social consequences of this necessary condition on subjectivation? Contra Butler, we have to be careful not to collapse the distinction between power and subordination here; however, if critical theory is to do justice to the complexity of the power relations that it aims to criticize, we must go further than Habermas in acknowledging the implications of the role that power plays in subjectivation processes. At the very least, Butler's account of psychic subjection can be understood as a necessary counterpart to Habermas's account of individuation through socialization, one that highlights the psychic obstacles to the exercise of autonomy that can arise in contexts of subordination.

However, there is a potentially more serious problem for Habermas's account of autonomy lurking in the background here. Because the child cannot discriminate between subordinating and nonsubordinating attachments, and because she will form an attachment to painful and subordinating modes of identity rather than not attach, her psychic attachment to subordination may well precede the development of her capacity for autonomy. In such cases, as Butler puts it, "power pervades the very conceptual apparatus that seeks to negotiate its terms, including the subject position of the critic."[110] For example, consider the fact that in societies that are structured by sex/gender systems, the very vehicles of recognition through which the infant's capacities for autonomy are nourished and developed—language and the familial relations into which infants are first socialized—are shot through with relations of dominance and subordination based on gender. Thus, power threatens to pervade not only the content of oppressive gender norms but also the very critical capacities that enable the gendered individual to reflect autonomously on such norms. The autonomous subject that reflects on the validity of gender norms is always already gendered, understands his/her gender to be integral to his/her identity as a person, and, thus, is heavily invested in that identity, despite his/her awareness of the ways in which gender is intertwined with relations of subordination. At the limit, such a subject is incapable of imagining what it is like to be ungendered without simultaneously imagining the disintegration of his/her identity. At the very least, this example calls into question Habermas's faith in the gendered adult's (let alone adolescent's!) ability retrospectively to liberate him/herself via a critical appraisal of the asymmetries that structured his/her own socialization.[111] Moreover, thinking through this type of example threatens to problematize the distinction between power and validity that Habermas takes to be so central to critical theory, for if the validity of certain norms is so woven into the fabric of our form of life, our language, and our sense of who we are that we literally cannot imagine ourselves independent of them, then these norms will remain stubbornly resistant to attempts discursively to assess their legitimacy.

Indeed, elsewhere, Habermas makes it clear that he rejects the kind of Nietzschean account of bad conscience offered by Butler for precisely this reason, because it leads ineluctably to a blurring of the distinction between validity and power.[112] According to Habermas, Nietzsche's claim that morality results from the will to power turning back against itself, coupled with his privileging of taste and aesthetic sensibility, leads him in the direction of "rebellion against everything normative."[113] As Habermas sees it, Nietzsche proceeds by means of a two-step deflation of both truth and normative rightness claims: first, he reduces these to value judgments or judgments of taste, then he reduces the latter even further to expressions of the will to power. The difficulty with this Nietzschean unmasking of the power relations that lurk behind and reinforce our normative judgments is this: "Once all predicates concerning validity are devalued, once it is power and not validity claims that is expressed in value appraisals—by what criterion shall critique still be able to propose discriminations? It must at least be able to discriminate between a power that *deserves* to be esteemed and one that *deserves* to be devalued."[114] To be sure, Nietzsche attempts to make such a discrimination by appealing to a distinction between active and reactive forces, but Habermas argues that, once he has reduced truth and normative rightness to power-laden value judgments, Nietzsche can no longer claim the status of truth for his totalizing genealogical critique of reason.

This critique of Nietzsche suggests a possible reason for Habermas's downplaying of the role that power plays in socialization processes, that is, of what Foucault and Butler diagnose under the heading of subjection. As we have seen, Habermas does not deny that power plays any role in these processes but he does seem to be utterly sanguine about the consequences of this role and, thus, utterly unwilling to acknowledge the psychic costs involved in socialization. As Johanna Meehan puts it, Habermas fails "to acknowledge that all socialization entails subjugation but that this is the cost of civilization, as Freud recognized."[115] I would suggest that Habermas's failure to acknowledge this point is no mere oversight. He needs to downplay the role that power plays in socialization precisely so that he can establish how the subject can break out of the circle that Butler is worried about, how it can be autonomous with respect to the contents of its lifeworld. Dwelling on the role that power plays in socialization makes a strong conception of postconventional autonomy according to which we are capable of being rationally accountable for—in the sense of being able to reflectively distance ourselves from—our moral and ethical-existential choices difficult to maintain. To be sure, even if we can distance ourselves from some aspects of our lifeworld, we can only do this by relying on other aspects that remain unquestioned and unthematized. As McCarthy puts it, "at every moment and in every situation unconscious factors [including relations of power] will inevitably play a role in shaping our interpretive and evaluative schemes."[116] The challenge for critical theory is to offer conceptions of autonomy and critique that acknowledge this inevitability without foregoing entirely the goal of emancipation.

The charge that Habermas screens power out of the lifeworld turns out to be not entirely fair, though it isn't entirely wrong, either. Habermas acknowledges a role for power in the lifeworld in his colonization thesis, though, as we saw, this account preserves the association between power and systemic imperatives and, thus, does not meet the full force of the original objection. The account of systematically distorted communication does a better job of considering how power can and does permeate lifeworld contexts themselves, though this account raises as many questions as it answers and is never developed into a satisfactory model of subjection. Implicit in Habermas's account of individuation through socialization is yet a third, largely unacknowledged, account of how power functions in the lifeworld: as a necessary condition on the formation of individual autonomy, which takes place via the internalization of parental authority and the translation of this internalized subjugation into postconventional reflexivity. At a purely descriptive level, this account dovetails with Nietzsche's account of bad conscience and with the Foucaultian and Butlerian accounts of subjection that were inspired by Nietzsche. But

Habermas strives to avoid what he perceives as the self-undermining and relativistic implications of this Nietzschean account. Perhaps for this very reason, he insists on downplaying the role that power plays in socialization, linking such power to notions of legitimate authority, conflating it with a thick account of normative reciprocity, and viewing the autonomy that is conferred through postconventional socialization processes as powerful enough to enable the autonomous individual to break free of whatever modes of dependency and asymmetry are responsible for its formation. It is in this sense that the charge that he screens power out of the lifeworld is not entirely wrong. Even when he admits power into the lifeworld, he does so in ways that blunt its effects and render it irrelevant to his norma-tive-philosophical project and to the conception of autonomy that forms its conceptual core.

This line of criticism raises the following questions: Does the acknowl-edgment that power necessarily plays a formative role in subjectivation lead to the reduction of validity to power, hence, to an undermining of all critique and to the impossibility of autonomy? Does it make it impossible to distinguish between what Fraser calls better and worse subjectivating practices? Or might it instead lead us to a reconsideration of how we do critique, to a more modest recasting of our conception of autonomy, to a less utopian and more pragmatic understanding of the normative under-pinnings of critical theory? These are questions that I will take up in the next chapter.

6

Contextualizing Critical Theory

THE MAIN argument of chapter 5 was that Habermas does not offer a satisfactory account of the ways in which power works through socialization processes to constitute individuals as subjects. For the most part, in his theory of communicative action, he examines power in the context of systems theory; his discussions of power in the lifeworld, whether in the context of his colonization of the lifeworld thesis or his analysis of systematically distorted communication, are not adequate to the task of developing an account of subjection. And although he does acknowledge, at least implicitly, a necessary role for power in the process of socialization, he is overly sanguine about the implications of this. Even his more complicated and differentiated analysis of power in *Between Facts and Norms*, which distinguishes social power, administrative power, and communicative power, fails to consider subjection as a mechanism for the reproduction and maintenance of certain forms of social subordination.

Recently, however, McCarthy has argued that although Habermas has not offered a satisfactory account of how cultural and symbolic power structures the lifeworld, including socialization processes, "there are tools available in Habermas's framework for constructing a more adequate approach" to such phenomena.[1] Some of these tools are to be found, he suggests, in Habermas's early work, prior to the development of the theory of communicative action. McCarthy points out that in *Knowledge and Human Interests*, for example, Habermas offered an account of the relationships between power, social practices, and subjectivity not unlike that found in Foucault, whose work, McCarthy admits, at least initially appears more suitable for constructing an analysis of racial and gender oppression. However, McCarthy also characterizes the account of the relationships between power, knowledge, and subjectivity in Habermas's early work as "non-totalizing" and, as such, preferable to Foucault's account.[2] Whereas McCarthy acknowledges that Habermas turned his attention away from this project when he began to develop his formal-pragmatic analysis of communication, his theory of social action, and his discourse theory of morality, law, and democracy, he also claims that "it would be worth the effort ... to start now from the fully developed theory of communicative action and return to the themes of [Habermas's] earlier work with the aim of developing a framework suitable for analyzing power relations across the range of phenomena highlighted by Foucault."[3] Specifically, McCarthy suggests that Habermas's account of symbolic reproduction in the lifeworld—in the domains of culture, society, and personality—provides a promising point of departure for a critical theory of the cultural, social, and psychological dimensions of racial/gender subordination and their complex interactions. Carrying out this project, according to McCarthy, will involve engaging in a form of ideology critique, a critique that will require us to reflect on "those race-based relations of power lodged deep in pretheoretical layers of cultural backgrounds, normative expectations, and socialization practices—in racial classifications and identifications, status differentials and role models, attitudes and perceptions, and so forth."[4]

I wholeheartedly agree with McCarthy that Habermas's framework needs to be expanded to encompass an account of the role that cultural/symbolic power plays in the formation of subordinated identities if it is to offer a truly critical theory of racial, gender, and sexual subordination. I further agree that incorporating something like Foucault's account of power into the social-theoretical framework of the lifeworld seems like a sensible way to go about expanding Habermas's view—though I would also argue that Foucault's account needs to be supplemented with some consideration of the psychic attachment to and investment in subordination that can be and often is instilled in subordinated subjects. Thus, the main question for this chapter is the following: What are the implications for Habermas's philosophical framework of this sort of theoretical move? Specifically, can Habermas's robust conception of autonomy remain unscathed by the incorporation of a Foucaultian account of subjection? Can his commitment to the context transcendence of validity claims and his staunch moral-political universalism be maintained in the wake of such a move?

In what follows, I will maintain that the answer to both of these questions is no. A basically Foucaultian account of power and subjection cannot be plugged into Habermas's social theoretical framework without putting some pressure on the all-important distinction between power and validity. This, in turn, poses challenges to Habermas's conception of postconventional autonomy and to his commitment to the context transcendence of validity claims. To assume otherwise would be to assume not only that Foucault offers nothing more than empirical insights into the workings of power, but also that there are no normative, social-theoretical, or philosophical implications that follow from these empirical insights. Such an assumption is grounded in a problematic separation between the formal (either transcendental or quasi-transcendental) and the empirical levels of analysis, an issue that I take up below. Nor should we assume that admitting a role for Foucault's insights into power will necessarily lead us down the garden path toward a totalizing abstract negation of reason and normativity that results in an infantile moral nihilism. This latter assumption is grounded in a fundamental misunderstanding of Foucault's philosophical project, a misunderstanding that I hope to have gone some way toward dispelling in chapters 2 and 3. The choice between a staunch Habermasian moral-political universalism and an infantile Foucaultian nihilism is, I maintain, a false antithesis. Taking seriously the role that power plays in lifeworld processes such as the constitution of autonomous subjects leads us back to the entanglement of power and validity, and to the worry that validity—and therefore autonomy—can never be completely purified of power. One obvious response to this worry would be to reduce validity to power and autonomy to disciplinary subjection; this is a strategy that is often imputed—incorrectly, as I argued in chapter 3—to Foucault. The other would be to insulate validity from the workings of power entirely; this latter strategy is arguably what Habermas attempts with his account of rational reconstruction and with his notion of the context transcendence of validity claims. But there is a third, and better, possibility: we could instead give up the demand for purity altogether.[5] Taking this third tack requires offering a more pragmatic and contextualist reading of Habermas's project. Doing so will clear the way for the construction of a critical-theoretical account of the relation between power and autonomy that draws on the insights of both Foucault and Habermas, even as it moves beyond them.

The Empirical and the Transcendental (Reprise)

Habermas, throughout his work on various topics, makes a consistent and clear distinction between formal and empirical levels of analysis. This shows up in his account of communication as a distinction between formal (or universal) and empirical pragmatics, in his account of subjectivation as a distinction between the ontogenesis of ego identity and moral consciousness and the psychodynamics of that formative process, in his moral theory as a distinction between universal moral norms (*Moralität*) and the empirically various forms of concrete ethical life (*Sittlichkeit*) in which they are embedded, and in his legal and political theory as a distinction between deliberative democratic procedures and the lifeworld contexts that must meet them halfway. Indeed, one might appeal to this distinction as grounds for an objection to the line of criticism I have been pursuing against Habermas in this book. One might insist, that is, that the empirical specifics of how power relations can and often do impact socialization processes have no bearing whatsoever on the formal account of individuation through socialization.[6] Fraser paved the way for this reading of Foucault when she praised his empirical insights while denying that there are any coherent normative or conceptual-philosophical consequences that follow from them;[7] this move has, I think, structured the critical-theoretical reception of Foucault ever since. However, the general worry that I have with this move is that it fails to take seriously enough the potential normative and philosophical implications of Foucault's analysis of power. The assumption seems to be that at the formal level, power plays no role at all, whereas at the level of purely empirical investigation, it does play a role, but one that is completely inconsequential for the formal or (quasi-)transcendental account. Neither of these positions takes seriously enough Foucault's account of how historically specific power relations are intertwined with our formal conceptions of and modes of understanding language, rationality, subjectivity, identity, and autonomy.

Moreover, such a reading of Foucault relies on a problematic bifurcation between form and content that has been questionable at least since Hegel. Indeed, it is ironic that such a bifurcation should be evident in Habermas's work since the overcoming of the split between form and content, between the transcendental and the empirical, between theory and practice, has long been an explicit aim of his work. As McCarthy points out, Habermas's early theory of cognitive interests can be usefully understood as an attempt "to open up and chart a territory lying between the realms of the empirical and the transcendental."[8] In *Knowledge and*

Human Interests, Habermas argues that there are three fundamental, anthropologically grounded human interests that underlie and inform our knowledge projects: the technical interest in mastery of external nature that guides the empirical-analytic sciences (including the natural and the more empirically minded social sciences), the practical interest in securing social relations based on mutual understanding that guides the historical-hermeneutic sciences (including the humanities and the more interpretatively minded social sciences), and the emancipatory interest in freedom from ideological domination that guides the critically oriented sciences (including psychoanalysis, philosophy, and critical theory).[9] The theory of cognitive interests, as Habermas points out, "like the transcendental logic of an earlier period ... seeks a solution to the problem of the a priori conditions of possible knowledge"; however, the rules uncovered by the theory of cognitive interests "have a transcendental function but arise from actual structures of human life: from structures of a species that reproduces its life both through learning processes of socially organized labor and processes of mutual understanding in interactions mediated in ordinary language."[10]

Thus, the three fundamental cognitive interests are rooted in what Habermas at this point maintains are the three fundamental structures of human life or anthropological givens: work, language/interaction, and power. This is made clear in his inaugural lecture in Frankfurt in a long passage that is worth quoting in full:

The specific viewpoints from which, with transcendental necessity, we apprehend reality ground three categories of possible knowledge: information that expands our power of technical control; interpretations that make possible the orientation of action within common traditions; and analyses that free consciousness from its dependence on hypostatized powers. These viewpoints originate in the interest structure of a species that is linked in its roots to definite means of social organization: work, language, and power. The human species secures its existence through violence, through tradition-bound social life in ordinary-language communication, and with the aid of ego identities that at every level of individuation reconsolidate the consciousness of the individual in relation to the norms of the group. Accordingly the interests constitutive of knowledge are linked to the functions of an ego that adapts itself to its external conditions through learning processes, is initiated into the communication system of a social lifeworld by means of self-formative processes, and constructs an identity in the conflict between instinctual aims and social constraints. In turn these achievements become part of the productive forces accumulated by a society, the cultural tradition through which a society interprets itself, and the legitimations that a society accepts or criticizes.[11]

At this point in the development of Habermas's view, these three structures of human life are taken to be equally basic. However, in the critical response to *Knowledge and Human Interests*, the status of the emancipatory interest, and thus that of the claim that power is a basic structure of human life, came under pressure. McCarthy puts the concern this way: "experiences of systematically distorted communication and attempts to remove such distortions through critical self-reflection do not, on the face of it, possess the same anthropological primordiality as the mastery of nature and the achievement of understanding in ordinary language communication."[12] Subsequently, Habermas came to acknowledge the force of this objection, and so he modified his account such that the technical and practical interests are held to be anthropologically basic while *"the emancipatory interest in knowledge* has a derivative status."[13] With this move, Habermas relocated the critique of power and ideology "within the sphere of interaction as distortions of 'the moral relationship.'"[14] McCarthy maintains that

> this characterization of the third interest as derivative should not ... be taken to mean that it is less important than the other two. The point of the comparison is not the relative importance but the relative invariance of the different conditions of human life. Whereas work and interaction are for Habermas invariant consituents of our sociocultural form of life, systematically distorted communication is not (or rather, one may adopt the "practical hypothesis" that it is not).[15]

However, what are the implications of adopting this view of the role of power in human sociocultural life? Is this not tantamount to the claim that it is possible to imagine a form of human sociocultural life that is completely free of the operations of power, that there is, as Foucault would put it, an outside to power? On what grounds would we be justified in accepting this claim, even as a practical hypothesis? After all, it would seem that we unfortunately have all the evidence we could ever hope for that power is an ineliminable actual structure of human life, an anthropological given. Even supposing that we could imagine a form of social life completely free from power, would such a form of life be recognizably human? Moreover, despite McCarthy's contention that the claim that this interest is derivative is not meant to signal its lesser importance, as a matter of fact, in subsequent elaborations of Habermas's social theory, power and ideology seem to fade into the background. Once power has been downgraded in status from an anthropologically basic structure of human life to an unnecessary distortion, the door has been opened to think of the operations of power and ideology as merely empirical issues that can be shunted off to the side in the elaboration of the formal-theoretical account.

At about the same time, and also in response to criticisms of his project in *Knowledge and Human Interests*, Habermas shifts the focus of his critical theory away from the unmasking of relations of power and ideology and toward the rational reconstruction of species competences. As he puts it:

> The studies I published in *Knowledge and Human Interests* suffer from the lack of a precise distinction between reconstruction and "self-reflexion" in a critical sense. It occurred to me only after completing the book that the traditional use of the term "reflexion," which goes back to German Idealism, covers (and confuses) two things: on the one hand, it denotes the reflexion upon the conditions of potential abilities of a knowing, speaking, and acting subject as such; on the other hand, it denotes the reflexion upon unconsciously produced constraints to which a determinate subject (or a determinate group of subjects, or a determinate species subject) succumbs in its process of self-formation.[16]

Henceforth, Habermas will be careful to disambiguate these two senses of reflection: the former becomes the quasi-transcendental rational reconstruction of species competences—including, most crucially, communicative competence—and of the developmental sequence that leads to their achievement, and the latter is downgraded to the status of an empirical-genetic inquiry into possible distortions of these competences or deviations from this formal developmental track. Rational reconstructions "have a status similar to a (universal-pragmatic) theory of language and of science, which today takes over the role of (a transformed) transcendental philosophy."[17] The systems of rules and implicit know-how that the reconstructive sciences uncover are neither "cognitive components of the life-praxis whose validity has been called into question; nor are they scientific theorems which are being accumulated in the process of corroborating truth claims."[18] As a result, the kind of knowledge yielded by rational reconstruction is not grounded in interests at all, be they practical or technical; instead, it claims "a special status; that of 'pure' knowledge."[19] The critique of ideology, then, becomes an impure, empirical, genetic science that has a derivative status with respect to the reconstructive sciences. "The 'critical' sciences such as psychoanalysis and social theory also depend on being able to reconstruct successfully general rules of competence. To give an example, a universal pragmatic capable of understanding the conditions of why linguistic communication is possible at all has to be the theoretical basis for explaining systematically distorted communication and deviant processes of socialization."[20]

However, as McCarthy argues, this distinction between rational reconstruction and critical self-reflection seems to reopen the very gap between the transcendental and the empirical, "between theory and practice, between reason and emancipation that *Knowledge and Human Interests* tried to close."[21] The difficulty is this: "'Transcendental' reflection appears to be an exception to the 'interest-ladenness' of cognition; it pursues neither the technical, the practical, nor the emancipatory interest. It is, in this sense, 'interest free'—and we are back to something like the traditional notion of disinterested reason,"[22] a notion that the Habermas of *Knowledge and Human Interests* had been, one might think, right to reject. So as we take a closer look at how this distinction between the formal/transcendental and the empirical is used by Habermas, we will have to be attentive to whether or not it recapitulates the gap between the empirical and transcendental in a new guise.

After *Knowledge and Human Interests*, the split between the formal and the empirical figures prominently in Habermas's work, particularly in the distinction between a formal (or universal) and empirical pragmatic account of language. However, given our focus on Habermas's intersubjective conception of the autonomous subject, we will concentrate on how the split between the formal and empirical appears in this context, namely, as the distinction between the ontogenesis of ego identity and the psychodynamics of this process. Although, as I discussed in chapter 5, Habermas relies heavily on Mead for the former, he is also critical of Mead's "fixation on the *formal* features of modern legal and moral development, and on the formal features of individualism in the domain of personality development" and of his correlative neglect of "the other side of this formalism," namely, "the price that communicative reason has to pay for its victory in the coin of concrete ethical life."[23] With this criticism, Habermas signals his aim of reconciling the tension between formal and empirical conceptions of the development of ego identity. However, the question remains: Does Habermas succeed in thinking through the implications of the relationship between the logic and the dynamics, between the transcendental and the empirical, in this context?

Perhaps the closest Habermas comes to tackling this issue head-on is in his 1974 essay "Moral Development and Ego Identity." There, Habermas criticizes ego psychologists for failing to theorize "the relation of the claimed logic of ego development to the empirical conditions under which it is realized in concrete life histories."[24] In this context, he acknowledges that the attainment of moral autonomy (understood in the highly formal and cognitivist developmental terms that Habermas borrows from Piaget, Kohlberg, and Mead) is not coextensive with true freedom. Freedom requires not only the attainment of moral autonomy but also "the ability to give one's own needs their due in these communication structures; as long as the ego is cut off from its internal nature and disavows the dependency on needs that still await suitable interpretations, freedom, no matter how much it is guided by principles, remains in truth unfree in relation to existing systems of norms."[25] In this way, Habermas goes beyond his intersubjectivist reading of Kant's notion of autonomy and brings this notion into conversation with Freud: true freedom results not from the Kantian repression of internal nature or inclination but from a communicative rapprochement between the subject and her internal nature.[26] Here, Habermas is critical of Kohlberg's cognitive developmental schema in particular on the grounds that it "screens out the psychodynamics of the formative process."[27] By paying attention to the psychodynamics of this process, we can see, for example, "the instrumental role that libidinous energies, in the form of a narcissistic attachment to the self, play in the development of ego ideals; we can also see the function that aggressive energies, turned against the self, assume in the establishment of the authority of conscience."[28] The proper account of ego identity would be attentive to what Habermas calls its "dual status," both in the sense of "the cognitive-motivational duality of ego development" and in the sense of "an interdependence of society and nature that extends into the formation of identity."[29] Accordingly, at the end of this essay, Habermas posits a seventh-stage moral development, beyond the attainment of Kohlbergian postconventional moral autonomy and the concomitant capacity to reflect critically on the status of normative principles through a formally legitimate discursive procedure. At this seventh stage, "inner nature is rendered communicatively fluid and transparent."[30] This does not entail the repression or subjection of inner nature to ego, but instead an expression of inner needs through communication. As he puts it, "Autonomy that robs the ego of a communicative access to its own inner nature also signals unfreedom."[31]

As Whitebook points out, Habermas is arguing here that Kohlberg's cognitivist account of moral development does not go far enough because it relies too heavily on the old Kantian opposition between duty and inclination: "Because needs are posited as naturally given, they are assumed to be inaccessible to cultural, rational, and communicative influence."[32] If

Habermas's postconventional subject is to have the flexibility and openness that he wants it to have, "it must be possible for inner nature to be more consciously drawn into the self-formation process."[33] Whitebook argues that the main problem with this attempt to bring some affective content back into the otherwise purely formal and cognitive account of subjectivation lies in Habermas's assumption that our inner nature—our unconscious—can be rendered communicatively transparent and fluid. This assumption is grounded in a prior assumption of the linguisticality of inner nature—an assumption that Habermas curiously shares with Lacan.[34] As Whitebook puts it, "the articulability of inner nature can be casually maintained with little argumentation, because the linguisticality of inner nature is in fact presupposed from the start."[35] Whitebook is critical of this assumption both on textual grounds—he maintains that it conflates Freud's distinction between word representations and thing representations—and, more important for our purposes, on conceptual grounds—he argues that this assumption leads Habermas to ignore the psychic imaginary and the psychic costs of socialization. Benjamin makes a similar point. She argues that Habermas fails to appreciate (or, at the very least, seriously downplays) the ineliminable role that negation, destruction, and omnipotence play in the process of subject formation; as a result, he fails to appreciate that destruction and negation are necessary and ineradicable elements of the dynamic of intersubjectivity.[36] As Benjamin puts it, Habermas provides "an entry into intersubjectivity, but without sufficient attention to the subject's destructive omnipotence."[37] As such, he underestimates the regressive potential of the psychic imaginary and its recalcitrance to rational direction. As Meehan put it in a passage that I quoted above, "all processes of socialization, no matter how benign or rational, require a psychic subjugation that is almost inevitably blind and furious," and the costs of that subjugation arguably resurface in the forms of violence, hatred, aggression, and irrationality that persistently frustrate our attempts to achieve justice. Moreover, Whitebook argues, drawing on Castoriadis's work, that Habermas overlooks not only the regressive but also the progressive potential of the psychic imaginary. "One essential source for visions of a better society—visions that could be debated in a just public sphere—is the psychic imaginary and its refashioning of the contents of cultural tradition. Without the input of the imaginary, any such debate, while possibly being just, is in danger of being empty."[38]

Although Habermas's attempt to close the gap between the transcendental and the empirical with respect to subjectivation runs into problems, at least at this relatively early point he was still willing to address this issue. In his later work, by contrast, both the seventh stage and the attempt to integrate discussion of the formal developmental process of subjectivation with a genetic psychodynamic account disappear entirely, and Habermas's account becomes much more straightforwardly Kohlbergian.[39] This move not only appears to reinstantiate the gap between the transcendental and the empirical that Habermas had earlier thought it was so important to close, and to insulate the formal-transcendental account from any groundedness in interest, power, or ideology; it also seems, by the terms of Habermas's own earlier argument, to fail to offer a paradigm of true human autonomy, since it focuses solely on the cognitive requirements for the development of moral autonomy to the neglect of the affective-motivational requirements for the exercise of that cognitive capacity.

To be sure, in his more recent work, Habermas acknowledges that "even if the passage to the postconventional level of moral judgment has been successful, an inadequate motivational anchoring can restrict one's ability to act autonomously."[40] Although he admits that "the question of whether structuralist theory can be combined with the findings of ego psychology in a way that would do justice to the *psychodynamic aspects of the formation of judgments* remains an open one," he seems to be optimistic that such an integration is possible.[41] He maintains that this difficulty is one that the Kohlbergian account "shares with any approach that distinguishes competence from performance."[42] Such accounts attempt to measure (formal) competence as distinct from (empirical) performance, but "competence can be captured only in its concrete manifestations, that is, only in performance."[43] Although these considerations would seem to lead in the direction of closing the gap between the formal and the empirical—and hence also toward attenuating the status of the claims made on behalf of the formal account—Habermas does not draw this conclusion. Instead, he appeals to the distinction between moral judgment—the subject of the formal, Kohlbergian account—and moral action or behavior. Although he acknowledges that "to consider moral judgment as an indicator of competence and moral action or behavior as an indicator of performance is of course a crude simplification," he nevertheless maintains that "the motivational anchoring of the capacity for postconventional judgment in homologous superego structures does represent an example of *supplementary* performance-determining factors without which moral judgments at this level could not become effective in practice."[44] With this distinction between moral judgment and moral behavior—a distinction that maps onto Habermas's important distinction between justification and application discourses[45]—Habermas not only fails to close the gap between the ideal and the real, between the transcendental and the empirical, between theory and practice, he reinscribes it.

In *The Philosophical Discourse of Modernity*, Habermas argues that the problem plaguing the philosophy of the subject from Kant forward was that the gap between transcendental reflection and the empirical realm, once opened up, proved to be unbridgeable. As Habermas puts it, "no mediation is possible between the extramundance stance of the transcendental I and the intramundance stance of the empirical I."[46] The shift away from transcendental philosophy and to the method of rational reconstruction is designed to close this gap:

> What earlier was relegated to transcendental philosophy, namely the intuitive analysis of self-consciousness, now gets adapted to the circle of reconstructive sciences that try to make explicit, from the perspective of those participating in discourses and interactions, and by means of analyzing successful or distorted utterances, the pretheoretical grasp of rules on the part of competently speaking, acting, and knowing subjects. Because such reconstructive attempts are no longer aimed at a realm of the intelligible beyond appearances, but at the actually exercised rule-knowledge that is deposited in correctly generated utterances, the ontological separation between the transcendental and the empirical is no longer applicable.... Consequently, we do not need hybrid theories any more to close the gap between the transcendental and the empirical.[47]

The methodological distinctions between rational reconstruction and what Habermas calls here "methodically carried out self-critique" and between developmental logic and developmental dynamics are part of the broader paradigm change that is designed to provide a way out of the subject/object dilemmas diagnosed by Foucault in *The Order of Things*.[48] Habermas insists that "it must be made clear that the purism of pure reason is not resurrected again in communicative reason."[49]

And yet, in this context, even Habermas admits that "it is not so simple to counter the suspicion that with the concept of action oriented to validity claims the idealism of a pure, nonsituated reason slips in again, and the dichotomies between the realms of the transcendental and the empirical are given new life in another form."[50] In response to this worry, Habermas insists that "there is no pure reason that might don linguistic clothing only in the second place. Reason is by its very nature incarnated in contexts of communicative action and in structures of the lifeworld."[51] This suggests that reason is by its nature not only situated but also impure, and, yet, Habermas does not completely dissolve the tension between the real and the ideal. Instead, as McCarthy puts it, he "relocat[es] the tension between the real and the ideal *within* the domain of social practice."[52] The key to this relocation is Habermas's notion of the context transcendence of validity claims. As Habermas puts it, validity claims—primarily claims to truth or normative rightness—"have a Janus face: As claims, they transcend any local context; at the same time, they have to be raised here and now and be de facto recognized if they are going to bear the agreement of interaction participants that is needed for effective cooperation."[53] Validity claims are raised here and now, in a given context, and yet "the validity claimed for propositions and norms transcends spaces and times, '*blots out*' *space and time*."[54] Thus, the tension between the ideal and real remains but is now located within discourse: even as participants to discourse reciprocally presuppose that the idealizing presuppositions of the ideal speech situation—that all those affected are able to participate and are given an equal opportunity to raise and to question validity claims without being subject to either external or internal constraint—are met to a sufficient degree, they recognize this presupposition as counterfactual.[55] Nevertheless, according to Habermas, we cannot do without these presuppositions; without them, our postconventional sociocultural form of life, the form of life of a community of beings who argue, would be impossible.[56] Hence, "we can by no means always, or even only often, fulfill those improbable pragmatic presuppositions from which we nevertheless set forth in day-to-day communicative practice—and, in the sense of transcendental necessity, from which we *have to* set forth."[57]

Habermas admits that "the task of justification, or, in other words, the critique of validity claims carried out from the perspective of a participant, cannot ultimately be separated from a genetic consideration that issues in an ideology critique—carried out from a third-person perspective—of the mixing of power claims and validity claims."[58] However, it is not clear that Habermas has fully acknowledged the consequences of this admission. Although he seems happy to admit that we must be attentive to the mixing of power and validity claims at the practical level of participation in actual discourses, he does not take seriously enough the possibility of the mixing of power and validity claims at the theoretical level. Indeed, he seems to think that he cannot take this possibility seriously without sacrificing his notion of validity itself. However, that this possibility is worth taking seriously seems to follow from Habermas's own conception of philosophy and of the social critic. After all, on his view, the distinction between participant and critical, philosophical observer cannot ultimately be maintained, for, as he claims elsewhere, "in a process of enlightenment there can only be participants."[59] Moreover, earlier in *The Philosophical Discourse of Modernity*, he acknowledges, in the context of his definition of ideology critique, that it is possible to show that "the validity of a theory has not been adequately dissociated from the context in which it emerged; that behind the back of the theory there lies hidden an inadmissible *mixture of power and validity*, and that it still owes its reputation to this."[60] This suggests that both at the level of discursive practice and at the level of theoretical elaboration, the task of justification cannot ultimately be separated from a genetic—and, one is tempted to add here, genealogical—critique of what I called earlier the entanglement of power and validity.

And yet Habermas is extremely dismissive of attempts by Foucault and others to raise genealogical questions about theoretical elaborations/defenses of the ideals of modernity on the grounds that such efforts are totalizing forms of critique that collapse entirely the distinction between power and validity.[61] By contrast, Habermas insists that "the categorial distinction between power claims and truth claims is the ground upon which *any* theoretical approach has to be enacted."[62] With respect to the first point, as I argued in chapter 2, it is not the case that Foucault offers a totalizing abstract negation of modernity; instead, his work is best understood as an immanent critique, a continuation-cum-transformation of the Enlightenment project. Habermas is too quick to dismiss Foucault's approach, particularly on the issue of the relation between the empirical and the transcendental. Moreover, one might wonder whether Habermas's conception of communicative reason is ultimately any better at maintaining the distinction between power and validity than is Foucault's genealogical approach. After all, it seems that he is only able to posit this as a categorial distinction via a highly questionable insulation of reason from power at the metatheoretical level, by claiming first that power is not an anthropological given and second that rational reconstruction is a "pure" form of inquiry that is not shaped by any interest whatsoever. Habermas's insistence that rational reconstructions are always hypothetical and the theories on which they are based are therefore fallibilistic thus does not go far enough. It isn't just that "there is always the possibility that they rest on a false choice of examples, that they are obscuring and distorting correct intuitions, or, even more frequently, that they are overgeneralizing individual cases."[63] Of course all that is possible, but the bigger worry is that the reconstructive science might be reconstructing rules or notions of competence that are thoroughly ideological.[64] Once this possibility is admitted, one might wonder which is worse, offering a "critique of ideology that attacks its own foundations," as Habermas claims the heirs of Nietzsche such as Foucault do,[65] or offering a critical theory that attempts to insulate its own theoretical foundations from critical scrutiny from the start?

These worries bring us back to the tension between the transcendental and the empirical, the ideal and the real—a tension that is, in a sense, constitutive for Habermas's philosophical project. The question for Habermas is whether this is a productive tension or an insurmountable gap. Is it possible for this tension to be relocated within the world and still be capable of performing the idealizing, universalizing, transcendental functions that Habermas needs it to perform? Recall that in the wake of his diagnosis of the empirical/transcendental doublet, Foucault responds by thoroughly historicizing and contextualizing the trancendental, by developing the notion of the historical a priori. Habermas, by contrast, wants to eat his cake and have it too, with the notion of the context transcendence of validity claims. The question remains, is this possible? Or might Habermas be compelled to admit that his own claims for the context transcendence of validity claims are themselves not only rooted in but also limited to a particular context, the context of late modernity?

The Context Transcendence of Validity Claims

The possibility of the context transcendence of validity claims is a major sticking point in the debates between Habermas and a host of his critics, including post-structuralists such as Foucault and Butler, but also including neopragmatists such as Richard Rorty, and neo-Hegelians such as Charles Taylor. In her recent book Cooke confronts this debate head-on. She argues that there are two fundamental normative impulses that undergird critical social thinking: a strong commitment to antiauthoritarianism (the flip side of which is the positive value placed on autonomy) and the articulation of a vision of the good society. The first impulse, evident already in the writings of both Rousseau and Kant, commits critical social theorists to the belief that "human beings must have reasons for the validity of their perceptions, interpretations, and evaluations, and for subjecting themselves to laws and political regimes, that they are able to *call their own*."[66] And although the second impulse may seem to have fallen out of favor as utopian energies have been exhausted, Cooke insists that "without some, more or less determinate, guiding idea of the good society, critical social thinking would be inconceivable; it would lack an ethical basis for its critical diagnoses."[67] It is this latter impulse that raises the issue of context transcendence, as some sort of validity is claimed on behalf of these visions of the good society, and usually this validity is construed in a context-transcending sense. However, precisely this claim to context-transcending validity is apparently in tension with the first impulse toward antiauthoritarianism. Cooke gives partial credit for this development to Foucault, whose genealogies raise the possibility that "claims to context-transcending validity, by obscuring their origins in particular epistemological and ethical orders [which are themselves entangled with power relations], collude in the dissemination and perpetuation of social repression."[68] Thus, the two normative impulses that Cooke takes to be fundamental for critical social thinking are revealed to be in tension with one another, and critical theorists are faced with the challenge of figuring out "how to maintain an idea of context-transcending, ethical validity without violating their own antiauthoritarian impulses."[69]

Of course one way to eliminate this tension would be simply to give up on the idea of context-transcending validity claims altogether. However, Cooke argues that this is not a viable option for critical social theory. She distinguishes four possible positions vis-à-vis the status of the ideals of the good society that guide critical social inquiry: conventionalism, radical contextualism, the context-transcending position, and authoritarianism.[70] Of these, only the second and third positions "are congruent with the self-understanding and concerns found in contemporary critical social theories";[71] thus, Cooke focuses her attention here, casting the debate between these two positions as the debate between radical contextualists such as Rorty and context-transcending theorists such as Habermas.

As Cooke sees it, both radical contextualists and context-transcendence theorists are committed to the notion of situated rationality, which she defines as "the view that the social theorist's critical perspective is inescapably conditioned by historical, cultural, social, and subjective factors: her perspective is not—and cannot be—neutral."[72] A commitment to situated rationality entails a commitment to the view that the social theorists' critical perspective is internal to the historical, social, and cultural context in which she works. The difference between radical contextualists and context-transcendence theorists is that the former see the critical perspective as "purely" internal to the sociocultural context, in the sense that "they have no purpose or rationality beyond this context," whereas the latter appeal to "normative ideas that are at once immanent to the sociocultural context in question and transcend it."[73] Although radical contextualist positions are more easily squared with the commitment to situated rationality, Cooke argues that such approaches are inherently unstable. Specifically, they fall prey to two intractable difficulties. First, they are "unacceptably restricted in scope: they are unable to offer a critical perspective *across* socio-cultural or historical contexts and must confine their critical observations to the immediate contexts in which they are situated."[74] In other words, they are, in Cooke's view, incapable of accounting for moral progress or of describing intercultural

exchanges as learning processes. Second, they "lack the conceptual resources necessary to conceive of challenges to the deep-seated, normative
intuitions and expectations, which are formative of identities in a particular social order, as *rational* disputes."[75] Radical contextualists rely on
an overly sharp dichotomy between "Reason"—understood as timeless,
ahistorical, and transcendent—and "reason"—understood as purely immanent and historically contingent. Cooke argues that this overly sharp
dichotomy ultimately breaks down as radical contextualists such as Rorty
"find a purely immanent approach inadequate and smuggle in ideas of
context-transcending validity such as truth."[76] Thus, Cooke concludes that
the radical contextualist attempt to ameliorate the tension between antiauthoritarianism and the context transcendence of validity by giving up
entirely on the latter idea is ultimately incoherent.[77] A central thesis of her
argument is that the tension between the antiauthoritarian and context-
transcending normative impulses of critical theory "should be negotiated
rather than eliminated."[78]

However, context-transcending approaches face their own difficulties, most notably, that their position on the capacity of validity claims
to transcend their context is, on its face, difficult to reconcile with their
avowed commitment to situated rationality.[79] Habermas's context-transcending account of validity is grounded in the idealizations that he posits
as constitutive of communicative action, idealizations that concern both
the procedure—all relevant parties are included in the discussion and are
allowed to raise and question validity claims, participants are oriented
toward reaching understanding, and assent is compelled solely by the
unforced force of the better argument—and the outcome of argumentation—it is presupposed that an agreement reached by means of a valid
procedure is itself valid.[80] As Cooke puts it, "the tension between the
normative promise contained in these idealizations and what happens in
everyday communicative practices provides a basis for criticism: in the
one case, they permit criticism of the ways in which the outcomes of argumentation are reached; in the other case, they permit criticism of the
outcomes from the point of view of moral validity."[81] Moreover, Cooke
emphasizes the point that, for Habermas, "this critical power is not purely
immanent to a particular sociocultural context. Since it is grounded in
universal features of language use, it expresses a critical perspective with
context-transcending force, in the sense that its validity would have to be
accepted by everyone, everywhere, irrespective of sociocultural context
and historical epoch."[82]

It is precisely this strong claim to the *universal* validity of the critical
power of the theory of communicative action that exposes Habermas to

the charge of authoritarianism. To be sure, Habermas's account is post-metaphysical and, in that sense, seems to be in tune with the nonauthoritarian impulse of critical social thinking.[83] He understands emancipation not as the result of an inexorable historical process, but instead as a potential whose realization is contingent on human practice; in that sense, he avoids what Cooke calls "ethical authoritarianism."[84] And his justificatory strategy for the theory of communicative action is nonfoundationalist and only quasi-transcendental—it sets forth hypotheses that rely on the reconstructive sciences for empirical confirmation—so, in this sense, he avoids what Cooke labels "epistemological authoritarianism."[85] Nevertheless, his formal pragmatics contains what Cooke calls an "authoritarian residue."[86] The reasons for this have to do with doubts about the accuracy of Habermas's claim that the idealizations that orient communicative practices are grounded in features of the communicative use of language that are truly universal. As Cooke puts it, "historical and cross-cultural studies suggest that certain of these idealizations orient communicative practice only in certain sociocultural contexts, as a result of certain historical developments."[87] For example, Habermas's conception of moral validity seems to emerge "only in sociocultural contexts in which knowledge has been desacralized, in which authority has been secularized, and in which the principle of universal moral respect has been internalized—in other words, under conditions of modernity."[88] More generally, "normative expectations concerning social inclusiveness and equality" appear to be "socioculturally specific" rather than invariant and universal features of communicative action.[89]

According to Cooke, doubts about the empirical accuracy of Habermas's formal-pragmatic claims regarding the universal features of communication leave him with the following problem: "If he wants to maintain an empirical basis for his critical perspective on forms of social exclusion and inequality, he must acknowledge the socio-cultural specificity of that perspective; but by doing so, he threatens to lose the conceptual resources necessary for the purposes of cross-cultural and transhistorical social criticism."[90] Habermas thus appears to be caught in a double bind: either he admits the sociocultural specificity of the formal-pragmatic account of communication that provides the normative basis for his critical theory, in which case Cooke fears that he runs the risk of lapsing into radical contextualism, or he reasserts the validity of his formal pragmatics in the face of empirical counterevidence, in which case he retreats substantially from the postmetaphysical, situated conception of inquiry. Thus, Cooke concludes that "formal pragmatics is at times inadequate and at times unsuitable for the purposes of justifying the critical force of Habermas's emancipatory perspective."[91] Nevertheless, she maintains that "Habermas does not have to abandon his formal-pragmatic strategy; instead he should historicize it, acknowledging that his linguistic reflections cast light only on the communicative practices of the inhabitants of modern societies."[92] If he were to make this move, then Habermas would no longer be able to justify his strong idealizations by means of a transcendental-pragmatic argument that appeals to universal presuppositions of communication; instead, he would have to justify them, as Cooke puts it, "through reference to the deep-seated, normative intuitions and expectations that are formative of the identities of the inhabitants of modernity."[93]

Of course, this would leave Habermas with the problem of how to avoid the difficulties that Cooke diagnoses in the radical contextualist position. In order to avoid these difficulties, he would need some alternative strategy for justifying the context-transcending validity of his idealizations. Cooke suggests that the best way for Habermas to fill in this gap is with "an account of what it means to see modernity as the result of an ethically significant learning process."[94] Cooke acknowledges that Habermas has already offered independent accounts of moral learning processes— grounded in his discussions of Kohlberg—and of modernity—articulated through his readings of philosophical accounts of modernity from Hegel to Bataille in *The Philosophical Discourse of Modernity*—but she argues that neither of these strategies is sufficient for the purposes of maintaining his context-transcending position. Habermas's Kohlbergian account of moral learning processes is open to empirical objections—particularly from feminists who charge it with gender bias. His account of modernity, by contrast, is initially "more promising"[95] than the Kohlbergian strategy, because "insofar as he successfully exposes the confusions and contradictions of these rival accounts of modernity, Habermas could be said to make the case for his own emancipatory account in a critical-hermeneutic manner that is more in tune with the idea of situated rationality than the universalist claims of formal pragmatics."[96] However, as Cooke argues, even if this critical-hermeneutic strategy was fully successful, it would only establish the relative superiority of his account of modernity and its achievements—specifically, the idealizations that undergird the theory of communicative action; thus, it would not get Habermas all the way to the context-transcending validity of those idealizations.[97]

In order to get there, Cooke proposes an alternative interpretation of the idealizing projections guiding Habermas's theory, in particular his ideas of the ideal speech situation and of a rationalized lifeworld that exists in a relation of harmony with the rationalized system. In the case of the ideal speech situation, for example, she suggests that we view it as "a representation of truth (or justice), in the sense of a constitutively inadequate, particular articulation of a transcendent object."[98] Understanding it in this way enables us to avoid the danger of a pernicious ideological closure—the danger of "immunizing a particular representation of truth or justice against critical interrogation, rearticulation, and reenactment in processes of political contestation"[99]—a danger to which, as I argued above, Habermas's own account of the ideal speech situation succumbs.[100] If it is understood as a constitutively inadequate representation of a transcendent object, then the ideal speech situation becomes a regulative idea that "imaginatively evokes the idea of a social condition in which the coordination of social action and the reproduction of social order would take place according to the norms of communicative rationality."[101] Moreover, as a regulative idea, the ideal speech situation has a fictive status: "It projects the idea of a social condition of self-sufficiency and self-transparency that can never be achieved by human beings."[102] However, this way of understanding the ideal speech situation leaves open the question of whether it is a useful or a pernicious fiction, an ideal or an illusion. Or perhaps it is both?

Cooke, for her part, maintains that the ideal speech situation is not a pernicious fiction. In her view, pernicious ideological closure with respect to regulative ideas such as the ideal speech situation "can be avoided by making two key moves: a self-conscious acknowledgement of their fictive character, coupled with their connection to validity claims that are inherently open to contestation."[103] The key to avoiding pernicious ideological closure is thus affirming the situatedness and openness to contestation of our normative idealizations. Thus, Cooke argues not only that "the link between validity and argumentation ... is a historically contingent one,"[104] inasmuch as it presupposes a committment to situated rationality, but also that "situated rationality is a conception of rationality that is itself situated."[105] Hence, as Cooke sums it up:

> The model that I propose acknowledges its own historicity, in this case, its indebtedness to core normative intuitions and expectations that shape modern identities. Accordingly, it is not merely committed to the idea of situated rationality, it also recognized the historical situatedness of that idea. This means that critical social theory must acknowledge that its deep commitment to normative ideas such as autonomous agency, universality, and contestability—ideas that are constitutive for its own self-understanding—has a historical location: the social imaginary of Western modernity.[106]

If situated rationality demands that all of the basic normative and philosophical commitments of critical social theory are themselves historically situated, then there is, as Cooke admits, "no escape from the contextualist circle."[107] However, she goes on to say that "this circle is cause for concern only to those who hold that knowledge of a reality independent of our descriptions, interpretations, and evaluations is possible."[108] Once we give up faith in that impossible epistemic and metaphysical ideal, then some version of contextualism is the only game in town.

I wholeheartedly agree. But this brings us back to Cooke's initial distinction between context-transcending social criticism and radical contextualism. Suppose, as Cooke argues, that context-transcending critical theory is predicated on two fundamental assumptions: "One of these is the assumption of an ineradicable gap between the transcendent object and its historical articulations.... A further important assumption is the assumption that the gap, though ineliminable, is not invariable: it can be narrowed."[109] However, if we combine these assumptions with the acknowledgment that these assumptions themselves have a "historically contingent character,"[110] then we are led to the conclusion that the very faith in context-transcending validity is itself rooted in and restricted to a specific sociocultural, historical context: the context of late Western modernity. On this view, it is constitutive of our late modern Western form of life that we posit this idealization, and, in that sense, idealizations such as this one are necessary for us, but only contingently so. This way of reading the notion of the context transcendence of validity claims is not completely deflationary, in that it acknowledges the crucial importance of such ideas for the normative horizon of our form of life, but it does thoroughly contextualize the idea of context transcendence itself. Thus, in the end, Cooke's account of context-transcend*ing* validity—and the gerund form is significant, as it indicates that such validity is a dynamic idealizing projection rather than a concrete or realizable end state[111]—might be better described as a more principled version of contextualism, one that recognizes the force of our normative ideals but also understands that they are inextricably rooted in our practices and forms of life. Such an account neither holds out hope for the possibility of actually transcending our rootedness in our context—of blotting out time and space, as Habermas puts it—nor does it seek to reduce our normative ideals to nothing more than illusions grounded in our power-laden practices.

Contextualizing Habermas

Cooke's vision of critical theory thus dovetails nicely with an account that recognizes that our ideas of reason—autonomy being foremost among them—are irreducibly *both* "unavoidable presuppositions of rational thought that must carefully be reconstructed" *and* "illusions of logocentric thinking that must tirelessly be deconstructed."[112] Just such an account has been offered by McCarthy, both a prominent defender and a sharp critic of Habermas's work. McCarthy's contextualist and pragmatic interpretation of Kant's ideas of reason thus offers us a way of reading Habermas's project that is much more compatible with the Foucaultian approach to critical theory than has been previously realized by commentators on the Foucault-Habermas debate—even by McCarthy himself.

McCarthy's pragmatic turn in critical theory is grounded in his critique of Habermas's theory of communicative action, a critique that turns on the charge that even Habermas's detranscendentalized ideas of reason remain too idealized. As McCarthy puts the point: "Habermas's conceptions of reason and rationalization, theory and discourse" are "stronger than his arguments warrant or his project requires."[113] It is possible to give the idealizations on which Habermas's normative project is grounded a much more pragmatic meaning and still have them do the work that Habermas needs them to do.

For example, with respect to Habermas's "developmentalist approach" to both individual ego development and societal modernization processes, McCarthy argues that "in this context he is working with a conception of the end point of the history of reason that fails to account for some of his own insights."[114] Although McCarthy does not question Habermas's guiding assumption that differentiation—the separating out of first, second, and third person speaker perspectives and the objective, intersubjective, and subjective world perspectives—is a developmental advance, he does emphasize that "the separation of domains of reality and types of validity claims, of an ego that stands over against nature, society, and its own feelings and desires, must eventually allow for a *nonregressive* reconciliation with self, others, and nature if the 'dialectic of enlightenment' is to lose its sway over our lives."[115] However, given Habermas's developmentalist approach, it is difficult to conceive of such reconciliation in anything other than regressive terms. The problem is that Habermas seems to presuppose that differentiation and the postconventional selves and societies that it makes possible are the end point of history. If, however, we cast doubt on this assumption, as McCarthy suggests that we should, then it follows that "we have things to learn from traditional cultures as well as they from us—not only things we have forgotten or repressed but something about how we might put our fragmented world back together again. This is not a matter of regression, but of dialogue, dialogue that is critical, to be sure, but not only on one side."[116]

McCarthy makes a similar critical point with respect to Habermas's discourse-ethical conception of morality. In this case, his argument is that Habermas's conception of practical discourse contains "a residue of the Kantian dichotomy between the phenomenal and the noumenal ... in the form of a tension between situated reasoning and the transcendence of situatedness required by his model of rational consensus."[117] This residue emerges as a function of Habermas's overly sharp distinction between the moral and the ethical.[118] McCarthy is concerned primarily with the distinction between moral discourse—which centers on the "general acceptability of the anticipated consequences of a norm for the legitimate satisfaction of needs" and interests[119]—and ethical-evaluative discourse—in which members of a shared form of life discuss "who we are and who we want to be" and "what kind of life we want to lead."[120] Habermas maintains that both kinds of conversations allow for rational criticisms and revisions of our values, even though only the former kind of discourse concerns universalizable norms. Within the horizon of ethical-evaluative discourse, "one may challenge, for instance, the truthfulness of an agent's expression of desires, preferences, feelings, and so forth. When this goes beyond questions concerning insincerity, conscious deception, manipulation, or the like to questions of inauthenticity, self-deception, false consciousness, and the like, we may enter into a form of discussion whose paradigm case, in Habermas's view, is therapeutic critique."[121] The crucial difference is that such discussions "do not involve the idealizing presuppositions of practical discourse but remain closely tied to the context of action and experience" in ways that moral discourses allegedly do not.[122] But it is this last point that McCarthy finds difficult to swallow. After all, ultimately the reasons that are offered in moral discourses appeal to the satisfaction of the needs and interests of those affected by a norm. But these needs and interests are not brute or immediately given; they are irreducibly grounded in sociocultural context and open to rival interpretations and political contestation.[123] The consequence of this for Habermas is that

> if judgments of the relative cogency of reasons that cite needs, interests, feelings, sentiments, and the like vary with interpretive and evaluative standpoints, and if there is no common measure by which to assess the relative weights of reasons articulated in different evaluative languages, then the distinction between argument and rhetoric, between convincing and persuading becomes less sharp than the discourse model allows.[124]

In other words, the distinction between the unforced force of the better argument and the ideological manufacturing of consent, the distinction that undergirds his distinction between validity and power, becomes less sharp than Habermas would like. McCarthy suggests that the tension between the real and the ideal, the phenomenal and the noumenal, is to be resolved in favor of the real and the phenomenal; such a resolution, in turn, compels the recognition of the impossibility of ever fully transcending our situatedness.

In this sense, McCarthy is willing to concede much more ground to poststructuralists such as Foucault than Habermas himself is. As McCarthy sees it, even if we grant Habermas the point that we are capable of becoming critically aware of previously unrecognized power-laden or ideological aspects of our lifeworld, we are by no means capable of bringing all of them to our critical consciousness simultaneously. "But this means that *at every moment and in every situation*, unconscious factors will play a role in shaping interpretive and evaluative perspectives and thus that the symbolic force of language will inevitably figure in judgments of cogency."[125] It also means that "there is no Archimedean point from which to judge whether what democratic majorities regard as the better argument is really better."[126] To be sure, McCarthy is unwilling to draw from these observations the skeptical conclusion that reason and argument are nothing more than pernicious illusions. Indeed, in the wake of this realization, he maintains that "dissenters can only continue the debate."[127] Thus, whereas McCarthy is more willing than Habermas to acknowledge that the ideas of reason guiding his project are open to the charge of dogmatism—or of what Cooke, following Laclau, calls "pernicious ideological closure"—he also emphasizes, against the skeptic, their subversive potential:

> Understood pragmatically, ... the unconditionality of validity claims ... runs counter to what contextualist critics suppose: it invites an ongoing critique of dogmatism, prejudice, self-deception, and error in all their forms. The tension between the real and the ideal it builds into the construction of social facts represents an immanent potential for criticism that actors can draw upon in seeking to transcend and transform the limits of their situations.[128]

Nevertheless, McCarthy wants to maintain a place for deconstructive critique in the methodology of critical theory: "a number of deconstructive motifs and techniques, stripped of their totalizing pretensions, could be integrated into a pragmatic approach to communication, where they might serve as antidotes to our deep-seated tendency to hypostasize ideas of reason into realized or realizable states of affairs."[129]

McCarthy, in his book-length debate with Hoy, attempts to flesh out his more pragmatic, contextualist, but still normatively principled approach to critical theory. McCarthy's guiding insight is this: "Many of the objectionable features of the classical critique of reason can be overcome by deabsolutizing ideas of reason through stressing their relations to social practice and building deconstructive concerns into reconstructive endeavors from the start."[130] However, like Cooke, McCarthy claims that "acknowledging the situatedness of knowledge is compatible with raising claims to situation-transcendent validity."[131] The key for McCarthy is to relocate the tension between the ideal and the real within the social realm itself, in the way that the Habermas of *Knowledge and Human Interests* had done. Once we make this move, it becomes possible to view the context transcendence of the ideas of reason as marking "a normative surplus of meaning that critical theorists can draw upon in seeking to transcend and transform the limits of their situations."[132]

McCarthy spells out this pragmatic alternative by means of an integration of Habermas's social theory with the insights of ethnomethodology.[133] However, McCarthy acknowledges that this move raises a potential problem; namely, the question of whether and how the "transcendence and idealization stressed by Habermas [can] somehow be reconciled with the indexicality and practicality emphasized by Garfinkel?"[134] McCarthy maintains that these two strains can be brought together, but only if we recast the notion of communicative rationality by understanding it "temporally (it is an ongoing accomplishment), pragmatically (which is never absolute but always for all practical purposes), and contextually (in ever changing circumstances)."[135] The temporal recasting of communicative rationality emphasizes that discourse is always open ended: "because validity claims are redeemed by the grounds or reasons offered in support of them, and not by agreement as such, ... any existing consensus is open to reconsideration."[136] The pragmatic point is the acknowledgment, discussed above, that "critical self-awareness is always only 'for all practical purposes' ... at every moment and in every situation unconscious factors—in this very broad sense—will inevitably play a role in shaping our interpretive and evaluative schemes."[137] The pragmatizing of communicative reason goes even further, however, for it is also tied to a scaling back of the strong claim to universality that Habermas made on behalf of the pragmatic presuppositions of communication. Unlike Habermas, McCarthy thinks that critical theory does not need to make such a strong claim: "Given that we must start from where we are, any presuppositions that are practically indispensable for participating in communication processes to which we have no alternative will figure as preconditions of our communication—whether or not they belong to the conditions of possibility of communication as such."[138]

The temporalizing, pragmatizing, and contextualizing of communicative rationality does not, however, lead in the direction of a radical contextualism that wholly refuses the notion of context transcendence. McCarthy insists that one can make such contextualist moves "*without surrendering* transcendence (it turns on validity claims that go beyond the particular contexts in which they are raised) or idealization (and rests on pragmatic presuppositions that function as regulative ideas)."[139] Indeed, as McCarthy makes clear in his critical discussion of Rorty, given that the ideal of the context transcendence of reason is a constitutive one for modernity, and given that we are working within the context of late modernity, we have no choice but to mobilize such ideals. As he puts it: "'Our' culture is permeated with transcultural notions of validity. If, in the absence of any God's-eye view, we have to start from where we are—for instance, to use the forms of justification actually available to us—this will involve, in many pursuits at least, offering arguments that claim validity beyond the confines of our culture."[140] Nevertheless, McCarthy is, I think, quite careful to specify the terms on which he is willing to defend this ideal. Like Cooke, he tends not to speak of "the context transcendence of validity claims" *as such*, which implies a validity that does in fact transcend the context in which it is raised. Rather, he tends to speak of context transcendence as an "idealizing projection of a horizon of unlimited validity" or a "promissory note issued across the full expanse of social space and historical time."[141] In other words, he speaks of the *claim to* context-transcending validity, a notion that can be understood, as I argued above, as both emerging from and bound to the context of late Western modernity. He sums up his case thus:

> The point, in short, is to reject the either/or opposition between decontextualized-because-generalized norms and values, on the one hand, and contextualized-because-particularized judgments, on the other. Especially in modern pluralistic societies, we cannot help but have it both ways, that is, agree upon *some* decontextualized—abstract, general, formal—norms, values, principles, rights, procedures, and the like which must then be ongoingly contextualized—interpreted, elaborated, applied—in particular situations.[142]

I would suggest that the way to go about this is to reject the false opposition between radical contextualism and the commitment to reason's actual capacity to transcend its situatedness by developing instead a principled form of contextualism that emphasizes our need *both* to posit context-transcending ideals *and* to continually unmask their status as illusions rooted in interest and power-laden contexts.

On this way of understanding McCarthy's pragmatic recasting of Habermas's project, the key difference that remains between his project and Foucault's is just the willingness to acknowledge explicitly that critique must draw on the normative resources of modernity. However, as I argued above, even though Foucault is not always clear on this point, his genealogical critique is best understood in just this way, as an immanent rather than a total critique of modernity. Unfortunately, McCarthy has a tendency to overstate the differences between his critical-theoretical project and the deconstructive approach of Foucault. For example, he claims that "in contrast to exclusively deconstructionist approaches, [the critical theory tradition] allows for a critical reconstruction of Enlightenment conceptions of reason and the rational subject, a kind of 'determinate negation' through which they are given sociocultural forms rather than simply dismantled."[143] Similarly, he refers to Foucault's critique of the subject as amounting to an "abstract negation of the conceptual apparatus of rationalist individualism."[144] In other words, McCarthy tends to misread Foucault in precisely the way that I argued against in chapter 2—to think that he is doing totalizing critique or abstract negation of ideals of modernity. Once we realize that this is not the case, it becomes clear that there is very little difference between Foucault and McCarthy's more pragmatic and contexualist version of the Habermasian project.

As Habermas himself has noted, the dispute between Foucault and his followers and Habermas and his followers is really a domestic squabble. As he puts it:

> The encounter between McCarthy and the followers of Heidegger, Dewey, and Wittgenstein is a domestic dispute over which side accomplishes the detranscendentalization [of the knowing subject] in the right way: whether the traces of a transcending reason vanish in the sands of historicism and contextualism or whether a reason embodied in historical contexts preserves the power for immanent transcendence.[145]

If the reading that I have offered of Foucault is convincing, and if we follow Cooke and McCarthy in the direction of a contextualized and pragmatized reading of Habermas, then this domestic dispute turns out to be based not on irreconcilable differences but on a misunderstanding (or perhaps, even more trivially, on the narcissism of small differences!). In other words, once we realize that Foucault is not offering a totalizing, abstract negation of reason and the normative ideals of the Enlightenment but is instead engaged in his own continuation-through-transformation of the Enlightenment project, and once we give up on Habermas's demand for the purity of his idealizations and accept instead a more contextualized notion of the context transcendence of validity, then the differences between Foucault's and Habermas's approaches to critical theory become so small as to be negligible. In other words, if we reject McCarthy's critique of Foucault but accept his recasting of the Habermasian project, then this project appears to be completely compatible with this characterization of critical thought that Foucault offered in a late interview:

> I think that the central issue of philosophy and critical thought since the eighteenth century has always been, still is, and will, I hope remain the question: What is this Reason that we use? What are its historical effects? What are its limits, and what are its dangers? How can we exist as rational beings, fortunately committed to practicing a rationality that is unfortunately crisscrossed by intrinsic dangers? ... If critical thought itself has a function—and, even more specifically, if philosophy has a function within critical thought—it is precisely to accept this sort of spiral, this sort of revolving door of rationality that refers us to its necessity, to its indispensability, and, at the same time, to its intrinsic dangers.[146]

The ideas of reason, our conception of rationality, our normative ideal of autonomy: these are all ideals that we must posit from within the horizon of modernity, ideals that are constitutive of our form of life, and yet, as McCarthy acknowledges, they harbor pernicious illusions of the eradication of power relations and the fantasy of self-transparency that we must continually expose and subject to critique.[147]

To be sure, there is an issue here of the possible end point of critique: (how) will we ever know if we've got it right? The answer—and on this point, Foucault, Butler, Habermas, Cooke, and McCarthy seem to be in agreement—is clear: we won't. But, this just means that there is always something for critique to do, that we must keep all of our substantive and procedural moral and political decisions open to contestation and revision. On this point, there is no disagreement as far as I can tell. The disagreement has only ever been about the status that Habermas has wanted to claim for his de-transcendentalized ideas of reason. Once these have been sufficiently contextualized, the major source of the disagreement has disappeared.

7

Engendering Critical Theory

IN A recent article, Benhabib, reflecting on her earlier exchange with Butler, contends that the most important theoretical issue at stake in this debate, and in the feminism/postmodernism debates more generally, is "the problem of the subject."[1] Benhabib suggests that the problem of the subject can be broken down into two distinct but related problems: first, "how does feminism alter our understanding of the traditional epistemological or moral subject of western philosophy?"; second, "can we think of political/moral/cultural agency only insofar as we retain a robust conception of the autonomous, rational, and accountable subject, or is a concept of the subject as fragmentary and riveted by heterogeneous forces more conducive to understanding varieties of resistance and cultural struggles of the present?"[2] In the initial exchange between Benhabib and Butler, the second of these two problems, which we might call "the agency problem," is the source of the major disagreement. Benhabib argues that the postmodernist death of the subject is "not compatible with the goals of feminism" inasmuch as it undermines "concepts of intentionality, accountability, self-reflexivity, and autonomy"[3] and thus also undermines moral and political agency. Butler responds by insisting that she does not endorse the death of the subject at all but instead wants to "ask after the process of [the subject's] construction and the political meaning and consequentiality of taking the subject as a requirement or presupposition of theory."[4] "We may be tempted," Butler continues, "to think that to assume the subject in advance is necessary in order to safeguard the agency of the subject. But to claim that the subject is constituted is not to claim that it is determined; on the contrary, the constituted character of the subject is the very precondition of its agency."[5] In other words, in their initial encounter, Benhabib criticizes Butler for endorsing a fragmented conception of subjectivity that is incompatible with agency and defends a more robust conception of the rational, autonomous subject designed to illuminate rather than obscure the possibility of agency.

Butler, in her recent work on subjection, as we saw in chapter 4, revisits the relationships between power, subjectivity, and agency. Foucault's account of subjection remains her point of departure, but now Butler argues that, as compelling as his account is, it fails to explain the psychic mechanisms that make subjection work, that is, it fails to explain how power "assumes a psychic form that constitutes the subject's self-identity."[6] Thus, her account of subjection, grounded in a fusion of Foucaultian and psychoanalytic insights, analyzes the ways in which subordinated individuals become passionately attached to, and thus come to desire, their own subordination. Such an account enables feminists to theorize how individuals become attached to gender identity, despite the role it plays in reproducing and maintaining gender subordination. Although this account of subjection may seem even more pessimistic than her earlier account, inasmuch as it presents individuals not only as constituted by power but also psychically attached to that constitution, Butler insists that agency and resistance are nonetheless possible.

In her recent work, Benhabib also reconsiders the problem of the subject, envisioning a somewhat more fragmented and less robust subject than before, but one that nevertheless remains capable of rationality, autonomy, and moral/political agency. In this way, she attempts to move beyond her earlier exchange with Butler and avoid the false antithesis presupposed by the formulation of the agency problem above. Benhabib proposes a narrative conception of subjectivity as an alternative to Butler's performative model and argues that the narrative model does a better job of accounting for the creativity and spontaneity that make agency and resistance possible while at the same time avoiding the dangers of essentialism attendant upon overly robust conceptions of subjectivity. She also argues that her conception of the self is useful for feminist theorizing inasmuch as it is capable of accounting for our constitution as gendered selves while preserving the possibility of autonomy vis-à-vis gender narratives.

However, I want to suggest that Benhabib's strong account of practical autonomy remains a bit too strong. Notwithstanding her own, quite convincing, early critiques of Habermas for offering an excessively rationalist conception of the self and of autonomy, Benhabib's work also retains a problematically rationalist core. After laying out her narrative conception of the self, I will argue that this conception retains a rationalist residue in the form of the presupposition of an ungendered core of the self. To the extent that this is the case, Benhabib fails to heed her own best insights; as a result, her account of the self tends to obscure rather than reveal the role that gendered relations of power play in the constitution of selves.

Benhabib's Critique of Habermas

Benhabib's critical appropriation of Habermas is grounded in the suspicion that Hegel's critique of Kant's ethics might prove useful for the project of communicative ethics.[7] Although Benhabib does not go so far as to argue for a Hegelian or Aristotelian alternative to Kantian ethics—as have communitarians such as Charles Taylor and virtue theorists such as Alasdair MacIntyre[8]—she does advance a more Hegelian version of discourse ethics, one that stresses the contextual, the ethical, the particular, and the concrete as crucial aspects of moral-political deliberation. In so doing, Benhabib develops a version of moral-political universalism that is attentive to the crucial importance of the particular in our ethical and political lives and that stresses the interaction between universal and particular in our collective processes of moral decision making.

Benhabib's central criticism of Habermas is that, despite his attempts to avoid the empty formalism of Kant's moral theory, his theory of communicative action and his communicative ethics remain excessively and problematically rationalist. This results, in her view, not from Habermas's stress on argumentation per se, but instead from "the assumption that such argumentation processes also have a motive-shaping and action-determining quality. Habermas is too quick in translating the rationality intrinsic to argumentation procedures into the rationality of action and life conduct."[9] In other words, the problem is not that Habermas stresses the rational potential implicit in processes of argumentation, it is that he overemphasizes this potential while simultaneously underemphasizing the other—nonrational, bodily, affective, concrete—aspects of our selves.

Benhabib aims to correct for Habermas's rationalist bias by concretizing and contextualizing his insights into the self, autonomy, and ethics. This leads her first to develop a set of criticisms that question the status of the idealizations that form the normative core of Habermas's moral-political universalism. Indeed, much like McCarthy, Benhabib maintains that Habermas's "program of a strong justification of communicative ethics cannot succeed."[10] Specifically, she takes issue with his claim that "the decentered worldview and the reflexive differentiation of value spheres" that are constitutive of modern, postconventional identity are "quasi-transcendental, irrevocable, and binding upon us."[11] There are three points to her critique.

The first concerns the status of rational reconstruction. Contra Habermas, Benhabib argues that rational reconstructions cannot establish transcendental or even quasi-transcendental conditions of possibility and still retain their claim to empirical fruitfulness.[12] Moreover, "if reconstructive accounts cannot claim necessity for themselves in some strong sense, then what distinguishes them from, and gives them priority over, other modes of narrative accounts? Why is a reconstructive account of the development of modern rationality structures as a cumulative learning process to be preferred to one that views this same process as one of *forgetting*?"[13] If this is the case, then we do not have good grounds for preferring Habermasian rational reconstruction over Nietzschean or Foucaultian genealogy. In the end, Benhabib maintains that even though the former approach cannot be understood as superior to the latter on the grounds of its ability to articulate quasi-transcendental grounds for modern rationality, we nevertheless do have good reasons for favoring it. As she puts it, "what distinguishes rational reconstructions from both hermeneutical and deconstructivist accounts is not their special philosophical status but their empirical fruitfulness in generating further research, their viability to serve as models in a number of fields, and their capacity to order and explain complex phenomena into intelligible narratives."[14]

However, one might argue, as I did in chapters 2 and 3 above, that Foucault's project is not unlike the project of rational reconstruction, in the sense that it too aims to uncover a set of historically and socioculturally specific conditions of possibility for subjectivity, agency, and autonomy. The main difference between the two accounts, then, concerns not so much the methodology itself but the decision to view the modern historical a priori as a developmental advance over premodern, traditional forms of life. As became clear in the previous chapter, this is perhaps the most problematic assumption of Habermas's entire project. Moreover, the claim that Habermas's developmentalist approach ought to be preferred over Foucault's more ambivalent reading of modernity on the grounds that the former is more empirically fruitful is highly suspect. When judged by criteria of fruitfulness alone, Foucault's analysis of disciplinary power seems to be, if not more, certainly no less fruitful than Habermas's account of communicative rationality. Indeed, Foucault's work has generated a great deal of further research and served as a model in a wide variety of fields, from sociology, political science, and historiography to cultural studies, feminist theory, queer theory, literary theory, and philosophy. It has even played a crucial role in giving birth to an entirely new and still emerging field of inquiry: gender studies. Thus, this way of cashing out the distinction between rational reconstruction and other approaches, though convincing, does not in fact establish the superiority of the Habermasian position in the way that Benhabib seems to assume.

Benhabib's second criticism of Habermas's idealizations concerns the status of reflexivity as a normative ideal. As I discussed in chapter 5, in the context of Habermas's critique of Mead, Habermas regards the capacity for reflexivity that emerges with the transition to postconventionality to be crucial to the superiority of this stage of development at both the individual and the sociocultural levels. Unlike Habermas, Benhabib acknowledges explicitly that increased reflexivity does not necessarily mean decreased repression; as Nietzsche, Freud, and Horkheimer and Adorno well understood, increased reflexivity may well be predicated upon increased repression. This raises the following question: On what grounds, then, may we use the degree of reflexivity as a basis for judging other cultures, either those that are historically past or those that are contemporaneous? Here, Benhabib admits that

> there is a circularity in our argumentation, but this is not a vicious circularity. It would be a vicious circle only if presuppositionless understanding, an understanding that could divest itself of its own contextuality, were possible. Since, however, this cannot be the case, it follows that reflexivity is binding for us. To want to divest ourselves of it may be like wanting to jump over our own shadows.[15]

As McCarthy also argued, we have no choice but to start from where we are, and we start from a place where reflexivity is one of the norms constitutive of our late modern form of life.

This leads Benhabib to her third point, which concerns Habermas's assumption that the modern, postconventional point of view represents an irreversible developmental advance. Unlike Habermas, but in line with the more contextualist readings of his work offered by Cooke and McCarthy that I discussed in the previous chapter, Benhabib acknowledges that this claim can only be made from "our" point of view. Indeed, this qualification is crucial, for without it, Habermas runs the risk of positing the end of history, a situation in which "the future projected by the theorist, and which is fundamentally open, is presented as if it were a necessary and 'normal' outcome of a course of development."[16] Moreover, the argument that Habermas occasionally makes, that more contextualist modes of ethical reasoning or postmodernist assessments of culture represent developmental regressions, is of no use here, for "it is only in this light [that is, the light of the end of history thesis] that deviations from the theory can be deemed 'regressions'" in the first place.[17]

Benhabib sums up these three criticisms of the status of Habermas's idealizations as follows:

> The constituents of communicative rationality like decentration, reflexivity, and the differentiation of value spheres can be said to have "universal significance and validity" only in a weak sense. One cannot claim that they are "quasi-transcendental," only that they are the outcome of contingent learning processes whose internal evolution we can cogently reconstruct: what was once learned for good reasons, cannot be unlearned at will. Furthermore, the "epistemological reflexivity" of modern belief systems gives rise to a hermeneutical circle which we cannot overcome or escape. Finally, these structures are "irreversible" in that the future we would like to see can only be realized by fulfilling their still unexhausted potential.[18]

As we will see in a moment, Benhabib's positive and significant contribution to critical theory consists of an attempt to develop Habermasian critical theory and communicative ethics, on the basis of these insights, in a more modest and self-consciously historical direction.

In addition to developing these three critical points with respect to the status of Habermas's idealizations, Benhabib offers a second set of criticisms, the focus of which is Habermas's notion of autonomy. Here, once again, the central point is that Benhabib accuses Habermas of "falling into a certain rationalistic fallacy of the Kantian sort, in that it ignores the contingent, historical, and affective circumstances which made individuals adopt a universalist-ethical standpoint in the first place."[19] Benhabib argues that Habermas's highly formal accounts of universal pragmatics and of the postconventional self are not *purely* formal; they have "a cultural-historical content built into them."[20] The acknowledgment of this fact is not necessarily a reason for giving them up—indeed, Benhabib is quite clear that she shares the normative presuppositions of universal respect and egalitarian reciprocity that she claims are implicit in Habermas's ideal speech situation[21]—but it should lead us to advance more modest claims about their status than does Habermas. As Benhabib puts it, our commitment to such norms "is not a consequence of conceptual analysis alone; rather, it reflects the commitments of a moral philosophy as practiced by individuals who are themselves members of a culture that cherishes universalism."[22]

What Habermas fails to do, and what Benhabib attempts in her 1992 book *Situating the Self*, is to develop a "post-Enlightenment defense of universalism," one that "would be interactive not legislative, cognizant of gender difference not gender blind, contextually sensitive and not situation indifferent."[23] Moreover, Benhabib argues that one can formulate such an "interactive universalism" "without committing oneself to the metaphysical illusions of the Enlightenment" such as "the illusions of a self-transparent and self-grounding reason, the illusion of a disembedded and disembodied subject, and the illusion of having found an Archimedean standpoint, situated beyond historical and cultural contingency."[24]

Benhabib delineates three steps that are involved in developing such an interactive universalism. First, following Habermas and Karl-Otto Apel, Benhabib offers a discursive and communicative, rather than a substantialist, conception of rationality. Second, she understands subjects of reason as "finite, embodied and fragile creatures, and not disembodied cogitos or abstract unities of transcendental apperception to which may belong one or more bodies."[25] Specifically, Benhabib articulates this idea in terms of a narrative conception of the self, which I will discuss in more detail below. Third, because she regards reason itself as "the contingent achievement of linguistically socialized, finite and embodied creatures," Benhabib reformulates the moral point of view as "the contingent achievement of an interactive form of rationality rather than as the timeless standpoint of a legislative reason."[26]

It is clear that even as the first aspect of Benhabib's post-Enlightenment defense of universalism draws on Habermas for inspiration, her second and third points push beyond his discourse-ethical framework. Indeed, Benhabib claims that her aim is "to save discourse ethics from the excesses of its own rationalistic Enlightenment legacy."[27] One way that she accomplishes this is, as I mentioned above, to develop a more "historically self-conscious" version of universalism.[28] Thus, Benhabib emphasizes that the normative principles of universal respect and egalitarian reciprocity

> are our philosophical clarification of the constituents of the moral point of view from *within* the normative hermeneutic horizon of modernity. These principles are neither the *only allowable* interpretation of the formal constituents of the competency of postconventional moral actors nor are they unequivocal transcendental presuppositions which every rational agent, upon deep reflection, must concede to.[29]

Benhabib admits that "[my] recognition of the historical and sociological 'contingency' of communicative ethics, both as a social practice and as a normative ideal, is what distinguishes the kind of self-consciously historical universalism I advocate from the stronger justification programs of Habermas" but insists that it does not compel her to endorse relativism.[30] Indeed, one might understand Benhabib to be developing the kind of principled contextualism that I discussed in the previous chapter. Benhabib's universalism is not only historically self-conscious but also interactive, in that the goal of her communicative ethics is not consensus (even as a counterfactual ideal) but instead "the idea of an ongoing moral conversation."[31] This crucial step in her version of communicative ethics is

> to ask not what all would or could agree to as a result of practical discourses to be morally permissible or impermissible, but what would be allowed and perhaps even necessary from the standpoint of continuing and sustaining the practice of moral conversation. The emphasis now is less on *rational agreement*, but more on sustaining those normative practices and moral relationships within which reasoned agreement *as a way of life* can flourish and continue.[32]

Thus Benhabib's interactive universalism, like Cooke's nonauthoritarian reformulation of context-transcending validity claims, McCarthy's pragmatic interpretation of Habermasian critical theory, Foucault's understanding of critique as always in the position of beginning again, and Butler's cautious endorsement of the idea of the universal, presupposes a completely open-ended model of discourse, one in which "even the presuppositions of discourse can themselves be challenged, called into question and debated."[33]

In addition to offering a more historically self-conscious, interactive, and open-ended version of communicative ethics, Benhabib also aims to articulate a specifically feminist version of Habermasian critical theory. In her first book, *Critique, Norm, and Utopia*, Benhabib raises the following question: "Can the theory of communicative action really explain the emergence of one of the most significant social movements of our times, namely, the women's movement?"[34] At this point, Benhabib suggests that the crucial consideration here is not whether Habermas gives a satisfactory account of the feminist movement—it is quite obvious that he does not—but whether his critical social theory "succeed[s] in generating future research hypotheses which are fruitful."[35] Benhabib maintains that it does. In *Situating the Self*, Benhabib clarifies what is at stake in the feminist assessment of Habermas. "Certainly," she writes, "a normative theory, and in particular a critical social theory, cannot take the aspirations of any social actors at face value and fit its critical criteria to meet the demands of a particular social movement. Commitment to social transformation, and yet a certain critical distance, even from the demands of those with whom one identifies, are essential to the vocation of the theorist as social critic."[36] Thus, it would be inappropriate "to criticize the critical theory of Habermas simply by confronting it with the demands of the women's movement."[37] Nevertheless, her recasting of Habermasian critical theory aims to "'engender' the subject of moral reasoning, not in order to relativize moral claims to fit gender differences but to make them gender sensitive and cognizant of gender difference."[38] This is part and parcel of her broader goal, which is "to situate reason and the moral self more decisively in contexts of gender and community, while insisting upon the discursive power of individuals to challenge such situatedness in the name of universalistic principles, future identities and as yet undiscovered communities."[39]

However, as I will argue in the remainder of this chapter, Benhabib fails in the end to heed her own best insights. Although she is critical of Habermas on the grounds that he has "dismissed all too quickly a central insight of Gilligan and of other feminists, namely, that we are children before we are adults, and that the nurture, care and responsibility of others is essential for us to develop into morally competent, self-sufficient individuals" and insists that "such networks of dependence and the web of human affairs in which we are immersed are not simply like clothes which we outgrow or like shoes which we leave behind. They are ties that bind; ties that shape our moral identities, our needs, and our visions of the good life,"[40] she does not draw all the relevant consequences from this. Benhabib's narrative conception of the self is developed in the attempt to do justice to these aspects of our selfhood, and it is situated within a larger theoretical project that aims to rescue the Habermasian project from its rationalist excesses. Nevertheless, as I shall argue, there is a rationalist residue in Benhabib's account of the self, and this rationalist residue inclines her to the implausible view that there is an ungendered core to the self, and that gender is like clothes we can outgrow or shoes we can choose to leave behind.

The Narrative Conception of the Self

Although Benhabib seems to have developed a greater appreciation for Butler's theory of performativity during the years since their initial exchange, she remains critical of it on the grounds of its inability to satisfactorily explain the creativity and spontaneity that make agency possible. As she puts it:

> Repetition and innovation, necessity and contingency are brought together in an interesting fashion here.... However, I think that one needs a stronger concept of human intentionality and a more developed view of the communicative-pragmatic abilities of everyday life to explain how speech acts are not only iterations but also innovations and reinterpretations, be it of old linguistic codes, communicative or behavioral.[41]

According to Benhabib, these capacities for innovation and reinterpretation can be better explained by a Habermasian account of "the communicative competence of social actors in generating situational interpretations of their lifeworld through communicative acts oriented to validity claims."[42] Benhabib suggests that there can be no resignification, and thus no resistance, without communication. Butler's view, according to Benhabib, rather than locating the source of creativity and agency in how individuals use language in communicative interactions, attempts to locate it outside individuals, in "the bounty of language itself."[43] Benhabib suggests that this move not only does not explain the possibility of human creativity and agency, it mystifies and obscures this possibility. The Habermasian view that Benhabib endorses, by contrast, pays attention to the perspective of the participants in communicative interactions and locates the source of linguistic and social innovation, creativity, and change in their communicative competence.[44]

Benhabib suggests that her narrative model of the self "has the virtue of accounting for that 'surfeit of meaning, creativity and spontaneity' that is said to accompany iteration in the performativity model as well but whose mechanisms cannot be explained by performativity."[45] Although an explicit articulation and defense of her narrative conception of the self only emerges in Benhabib's recent work, elements of this conception have been evident in her work for quite some time. For example, in her classic critique of the Gilligan-Kohlberg debate, she criticizes the social contract tradition in moral philosophy for failing to realize that "the self is not a thing, a substrate, but the protagonist of a life's tale."[46] Her commitment to a narrative conception of selfhood is also evident in her initial critique of Butler, in which she argues that "a subjectivity that would not be structured by language, by narrative and by the symbolic structures of narrative available in a culture is unthinkable. We tell of who we are, of the 'I' that we are by means of a narrative."[47] And in her book on Arendt, Benhabib argues that one of Arendt's most important contributions to twentieth-century philosophy is her idea of the web of relationships and narratives as forming the space of human appearance.[48]

In her recent work, Benhabib expands upon and deepens these earlier insights. She argues that "to be and to become a self is to insert oneself into webs of interlocution; it is to know how to answer when one is addressed and to know how to address others."[49] As Benhabib notes, we are all thrown, in the Heideggerian sense, into various webs of interlocution or narrative—familial narratives, gender narratives, narratives of ethnic, racial, religious, and national identity, and so forth—and "we become who we are by learning to be a conversation partner in these narratives."[50] Moreover, although we are thrown into these ongoing narratives and thus are not in a position to choose them or our interlocutors, "our agency consists in our capacity to weave out of those narratives and fragments of narratives a life story that makes sense for us, as unique individual selves."[51] We are, in other words, not just the protagonist but also the author of our own stories.

This notion of "webs of interlocution" clearly resonates with Benhabib's reading of Arendt, but she borrows the term from Charles Taylor. Although her conception of the self is similar to his, she is critical of Taylor's claim that strong evaluative commitments are integral to human personhood. This disagreement with Taylor allows Benhabib to emphasize the antiessentialist nature of her narrative conception of the self. Accusing Taylor of conflating the distinction between "conditions of possible human agency" and a "strong concept of moral integrity," Benhabib argues that "there are lives that lack a horizon of strong evaluations and evaluative commitments. Such lives may lack a certain depth, a certain integrity, a certain vibrancy and vitality, but we know that they can be and are lived by some. It just seems wrong to say that they are not human life stories at all; should we rather not say that they are not very desirable, deep, or worthwhile ones?"[52] Rather than thinking of the continuity and coherence of the self as being provided by an ongoing commitment to a strong evaluation, Benhabib suggests that we think in terms of "the *capacity to take and adopt an attitude* toward such goods, even if, and particularly if, this attitude means noncommitment.... In the language of narration, it is not what the story is about that matters but, rather, one's ability to keep telling a story about who one is that makes sense to oneself and to others."[53] In response to "postmodernists" who claim that any conception of core identity is "essentialist, ahistorical, and implausible,"[54] Benhabib argues:

If we think of the identity of the self in time not in terms of a set of strong evaluative commitments but rather in terms of an ability to make sense, to render coherent, meaningful, and viable for oneself one's shifting commitments as well as changing attachments, then the postmodernist objection loses its target. The issue becomes whether it is possible to be a self at all without some ability to continue to generate meaningful and viable narratives over time. My view is that, hard as we try, we cannot "stop making sense." ... We *will* try to make sense out of nonsense.[55]

By insisting that the core of the self consists not in any substantive commitments but in an ability or capacity to make sense of our lives by fitting our experiences into a coherent narrative, Benhabib attempts to salvage coherence for the self without essentializing it. By construing the core of identity as an ability rather than a substance, Benhabib is also able to bring out the temporal dimension of identity; the process of achieving narrative coherence is "an interminable task, for narration is also a project of recollection and retrieval."[56] Particular events in our past take on new significance in the light of present events, new characters get written in and written out of our life stories, and so forth, all of which prompt us continually to reconstruct our narrative identity.

However, Benhabib emphasizes that she makes no strong claims about the mastery of the narrative self. She notes that "others are not just the subject matters of my story; they are also tellers of their own stories, which compete with my own, unsettle my self-understanding, and spoil my attempts to mastermind my own narrative."[57] Thus, we are never in complete control of our own narratives, as they must attain some degree of fit with the continually unfolding narratives of those others with whom our own life stories are inextricably intertwined. Moreover, Benhabib agrees with the psychoanalytic insight that the I is not the master of its own house, for "every story we tell of ourselves will also contain another of which we may not even be aware; and, in ways that are usually very obscure to us, we are determined by these subtexts and memories in our unconscious."[58] However, she insists that this does not give us cause "to get rid of the I as an instance of coherent mastery and ordering altogether."[59] Whatever mastery the I retains consists in its ability to weave these bits of its psychic past and its relationships with others into its own story.

Benhabib offers a rich and subtle account of the self, one that stakes out a plausible middle ground between, on the one hand, an overly robust, essentialist conception of the self that guarantees autonomy and agency at the cost of assuming an illusory unity and mastery of the self and, on the other hand, an antiessentialist but overly fragmented conception of self that renders autonomy and agency unthinkable. Conceiving of the core of the self in terms of a capacity to make sense of our lives by weaving together a unique life story from the competing narratives in which we find ourselves thrown allows Benhabib to offer a strong conception of practical autonomy, according to which practical autonomy is defined as "the capacity to exercise choice and agency over the conditions of one's narrative identifications."[60] Such a capacity would rather obviously explain the possibilities of resistance to and transformation of gender subordination and other objectionable forms of narrative identification. However, as I argue below, Benhabib is able to provide such a strong conception of practical autonomy only by downplaying the depth of the hold that gendered modes of subjection have on individuals who are thrown into societies structured by pervasive gender subordination. Ultimately, and despite her attempt to move beyond the narrow rationalism of Habermas's version of communicative ethics, Benhabib's narrative conception of the self retains a problematic rationalist core.

Gender, Power, and Narrative

The root of the problem, I shall argue, is that Benhabib conceptualizes gender itself as a narrative—akin to cultural, familial, or religious narratives—that individuals weave into the complex story of their lives. This assumption is evident in Benhabib's repeated references to gender as an element of our narratives, or to "gender narratives." For example, in *Situating the Self*, Benhabib argues that "identity ... [refers] to how I, as a finite, concrete, embodied individual, shape and fashion the circumstances of my birth and family, linguistic, cultural and gender identity into a coherent narrative that stands as my life's story."[61] More recently, she claims that "we are born into webs of interlocution or narrative from familial or gender narratives to linguistic ones and to the macronarratives of collective identity," and she refers to the "master narratives of family structure and gender roles into which each individual is thrown."[62] As a result of conceptualizing gender as a narrative, however, Benhabib must presuppose a core identity to the self that precedes or transcends gender. After all, a self that chooses *how* to weave the existing gender narratives into which it is thrown into its life story is not itself already gendered. Moreover, Benhabib's assumption of an ungendered core of the self is indicated by the gender-neutral language that she uses to describe the self. For example, in a passage that argues for the "importance of a coherent core of individual identity," Benhabib writes:

> We can think of coherence as a narrative unity.... As Hannah Arendt has emphasized, from the time of our birth we are immersed in a "web of narratives," of which we are both the author and the object. The self is both the teller of tales and that about whom tales are told. The individual with a coherent sense of self-identity is the one who succeeds in integrating these tales and perspectives into a meaningful life history.[63]

The significance of this gender-neutral language for describing the narrative ability that constitutes the core of identity for Benhabib is made clear in her more recent comments on Virginia Woolf's novel *Orlando*. Benhabib interprets the novel as suggesting that "fixed sexual identity, as defined by rigid gender roles and categories, is not central to the core identity of the self.... The sources of the self as a unified being, if there are any at all, suggests Woolf, lie deeper."[64] Although Benhabib acknowledges that Woolf's novel is somewhat equivocal on this issue, she nonetheless emphasizes that Woolf "sometimes suggests that the core identity of the self is formed by a set of gender-transcending characteristics that in old-fashioned language would be called 'character.'"[65]

These assumptions about gender as a narrative and the nongendered core of the self, when combined with Benhabib's understanding of practical autonomy, offer an initially appealing but ultimately excessively rationalistic account of the self and, thus, an overly optimistic account of what is required in order to exercise autonomy with respect to gender narratives. If practical autonomy is the ability to choose the conditions of our narrative identifications, then the practically autonomous narrative self has the ability to choose the conditions of its identification with gender narratives. This suggests that we are to imagine the autonomous core self—a self that is as ungendered as the Kantian noumenal self—asking questions such as the following: Ought I to identify with the gender narratives that predominate in my culture, my religious traditions, my family? If so, with which ones should I identify? How shall I weave gender into my overall life story?

To be sure, Benhabib's view is more complex than this. She acknowledges that the narratives that we have to choose from in constructing our life stories "are deeply colored and structured by the codes of expectable and understandable biographies and identities in our cultures."[66] Furthermore, she grants that "the codes of established narratives in various cultures define our capacity to tell the story in very different ways; they limit our freedom to 'vary the code.'"[67] And she quotes approvingly the work of a pair of social theorists who conclude that "which kinds of narratives will socially predominate is contested politically and will depend in large part on the distribution of power." [68] These admissions allow Benhabib to argue that we are presented with a limited range of options with respect to gender narratives, options that are structured in such a way as to further the exploitation and oppression of women. This provides Benhabib with a way of granting the point that power plays a crucial role in the constitution of gender identity without undermining our ability to resist and transform those gender narratives and the power relations with which they are linked. Thus, Benhabib always insists on the ability of the individual to choose whether and how to take up those narratives:

> We always have options in telling a life story that makes sense to us. These options are not ahistorical; they are culturally and historically specific and inflected by the master narrative of the family structure and gender roles into which each individual is thrown. Nonetheless, just as the grammatical rules of language, once acquired, do not exhaust our capacity to build an infinite number of well-formed sentences in a language, so socialization and accumulation processes do not determine the life story of any unique individual in his or her capacity to initiate new actions and new sentences in a conversation.[69]

But this way of conceptualizing the role that gender and power play in the constitution of narrative identity does not, in my view, go far enough. After all, is not the I who asks "(how) ought I identify with this or that gender narrative," insofar as it is embodied and concrete, already gendered?[70] Does it make sense, then, to think of gender as a narrative that we can choose how to weave into our own life story? Or, rather, is gender in some sense a (culturally and historically specific) precondition for the telling of any narrative whatsoever? If that is the case, and if, as Benhabib herself maintains, gender difference is intimately bound up with power inasmuch as all known gender-sex systems function to exploit and oppress women,[71] then does it make sense to think of power as merely structuring the available options from which we choose when constructing our gendered life stories? No doubt it does that too, but does it not also go deeper into the self than this, structuring the very I who chooses how to enact his or her gender?

The sense in which gender is a cultural and social precondition for telling any narrative whatsoever can be made clear by examining the literatures on gender development and on the autobiographical or narrative self in developmental psychology. Although one might think that drawing on this literature in this context represents a confusion of theoretical and empirical levels of analysis, Benhabib herself argues that "to embark on a meaningful investigation" of gender and identity constitution requires "a serious interchange between philosophy and other social sciences like socio-linguistics, social interactionist psychology, socialization theory, psychoanalysis, and cultural history, among others."[72] Indeed, she criticizes Butler for ignoring this empirical literature in her discussions of gender identity.[73] Thus, it seems reasonable to consider how Benhabib's narrative conception of gender identity coheres with the existing empirical literature.

The consensus among researchers in developmental psychology is that gender becomes salient at least by age two, at which point children can recognize and differentiate between male and female figures and can consistently label themselves as either male or female.[74] But some research suggests that gender may become salient even earlier. Many empirical studies establish that adult caregivers interact differently with male and female infants. As Susan Golombok and Robyn Fivush put it in their study of gender development: "Boys are played with more roughly than girls, beginning in infancy and throughout the childhood years. Further, parents assume their infant girls will be more vocal and more interested in social interaction than their infant boys, and parents work harder to engage girls in mutual social interaction, such as eye-gazing and reciprocal emotional expressions."[75] Further studies indicate that these perceptions on the part of parents and these patterns of interaction are not formed in response to any actual differences between male and female infants themselves. The "Baby X" studies show very clearly that adults interact with babies differently and interpret infants' emotional responses differently depending upon the *perceived* gender of the infant. In one such experiment, subjects viewed a videotape of a baby being startled and crying; those who were told the baby was a girl described the response as fear, whereas those who were told it was a boy described the very same response as anger.[76] A more recent review of gender-labeling studies found that "labeled females received more vocalizations, more interpersonal stimulation, and more nurturant play than labeled males did. In contrast, labeled males received more encouragement of activity and more whole body stimulation than labeled females did."[77] On the basis of these studies, Golombok and Fivush speculate quite reasonably that these differences in the ways adults react to and interact with infants on the basis of their *perceived* gender "will have important consequences for how children come to understand their own … experiences."[78] This suggests the source of our sense of our selves as gendered beings may extend all the way into infancy.

Be that as it may, however, even if we assume that gender does not become salient until age two, this is still long before children have developed the kind of narrative abilities that Benhabib considers to be necessary conditions for selfhood.[79] Research in developmental psychology links the achievement of a narrative self to the development of autobiographical memory, which does not begin to emerge until about age three or four, long after gender identity has been consolidated.[80] In contrast with episodic memory, which refers to the ability to recall particular one-time events, such as what I had for lunch yesterday, autobiographical memory refers to the ability to fit my recollections of past experiences into my personal life story. This ability is clearly linked to the emergence of a narrative sense of self (indeed, developmental psychologists tend to use the terms "autobiographical self" and "narrative self" interchangeably). As one pair of researchers put it, "memories of the past and sense of self develop dialectically, such that over the course of the preschool years, children construct a sense of self in time and a sense of autobiography that culminates in an autobiographical self that allows for the organization of self-referenced, coherently organized memories of personally experienced events that may be retained over a lifetime."[81]

The capacity for autobiographical memory and the ability to generate narratives are developed through social interactions with adult caregivers; in some sense, then, both autobiographical memory and the narrative self are socially constructed. As Fivush explains, "children learn the conventionalized narrative forms of describing the past through parent-guided conversations."[82] Such conversations do more than teach children conventional narrative forms; the child's emerging autobiographical self-conception is also shaped by the particular events upon which parents tend to focus during these reminiscences.[83] Thus, Fivush maintains, "autobiography is not memory of what happened; it is the way we make sense of what happened, and this is fundamentally a social-cultural process."[84] However, given the extent to which gender shapes our social and cultural reality, autobiography is deeply gendered as well. Indeed, in light of the studies cited above that show that parents interact with infants and young children in ways that correspond to gender stereotypes, we should expect to see gender differences in the construction of autobiography and narrative, and empirical evidence in fact bears this out. One study found that girls' and boys' narratives tend to be different in both their content and, perhaps more significantly, their structure:

> Structurally, girls' narratives were longer, more temporally-causally connected and more highly embellished with descriptive detail than were those of boys. In terms of content ... girls were more likely to narrate an interpersonal experience than were boys. Moreover, even when placing a past

experience within an interpersonal context, girls' narratives included more affiliation themes, more emotion, and more references to both specific and non-specific others than those of boys.[85]

In other words, not only the content of our narratives but also their structure and form varies along gender lines, and this variation tends to reproduce individuals who conform to gender stereotypes: girls who are concerned with relationships and connection, and boys who are concerned with individuation and autonomy.

So, what conclusions can be drawn about Benhabib's narrative conception of gender identity on the basis of this detour through the empirical literature? I want to tread very lightly here. It seems to me that this literature points to the conclusion that the idea of gender as a narrative and the related assumption of a nongendered core self that has the ability to autonomously choose whether and how to take up gender narratives are implausible. There is some reason to believe that social and cultural notions of gender difference—hence of gender dominance as well—are already a salient feature of our experience of our protoselves in infancy. Regardless of whether or not this is true, it is clearly the case that young children have mastered the concept of gender difference—both as a way of carving up their social world into people of two distinct types and as a way of understanding themselves as either a boy or a girl—long before they have attained the narrative capacities that are the hallmark of selfhood for Benhabib. Inasmuch as gender difference is connected to gender dominance in almost every culture of which we are aware, as Benhabib herself admits, this would suggest that they have a pretty good handle on gender dominance as well (though certainly without recognizing it as such). The fact that gender difference and dominance have an impact on not only the content but also the form of our narratives suggests, furthermore, that gender structures not only the substantive content of our narratives but also our very narrative capacities, thus, our narrative selves as well. All of the preceding suggests that, at the very least, the language that Benhabib uses to lay out her narrative conception of identity and to use this conception to ground an analysis of gender is seriously misleading.

However, I suspect that what is at issue here is more than a mere poor choice of words on Benhabib's part. Consider her insistence, in the context of her debate with Butler, on a distinction between "the historical study of culturally diverse codes which define individuality" and "the study of those social processes through which a human infant becomes the social self, regardless of the cultural and normative content which defines selfhood in different socio-historical contexts."[86] The former sort of analysis aims at "historical and hermeneutic processes of signification and meaning-constitution," the latter at "*structural processes* and *dynamics of socialization and individuation*."[87] Benhabib accuses Butler of conflating these two types of analysis, of inappropriately drawing conclusions about the general structure of processes of socialization and individuation from premises that concern the particular cultural and normative content that defines subjectivity in our own cultural and historical context. The implication is that at the structural level of analysis of the dynamics of socialization and individuation, discussions of particularities such as gender and power are irrelevant. At this level, what must be explained is

> how a human infant can become the speaker of an infinitely meaningful number of sentences in a given natural language, how it acquires, that is, the competence to become a linguistic being; furthermore, we have to explain how every human infant can become the initiator of a unique life story, of a meaningful tale—which certainly is only meaningful if we know the cultural codes under which it is constructed—but which we cannot predict even if we knew these cultural codes.[88]

This distinction in Benhabib recalls the problematic relationship between the formal and the empirical levels of analysis in Habermas discussed in the previous chapter. Here, a version of the question that we posed to Habermas may be put to Benhabib as well: If we take seriously the empirical literature that suggests that both the capacity for autobiographical memory and the ability to construct a narrative are developed through social interactions with adult caregivers whose attitudes toward and interactions with their children are shaped by gender stereotypes that tend to reinforce women's subordination, then how can we justify screening gender and power out of this discussion? Refusing to do so does not commit us to the deterministic view that once we know the cultural codes under which a life story is constructed, we will be able to predict how that story goes. But it does require us to take much more seriously than Benhabib does the ways in which our basic capacities, including our capacities to tell our own life stories and to reflect critically on those stories, though they may be biologically rooted, are necessarily socially and culturally elaborated and developed. Given how pervasively our social and cultural reality is shaped by gender difference and dominance, we would expect these capacities to be gendered as well and thus to reflect and reinforce gendered asymmetries of power. Simply appealing to structural processes of individuation and socialization or formal capacities of the self does not take us above the fray. As we have already seen, such formal and structural processes are themselves articulated from a situated and contextualized point of view, one shaped by gendered relations of power. Indeed, this is related to the critique Benhabib makes of Habermas, when she argues for a more historically self-conscious version of communicative ethics.

From a political point of view, such a conception of the role that gender and power play in the constitution of the self undoubtedly places limitations on how we can understand the possibilities for critical reflection upon, resistance to, and transformation of the gender-sex system. For, ultimately, it is Benhabib's assumption of a nongendered core self that allows her to be relatively optimistic about the possibilities for resistance to and transformation of existing gender subordination. If, however, it is not enough to say that the core self is always *situated within* narratives of gender (along with those of race, ethnicity, family, nation, and culture), if, instead, our very ability to narrate our lives is *constituted* in and through social-cultural relations that systematically reinforce a gender-sex system that subordinates women, then although critical resistance and progressive self-transformation are certainly not impossible, the task of achieving them will be different and probably more difficult than Benhabib imagines. If the roots of gender identity lie deeper than those of the narrative ability that Benhabib views as the source of spontaneity, creativity, and agency, then interrelated assumptions about gender difference and gender dominance are so basic to our sense of ourselves that they are likely to be extremely resistant to critique and to change.

Benhabib is no doubt right to argue that the challenge for feminist critical theorists is to address the following question: "How can one be constituted by discourse without being determined by it?"[89] However, insofar as her account obscures the role that gender and power play in the constitution of the narrative self, it underestimates both the depth of the problem and what it will take to overcome it.

The limitations of Benhabib's account seem to be a result of Benhabib's failing to heed her own best insights and to realize what is demanded by the more historicized and contextualized version of Habermas's discourse ethics that she defends. Despite her compelling critique of the overly rationalist residue of Habermasian discourse ethics, Benhabib's work also retains a problematically rationalist core, evident in her assumption of an ungendered core self that chooses which narratives of gender—albeit from a constricted range of options—to enact. This assumption leads her to presuppose too facile a distinction between power relations and human capacities such as the capacity for narrative. It also leads her to offer a strong conception of autonomy vis-à-vis gender norms, but one that is ultimately too strong, inasmuch as it does not take seriously enough the ways in which our basic narrative and critical capacities are shaped and structured by social and cultural realities, including gender subordination.

Another way to put this point is to say that among the "contingent, historical, and affective circumstances which made individuals adopt a universalist-ethical standpoint in the first place"[90]—circumstances that Benhabib was right to criticize Habermas for failing to theorize—are the child's subjugation to the power of the parent in the context of heterosexist and patriarchal family structures and the gendered nature of language. The first fact—which may not even be contingent, given the relatively lengthy period of radical dependency of human infants on their adult caregivers—leads to a psychic and affective situation in which we are extremely vulnerable to subordinating forms of subjection. The second—which is contingent—means that gender competence is a precondition for linguistic competence, thus, that the very language that we use to articulate our critique of gender subordination is relentlessly structured by the same. These two considerations suggest that gender is not like a narrative that we (ungendered core selves) can choose how to weave into our life story. It is more like a deep psychic and linguistic investment that structures not only how we understand the world but also how we understand and narrate our selves.

The best account of the relationships between power, autonomy, and gender in the constitution of the self, then, would take seriously the fact that the self is gendered all the way down and that it forms deep psychic attachments to its gender while preserving a robust but realistic conception of the possibility of autonomy with respect to gender. However, such an account will have to make do with a somewhat less robust conception of autonomy than Benhabib articulates. Reflecting autonomously and critically on gender norms will still require us to make distinctions between power and validity, or between power and capacity, but this will always be from a position within social practices, thus, from a position within power relations. Although this is a less robust conception of autonomy than the one that Benhabib defends, particularly in the context of her debate with Butler, it is not incompatible with her relatively modest, historically self-conscious, moral-political universalism.

Concluding Reflections

AS I discussed in the introduction, critical theory has two principal aims: the first is to offer an empirically grounded diagnosis of the central crisis tendencies and injustices of the present age; the second is to chart paths of progressive social transformation. Accomplishing the first task requires the development of an account of power in all its depth and complexity, including how it functions through the mechanism of subjection to constitute subordinating modes of subjectivity and identity. The task of analyzing subjection is crucially important for analyzing gender subordination and its complex interrelations with race and sexuality. Accomplishing the second task requires the development of an account of autonomy, understood both as the capacity for critical reflection on the power relations that constitute us and as the capacity for self-transformation. Subjection and autonomy are thus the two sides of the politics of our selves. And yet these two aspects of the politics of our selves are often thought to be in tension with one another: theorists of subjection such as Foucault and Butler are accused of denying or undermining the possibility of agency and autonomy, whereas defenders of autonomy such as Habermas and Benhabib are accused of being blind to the complexities of power relations. The principal aim of this book has been to develop a framework that does justice to both aspects of the politics of our selves: a framework that theorizes subjection without sacrificing the possibility of autonomy and that theorizes autonomy without denying the reality of subjection.

For the analysis of power and subjection, I turned first to Foucault. Whereas many of Foucault's feminist and Habermasian critics charge him with embracing the death of the subject, in chapter 2, I argued that this charge is based on a misreading of his work. Not only does Foucault not endorse the death of the subject, he is, I maintain, correct to claim that it is the subject, rather than power, that is the general theme of his research. His oeuvre is best understood as an immanent critique of the Kantian notion of the transcendental subject; its overall aim is to interrogate the historically, culturally, and socially specific conditions of possibility of subjectivity in the modern era, with an eye toward analyzing the contingent modes of constraint embedded in those conditions and envisioning new, freer practices of the self.

Once Foucault's project is understood in this way, it becomes clear that his late work on practices of the self is consistent with his early calls for the death of man. Not only that, but, as I argued in chapter 3, there is an account of autonomy that is implicit and sometimes explicit in Foucault's late work that is consistent with his analyses of power and subjection. Foucault understands autonomy—both in the sense of the capacity for critical reflection and in the sense of the capacity for deliberate self-transformation, both of which are implicit in his notion of technologies of the self—as always bound up with power. His immanent critique of the Kantian notion of autonomy both emphasizes the contingency of what is taken to be necessary and acknowledges the impurity of practical reason. This means that, for Foucault, we have to give up the hope of ever acceding to a point of view that is outside of power from which the critique of power can be launched. We have to give up, in other words, the demand for purity. This does not mean, however, that critique is futile or that autonomy is impossible. Rather, it means that critique is always open ended and ongoing—as Foucault put it, "we are always in the position of beginning again"[1]—and that self-transformation necessarily involves taking up in a subversive way the relations of subjection that have made us who we are.

Butler's analysis of subjection extends the Foucaultian notion by developing its psychoanalytic backstory; this enables Butler to analyze why subordinated individuals take up and reinscribe the disciplinary norms that subordinate them. As she understands it, subjection works at the psychic level by exploiting our primary narcissism, our basic desire for recognition. This desire is so powerful that we are willing to accept recognition on any terms; we prefer recognition that is predicated on our adherence to subordinating modes of identity over no recognition at all. For Butler, this explains how subordinated individuals come to be psychically invested in and attached to their subordination. In chapter 4, I argued that this analysis is extremely useful for analyzing certain aspects of gender subordination: in particular, it offers a way of understanding the curious recalcitrance of such subordination in the wake of decades of feminist critique and activism. Feminists have tended to assume that the key to dismantling gender subordination lies in revealing sex and gender to be contingent, historically emergent social categories that systematically subordinate some people to others and that are intertwined with other subordinating categories such as race and sexuality. And yet, more than fifty years after Simone de Beauvoir inaugurated this line of feminist criticism in her landmark book *The Second Sex*, gender and sex categories remain as socially and culturally salient as ever and gender subordination is far from a thing of the past. Butler's analysis of subjection gives us a way of understanding why this is the case: if gender subordination reproduces itself in part through the mechanism of psychic subjection, then the result is subjects who are psychically attached to their sex/gender identity, whether they perceive that identity to be subordinating or not. Changing the way we *think* about gender and sex will not be enough to undo such subordination; if we are to make it possible to form less subordinating attachments, we will also need to reorient our desire. In order to think through this possibility, we will need to theorize, for example, the ways in which literary and artistic counterpublic spheres and collective social movements imagine and create alternative structures of social recognition that in turn generate new, potentially less subordinating modes of attachment. I'll return to these examples below.

However, as I argued in chapter 4, Butler's ambivalence about the possibility of mutual recognition makes it difficult for her to envision recognition's transformative potential. In the end, both Butler and Foucault rely on an overly narrow conception of the social, one that tends to equate all social relations with strategic relations of power. Foucault consistently defines power in strategic terms and indicates that he sees power as emerging from all social relationships; a similar assumption seems to be behind Butler's suspicion that recognition is always a trap, that it is nothing more than a mask for relations of subordination. With respect to both Foucault and Butler, I argued that their lack of a broader conception of social relations undermines their ability to offer an adequate account of resistance to subjection; specifically, it makes it difficult for them to adequately distinguish resistance from the reinscription of subordination. Thus, and this is an important point, this critique of Foucault and Butler is not an external one, based on considerations that are extrinsic to their theoretical positions; on the contrary, there are reasons internal to their views that motivate the development of a broader conception of social relations.[2] The trick, of course, will be to develop a broader conception of the social that includes the possibility of normative reciprocity and mutual recognition but that does not posit an outside to power. This is necessary if such an account is to be consistent with Foucault's and Butler's analyses of subjection. I will say more about how this can be done below, but for now I will simply note that there are tentative and undeveloped gestures toward a vision of normative reciprocity in Foucault's late work and in Butler's recent discussions of recognition. Thus, there seems to be some room for introducing notions of normative reciprocity or recognition into the discussion here.

The need to offer a broader conception of the social but one that can be made compatible with the view that there is no outside to power is part of what motivates the turn to Habermas in chapter 5. Habermas offers a broad view of the social that encompasses both strategic and communicative interactions, but he is also committed to the idea of what McCarthy calls the "impurity of reason" or what Cooke calls "situated rationality." The other major motivation for turning to Habermas is the central role that his critical social theory gives to the notion of autonomy. Indeed, these two aspects of Habermas's thought are closely related: he understands the socialization processes that form the autonomous individual as rooted in the communicative relations of the lifeworld and grounded in relations of mutual recognition and normative reciprocity. This understanding of individuation through socialization—where socialization is understood to take place in the context of the normatively and communicatively structured domain of the lifeworld—allows Habermas to offer a robust conception of autonomy, according to which autonomous individuals are capable of reflecting critically on the norms, practices, institutions, cultural meanings, and social structures that have made them who they are. But, as I argued in chapter 5, this account is ultimately too robust, as it downplays the role that power necessarily plays in the formation of the autonomous individual. Although Butler goes too far when she suggests that subordination is central to the becoming of the subject, Habermas is overly sanguine about the psychic costs of the subjugation to the (from the child's perspective, completely arbitrary) will of the parent that is necessary for socialization. One of the costs of this is a vulnerability to subordinating forms of subjection, a tendency to become psychically attached to and invested in subordinating modes of identity.

Habermas seems to want to avoid this Nietzschean and Butlerian line of thought regarding the formation of bad conscience because it makes it difficult to disentangle validity from power, and Habermas's mature social theory rests on the ability to separate these two. Whereas the Habermas of *Knowledge and Human Interests* had viewed power as a basic, anthropological given, an ineradicable feature of human social life, in his later work, Habermas understands power as a phenomenon that is derivative from the more anthropologically basic communicative interaction. However, as I argued in chapter 6, this attempt to view power as a derivative phenomenon in social life is unconvincing, for two reasons: first, because it implies the possibility of a form of human social life that is devoid of power; second, because it reopens the gap between the real and the ideal, the transcendental and the empirical, theory and practice, that Habermas's earlier work had rightly attempted to close. Not only is Habermas's problematic positing of the possibility of a human social world beyond power not convincing, it is not necessary: it is possible to admit the impurity of reason and the entanglement of power and validity without undermining the critical edge of critical theory. The key is to give up on the demand for purity and to develop the Habermasian critical-theoretical project in a more contextualist and pragmatic direction. In this way, it is possible to salvage the normative content of that project but without making the overly strong metatheoretical claims that Habermas makes regarding the status of his normative idealizations.

Benhabib's critique of Habermas's communicative ethics echoes some of these concerns, and her notion of interactive universalism develops his insights in a more historically self-conscious and situated way. In chapter 7, I argued that Benhabib is rightly critical of Habermas's overly strong claims as to the status of his idealizations and his overly robust conception of autonomy. Her more particularist and historically self-conscious defense of the ideals of the Enlightenment and more situated, concrete, and embodied account of the self not only are more plausible in themselves but also are more compatible with some of the central insights of feminist theory. However, when she develops her own account of autonomy in the context of her narrative conception of the self, Benhabib fails to heed her own best insights. Her view of gender as one among many sorts of narratives from which the individual must weave his or her own life story presupposes (and at times Benhabib is explicit about this) an ungendered core of the self. This assumption not only entails an implausible account of the formation of gender identity, one that fails to cohere with the existing empirical literature on the topic, it also leads Benhabib to downplay the role that power plays in the constitution of the gendered self and to underestimate what is required for progressive transformation of sex and gender. In the end, and despite her own aim of saving Habermasian critical theory from its rationalistic excesses, in part in an effort to make it more responsive to the concerns of feminist theory, there is a problematic rationalist residue to Benhabib's conception of the self.

What I hope these critical engagements with Foucault, Butler, Habermas, and Benhabib show is both the possibility and the necessity of doing justice to both aspects of the politics of our selves. With Foucault and Butler, we can understand the subject as constituted through relations of power and subjection and also as potentially attached to and invested in those subordinating modes of identity. But this does not commit us to a denial of subjectivity, agency, or autonomy. What it does commit us to is the idea that there is no outside to power, that practical reason and autonomy are inescapably shaped by our social situatedness, thus, potentially by power relations as well. It is in this sense that they are impure. But this does not mean that critique is futile or that autonomy is impossible. It just means that there is no Archimedean point, no point wholly outside power relations from which our critique of power can be launched or our transformative vision of a better future can be articulated. As both Benhabib and Cooke pointed out, this will seem like a problem only to those who still have faith in that impossible point of view. With Habermas and Benhabib, we can understand autonomy as a crucially important, socially and intersubjectively developed capacity that makes it possible for us to take up a critical perspective on power relations. Moreover, Habermas acknowledges the role that power necessarily plays in the development of this capacity, even if he does not seem to recognize that this acknowledgment pushes in the direction of a less robust and more ambivalent notion of autonomy than the one he defends. And whereas Habermas's own understanding of the anthropological givens of human social life (at least after *Knowledge and Human Interests*) and of the status of his normative idealizations is inconsistent with the idea that there is no outside to power, the more contextualist and pragmatic interpretations of his project offered by Cooke, McCarthy, and Benhabib are not. Thus, by reading Foucault in a way that emphasizes his connection to the Kantian Enlightenment tradition and by interpreting Habermas in a more historicized, contextualist, and pragmatic direction, it is possible to stake out a productive and fertile middle ground between these two theorists whom commentators often take to be diametrically opposed. On the basis of this middle ground, we can envision subjects as both socially and culturally constructed in and through relations of power and subjection and capable of critique and of critically directed self-constitution and social transformation.

However, two major conceptual difficulties remain unresolved. The first of these concerns my use of the notion of recognition. On the one hand, I have criticized Foucault and Butler for having an overly narrow conception of the social, for not theorizing the important role that relationships of mutual recognition and normative reciprocity play in social life. On the other hand, I have accepted Foucault's and Butler's claim that there is no outside to power and, on this basis, have criticized Habermas for thinking of power as derivative from the anthropologically more basic reciprocal, communicative relations, on the grounds that this leads him to presuppose that there is an outside to power. But if I accept that there is no outside to power, then how can I maintain that relations of mutual recognition and normative reciprocity are even possible? Doesn't accepting that there is no outside to power commit me to saying that when you scratch the surface of any apparently mutual, consensual relationship, you will find that what is really happening is a power relationship? Foucault sometimes seemed to think so, which would explain why he was hesitant about endorsing the normative notion of consensus that is central to Habermas's work; as he put it, "the farthest I would go is to say that perhaps one must not be for consensuality, but one must be against nonconsensuality."[3] To the extent that this sentence makes any sense at all (how could one be against nonconsensuality without being for consensuality?), it does so only if one assumes that relations of apparent consensus are always in fact relations of power. This assumption would also explain Butler's criticism of Benjamin on the grounds that she fails to realize that destruction and aggression "constitute recognition essentially."[4]

How, then, can I have it both ways? How can I help myself to the notion of mutual recognition while still agreeing with Foucault and Butler that there is no outside to power? One way to respond to this worry would be to argue, as Richard Lynch has done, that although Foucault claims that power relations are omnipresent, this claim "entails neither that power relations are the only omnipresent relation nor that power relations are the most important relations in social situations."[5] As Foucault puts it: "The omnipresence of power: not because it has the privilege of consolidating everything under its invincible unity, but because it is produced from one moment to the next, at every point, or rather in every relation from one point to another. Power is everywhere; not because it embraces everything, but because it comes from everywhere."[6] This way of understanding the claim that there is no outside to power leaves open the possibility that other kinds of social relations are possible and may, at times, be more salient as a feature of social-theoretical analysis than power relations are. Lynch concludes from this that Foucault's view is that analyzing power relations is necessary for social-theoretical analysis, but it is not sufficient; a full social-theoretic analysis will need to encompass other kinds of social relations. Whereas this reading seems to make more room for the kind of broader conception of the social that I have claimed Foucault and Butler need, it also seems to support the conclusion that power relations are at least immanent in all social relations, including relations of mutual recognition and reciprocity. Thus, it does not fully resolve the problem at hand.

A better way to deal with this problem is to interpret the claim that there is no outside to power not to mean that power is present in any and all social relationships but instead as the more innocuous contention that power is an ineradicable feature of human social life. In other words, one could drop the omnipresence claim but retain the idea that there is no outside to power in the sense of no possible form of recognizably human social life from which power has been wholly eliminated. Interestingly, Foucault himself seems to have moved in this direction late in his life. For example, in the late essay "The Subject and Power," Foucault maintains that "power relations are rooted deep in the social nexus, not reconstituted 'above' society as a supplementary structure whose radical effacement one could perhaps dream of.... A society without power relations can only be an abstraction."[7] But in this essay he also distinguishes between power relations and relations of communication, and he claims that although these do not represent two distinct social domains, they are distinct "types of relationship which in fact always overlap one another, support one another reciprocally, and use each other mutually as means to an end."[8] If, as I suggested in chapter 4, we stress the temporal and dynamic nature of human relationships and think of mutual recognition and normative reciprocity not as static end states but as moments *within* such relationships, then this seems perfectly compatible with claiming that there is no outside to power in this sense. Following Benjamin, we could understand mutual recognition not as a possible state of social relations from which power relations have been permanently and completely expunged but as a permanent though temporally fleeting possibility within dynamically unfolding human relationships. Mutual recognition, then, can be thought of as an ideal that is immanent to social life; it provides a foothold within social practice for normative critique. It is only a pernicious illusion if we posit an end state of social life from which power has been expunged and in which social relations are structured by mutual recognition alone.

This leads me to the second unresolved conceptual issue, which concerns the possibility of satisfactorily grounding the various normative judgments that I have made throughout this book—between, for example, resistance and the reinscription of relations of subordination, between dependency and subordination, between better and worse subjectivating practices, and so forth—in light of my acknowledgment of the pervasive entanglement of power and validity. If validity cannot ultimately be insulated from power even by means of Habermas's formal-pragmatic procedural account, then does this not undermine any and all attempts to make normative judgments? Do not all such judgments ultimately just collapse into power plays of one kind or another?

The answer here lies in filling out the idea of principled contextualism that I discussed in chapter 6. It is a mistake to assume that our only options are either to hold on to the dangerous illusion of genuine context transcendence—an illusion whose danger is evident from the fact that it has so often been used to justify the colonizing of those others who are perceived to be less morally or politically enlightened than "we" are—or to accept a radically contextualist form of relativism. Instead, as Benhabib has shown, we can rely on the normative ideals of universal respect and egalitarian reciprocity in making normative judgments while at the same time acknowledging that these are ideals that are rooted in the context of late Western modernity. We may take them to be universal and context transcendent, as long as we recognize that the notions of universalizability and context transcendence are themselves situated in the context of late Western modernity. In other words, once we accept that there is no outside to power in the sense that I delineated above, then we have to accept that it may turn out from some future vantage point that our normative ideals are themselves, in some way that we have yet to realize, pernicious and oppressive. This requires us to be more historically self-conscious and modest about the status of our normative principles than Habermas himself has tended to be, but it does not in any way entail that we are incapable of making normative judgments in light of such principles.

Having addressed these two conceptual difficulties, there is one remaining practical-political issue, namely, how to make the conceptual framework that I have developed here useful for the project of analyzing gender domination and the possibilities for transforming it. I hope that chapters 1, 4, and 7 will have gone some way toward addressing this issue, but, in conclusion, I'd like to tie together some of the threads from those discussions.

Consider, for example, the argument advanced by Joan Jacobs Brumberg in her book *The Body Project: An Intimate History of American Girls*. Using girls' diaries as her primary source material, Brumberg details the shifts in American girls' self-conceptions from the late 1800s to the late 1990s. Her main thesis is that whereas late-nineteenth-century girls tended to understand themselves in terms of their moral character, girls at the end of the twentieth century tended to center their self-conception on their bodies and to view the attainment of bodily perfection as their most important project. Brumberg puts a quasi-Foucaultian spin on this development, though she makes no explicit reference to Foucault. After describing contrasting images of a late-nineteenth-century girl in a corset and heavy, full-length Victorian dress and a late-twentieth-century girl in a thong bikini, Brumberg notes: "These contrasting images might suggest a great deal of progress, but American girls at the end of the twentieth century actually suffer from body problems more pervasive and more dangerous than the constraints implied by the corset. Historical forces have made coming of age in a female body a different and more complex experience today than it was a century ago."[9] Brumberg argues that what looks like enhanced freedom of expression and autonomy for late-twentieth-century girls is actually a thoroughgoing subjection to pernicious norms of feminine beauty.

In my view, the most interesting passages in the book are those in which Brumberg discusses the students in her women's studies seminar at Cornell University, whom she describes as extremely knowledgeable about feminist theory and capable of deploying their knowledge of theory in the form of sophisticated critiques of cultural images of women and femininity. And yet, as Brumberg notes, "they had internalized the contemporary imperative for a perfect body, even as they stood apart from it and tried to understand it as a social and cultural phenomenon."[10] In other words, these are young women who identify themselves as feminists, who understand and endorse feminist critiques of the norms and ideals of feminine beauty and the multibillion-dollar-a-year industry that exploits women's desire to live up to those impossible ideals and their shame at failing to do so, and who nonetheless find their own sense of self shaped (negatively) by how much they weigh, what size they wear, and how big their thighs are. As Brumberg puts it, "they invariably wanted to be thinner, a desire that motivated them to expend an enormous amount of time and energy controlling the appetite and working on their bodies, all the while thinking about food.... Almost all of them admitted that they did battle, on a daily basis, with what therapists in the eating disorder world call 'bad body fever,' a continuous internal commentary that constitutes a powerful form of self-punishment."[11]

Now, on the one hand, understanding this example simply in terms of power and how power constitutes the subject is unsatisfactory as it might seem to suggest that Brumberg's students are mere cultural dopes or passive victims of sexism. But this does not seem to cohere with their critical feminist engagement with the norms of femininity that have constituted them. On the other hand, analyzing this example simply in terms of autonomy and choice does not quite work either. Of course these women are in some sense choosing to subject themselves to the demands of normative femininity, but they are doing so despite their own critical awareness that those demands are mechanisms of their own subordination. As a result, this example demonstrates the necessity of thinking through both aspects of the politics of our selves and their complex interconnections.

To be sure, one might claim that the choice that Brumberg's students make is, in fact, completely rational, given their limited range of options. One might argue, as Joseph Heath has done, that women who conform to norms of feminine beauty that they know to be oppressive do so not because they are in the grips of some pervasive gender ideology but rather because of a collective action problem. Because beauty has an inherently competitive structure, the goal being not to attain some absolute standard of beauty but to be judged to be more beautiful than other women, it is in the rational self-interest of each individual woman to conform to norms of beauty, even if it is in the interests of women as a group to flout them.[12] Alternatively, one might suggest that Brumberg misinterprets the behavior of her students. After all, the mere fact that women remain faithful in some way to norms of femininity does not necessarily indicate that they are merely reinscribing their subordination. Their acceptance of the demands of normative femininity might be an attempt to rework subjection from within, to turn, as Butler puts it, the power that constitutes them into the power they oppose. Perhaps these students view working on their bodies as a way of critically and autonomously reworking their subjection. Perhaps Brumberg's dismay over their adherence to the bodily requirements of normative femininity is rooted in her *misrecognition* of their selfhood and their capacity to decide for themselves how to enact the demands of normative femininity.

Although both of these readings of the example have some initial plausibility, neither neither is capable of explaining why girls and women feel so bad about themselves for not living up to those norms. If it were really simply a matter of rational choice, then why would they feel so ashamed and berate themselves so much for not measuring up? Why would they hate their bodies and, by extension, themselves for failing to achieve the ideal of feminine bodily perfection that American popular culture demands? From a more theoretical perspective, what makes this example so interesting is precisely that these students are *both* critically aware that by accepting normative femininity they are capitulating to their own subordination *and* at the same time feel intensely guilty and ashamed for failing to capitulate thoroughly enough. This example thus brings to light not only the ways in which subjection and autonomy are deeply intertwined but also the limits of autonomy understood solely as the capacity for rational critique. As we learned from Butler, power and subjection take hold of subordinated subjects at the psychic and affective level, producing an attachment to subordinating modes of identity that is capable of surviving even after such modes have been rationally demystified. And, as the early Habermas and Benhabib both suggested, genuine autonomy requires not only the rational capacity to reflect critically on the contingencies that have made us who we are (to paraphrase Foucault), but also the motivational capacity to change who we want to be.

The foregoing considerations suggest that progressive self and social transformation for women will entail a number of things. First and foremost, it will entail expanding the overly narrow range of options from which women are at present compelled to choose (for example, either attempt to live up to the impossible demands of normative femininity or live with the guilt and shame that come with not living up to them). It may also entail changing how we think about gender, sex, and normative femininity. But, in order to undo the guilt, shame, and self-beratement, it will not be sufficient to change how we *think* about gender, sex, and normative femininity; we will have to transform not only our beliefs but also our fantasies and desires.

Figuring out how to accomplish this sort of transformation is no easy matter. In closing I would like to suggest two possible sources of such transformation. First, we might think through the ways in which collective social movements such as the feminist movement or the queer liberation movement generate conceptual and normative resources on which individuals can draw in their own attempts at critical resistance. I borrow the phrase "conceptual and normative resources" from Jane Mansbridge, who has argued that "in the United States since about 1967, the feminist movement has generated new ideas about the possibility of different gender relations, the causes of gender differences, and the content of ideals that should apply to relations between men and women."[13] These ideas and ideals serve as conceptual and normative resources for women—whether they are active in or even identify with the feminist movement or not—"to help make sense of and to change their lives."[14] Following Mansbridge, one might hypothesize that such social movements, via experimentation with alternative modes of self-understanding and ways of living together, also can provide alternative possibilities for attachment and sources of recognition that can help individuals to form less subordinating modes of attachment.

A second possible source of social transformation is to be found in the realm of the cultural and social imaginary, as represented, for example, in literature, film, and art. As María Pía Lara has argued, the feminist narratives embedded in literary fiction and autobiography can generate new cultural understandings of concepts such as democracy, equality, the good life, and the public sphere, and the cultural transformations brought about by such narratives in turn make possible social and institutional change. As Lara puts it, "emancipatory narratives can themselves create new forms of power, configuring new ways to fight back against past and present injustices, thus making institutional transformations possible."[15] Lara argues that new political forms "have to be imagined before they can be achieved," and the feminist narratives generated in literary and artistic counterpublics are an important source of such imagination.[16] Such narratives can envision and make possible new forms of subjectivity, modes of self-understanding, possibilities for recognition, patterns of attachment and identification, and ways of living together.

Both of these visions of possible social transformation have in common the assumption that we have no choice but to start from where we are, as gendered subjects who are constituted by power relations, but they also suggest ways in which it is nonetheless possible to resist, subvert, and transform those relations from within. What shape such transformations will ultimately take must be left up to what Foucault once called "the undefined work of freedom."[17]

1. Introduction

1. Foucault, "About the Beginnings of the Hermeneutics of the Self," p. 203.
2. Ibid.
3. Ibid.
4. Foucault, "What Is Enlightenment?" p. 319.
5. Benhabib, *Critique, Norm, and Utopia*, p. 226.
6. At least one of the participants in the debate also indicates that she takes this to be the central issue. See Benhabib et al., *Feminist Contentions*, pp. 107–18.
7. Ibid., p. 21.
8. Ibid., p. 42. Butler also argues that Foucault never negates or repudiates the subject (see Benhabib et al., *Feminist Contentions*, pp. 46–48). I agree with Butler on this point, but I think that more needs to be said than she does here, particularly about how to reconcile this claim with Foucault's archaeological works, in order to make a convincing case for this claim. I take up this issue in chapter 2.
9. Ibid., p. 46. Butler is less sanguine about the ideal of autonomy, which she claims here is an illusion, the "logical consequence of a disavowed dependency, which is to say that the autonomous subject can maintain the illusion of its autonomy insofar as it covers over the break out of which it is constituted" (Benhabib et al., *Feminist Contentions*, p. 46). Given the contrast with dependency, it seems as if Butler is understanding autonomy here as independence or self-reliance. Although this conception of autonomy may well be incompatible with the Foucaultian conception of subjection that Butler is working with here, it does not

follow that all conceptions of autonomy are. As a matter of fact, Butler's own Foucaultian concept of critique seems to presuppose autonomy in at least one sense, a point that I discuss below, and in more detail in chapters 3 and 4.

10. Ibid., p. 28.

11. Ibid.

12. Ibid., p. 39; emphasis in original.

13. Ibid.

14. See ibid., p. 56, n. 4. Butler, in her reply to the initial exchange, even after being accused by Fraser of normative confusion, refuses to back down from this point: "'Critique' ... always takes place *immanent* to the regime of discourse/ power whose claims it seeks to adjudicate, which is to say that the practice of 'critique' is implicated in the very power-relations it seeks to adjudicate. There is no pure place outside of power by which the question of validity might be raised, and where validity is raised, it is also always an activity of power" (Benhabib et al., *Feminist Contentions*, pp. 138–39; emphasis in original).

15. Ibid., p. 66; emphasis in original.

16. Ibid.

17. Ibid., p. 67.

18. Ibid., p. 68.

19. Ibid., p. 69.

20. Ibid., p. 161; emphasis in original.

21. Ibid.

22. Ibid., p. 162.

23. See ibid., p. 164.

24. Anderson, *The Way We Argue Now*, p. 23.

25. Ibid.

26. See Fraser, "Foucault on Modern Power."

27. Benhabib et al., *Feminist Contentions*, pp. 166–67.

28. On this point, see also Meehan, "Feminism and Habermas's Discourse Ethics," and Allen, "Reconstruction or Deconstruction?"

29. Anderson, *The Way We Argue Now*, p. 1.

30. Ibid., p. 7.

31. Ibid., p. 17.

32. Ibid., p. 173.

33. See, for example, Habermas, *Moral Consciousness and Communicative Action*, p. 207.

34. Habermas, to his credit, does not sidestep this problem but confronts it head-on in his reply to the charge of ethnocentrism. See, for example, Habermas's essay "Discourse Ethics: Notes on a Program of Philosophical Justification," in *Moral Consciousness and Communicative Action*. I discuss this issue in more detail in chapter 6.

35. Anderson, *The Way We Argue Now*, p. 151.

36. See Habermas, *The Philosophical Discourse of Modernity*, pp. 322–23.

37. Brown, *States of Injury*, p. 64.

38. Ibid.

39. Of course, given Foucault's extensive and incisive critique of psychoanalysis, this might seem like a controversial move for Butler to make. For Foucault's critique of psychoanalysis, see *Histoire de la folie à l'âge classique*, published in an

abridged translation as *Madness and Civilization: A History of Insanity in the Age of Reason*, and *An Introduction*, vol. 1 of *The History of Sexuality*. Indeed, as Joel Whitebook has argued, one might view Freud (rather than, say, Sartre) as Foucault's main intellectual and philosophical rival. See Whitebook, "Freud, Foucault, and 'the Dialogue with Unreason.'" I, however, am won over by Butler's claim that a full illumination of the phenomenon of subjection entails "thinking the theory of power together with a theory of the psyche" (*The Psychic Life of Power*, p. 3). This no doubt involves moving beyond a strictly Foucaultian framework, but, as will become clear throughout this book, I do not see such a move as inherently problematic.

40. Butler, *The Psychic Life of Power*, p. 3.
41. Brown, by contrast, does acknowledge the limitations of the Nietzschean framework for thinking about transformation and the importance of collective action. See Brown, *States of Injury*, p. 74.
42. Cooke, *Re-presenting the Good Society*, p. 38.
43. Habermas, "Moral Development and Ego Identity," p. 78.
44. Cooke, "Habermas, Autonomy, and the Identity of the Self," p. 279.
45. Zerilli, *Feminism and the Abyss of Freedom*, p. 11.
46. Ibid., p. 12.
47. See ibid.
48. As Butler puts it in her influential formulation, "Identity categories are never merely descriptive, but always normative, and as such, exclusionary" (Benhabib et al., *Feminist Contentions*, p. 50).
49. Zerilli, *Feminism and the Abyss of Freedom*, p. 30.
50. See ibid., p. 28.
51. Ibid., p. 34.
52. Ibid., p. 35.
53. Ibid., p. 39.
54. See ibid., pp. 131, 140–41, 148.
55. Ibid., p. 162.
56. On this point, see Habermas, *The Philosophical Discourse of Modernity*, pp. 185–210. For a much more developed critique of Habermas on this point, see Wellmer, *The Persistence of Modernity*. For an extension of Wellmer's critique in the context of feminist theory, see Lara, *Moral Textures*.
57. On this point, see Anderson, *The Way We Argue Now*, chapter 1.
58. Arendt, *The Human Condition*, p. 52, quoted in Zerilli, *Feminism and the Abyss of Freedom*, p. 14.
59. Zerilli, *Feminism and the Abyss of Freedom*, p. 16, quoting Arendt, "What is Freedom?" p. 160.
60. Zerilli, *Feminism and the Abyss of Freedom*, p. 171.
61. Ibid., p. 148.
62. Ibid., p. 181.
63. Ibid., p. 172.
64. Ibid., p. 173.
65. Ibid., p. 177.
66. Ibid., p. 167.
67. Ibid., p. 65.
68. Ibid., p. 168.

2. Foucault, Subjectivity, and the Enlightenment

1. See, for example, Alcoff, "Feminist Politics and Foucault"; Habermas, *The Philosophical Discourse of Modernity*, lectures 9 and 10; Hartsock, "Foucault on Power"; Honneth, *The Critique of Power*; McCarthy, "The Critique of Impure Reason: Foucault and the Frankfurt School," in McCarthy, *Ideals and Illusions*.
2. Benhabib, *Situating the Self*, p. 213.
3. Ibid.
4. Honneth, *The Critique of Power*, p. 112.
5. See, for example, Foucault, "The Ethics of Concern for the Self as a Practice of Freedom," p. 290.
6. Foucault, "Afterword: The Subject and Power," pp. 208, 209.
7. See, for example, Dews, "The Return of Subjectivity in the Late Foucault"; Grimshaw, "Practices of Freedom"; McCarthy, "The Critique of Impure Reason," in McCarthy, *Ideals and Illusions*; McNay, *Foucault and Feminism*.
8. I borrow this phrase from Thomas McCarthy. See, for example, Hoy and McCarthy, *Critical Theory*, p. 2.
9. At the very least, Habermas himself seems to understand it this way. See Habermas, *The Philosophical Discourse of Modernity*, lectures 9 and 10.
10. Foucault, "The Art of Telling the Truth," p. 146.
11. Ibid., pp. 147–48.
12. Foucault, "What Is Enlightenment?" pp. 319, 311.
13. Ibid., pp. 313, 319.
14. Ibid., pp. 315–16.
15. Schmidt and Wartenberg, "Foucault's Enlightenment," p. 283.
16. Foucault, *Discipline and Punish*, p. 30. This criticism of Kant shouldn't be too surprising since *Discipline and Punish* is clearly inspired by the second essay of Nietzsche's *On the Genealogy of Morals*, the main target of which is Kantian moral philosophy.
17. Habermas, "Taking Aim at the Heart of the Present," p. 150; emphasis in original.
18. Ibid., p. 152.
19. Ibid., p. 154. Christopher Norris suggests a similar reading of Foucault's relationship to Kant when he writes: "Foucault came around to a viewpoint [on Kant] strikingly at odds with his earlier (skeptical-genealogical) approach, and … one major consequence … was a radical re-thinking of the subject's role in relation to issues of truth, critique, self-knowledge, and practical reason" ("What Is Enlightenment?" p. 179).
20. Schmidt and Wartenberg, "Foucault's Enlightenment," p. 287.
21. Ibid., p. 283.
22. Ibid., p. 303.
23. Hoy, "Foucault: Modern or Postmodern?" p. 32. See Foucault, *The Archaeology of Knowledge*.
24. Ibid., pp. 26–27.
25. Ibid., p. 32.
26. On this point, see also Norris, "What Is Enlightenment?" I wholeheartedly agree with Norris's argument that Foucault's work is neither a simple return to Kant nor a straightforward postmodern repudiation of Kantian ideas, but I disagree with the sharp contrast that Norris draws between Foucault's early and late views on Kant.

27. This is not to suggest that there are no contradictions in Foucault's thought, just that his stance vis-à-vis Kant is not one of them.
28. Kant, *Anthropology from a Pragmatic Point of View*, p. 3.
29. Foucault, *Introduction à l'anthropologie de Kant*, p. 52. All translations are mine. For other references to Kant's use of the terms *kann* and *soll* to describe the object of pragmatic anthropology, see also Foucault, *Introduction à l'anthropologie de Kant*, pp. 39–40, 55, 63.
30. Ibid., p. 43.
31. For helpful discussion of this point, see Gregor's introduction to the English translation of Kant's *Anthropology* (Kant, *Anthropology from a Pragmatic Point of View*, pp. xvii–xviii).
32. On this point, see Kant's division of ethics into the empirical part (pragmatic anthropology) and the rational part (metaphysics of morals) in Kant, *Grounding for the Metaphysics of Morals*, pp. 1–2.
33. Foucault, *Introduction à l'anthropologie de Kant*, pp. 3–4.
34. Ibid., p. 4.
35. Ibid., p. 56.
36. Ibid.
37. Ibid., p. 24.
38. Ibid.
39. Ibid., p. 57.
40. Ibid., p. 92.
41. Ibid., p. 89.
42. See ibid., p. 121.
43. Here Foucault is clearly pushing Kant in the direction of Hegel. Indeed, one might suggest that as soon as Foucault begins to think of the a priori as historical, he sounds much more Hegelian than Kantian. I would not disagree that both Hegel and Kant had a profound influence on Foucault's thought. However, Foucault seems interested in exploring the ways in which Kant's own thought can be seen, when viewed from a certain perspective, to move in the direction that Hegel later took. In any event, it seems worth taking seriously Foucault's self-understanding as an heir to the Kantian Enlightenment tradition, even if his own contribution to that tradition is influenced by post-Kantian philosophical developments. I am grateful to Sally Sedgwick for pressing this point with me.
44. Foucault, *Introduction à l'anthropologie de Kant*, p. 105.
45. Ibid., p. 106.
46. Foucault, *Dits et écrits*, vol. 1, p. 26.
47. Foucault, *The Order of Things*, p. 310.
48. Ibid., p. 312.
49. Ibid., p. 318.
50. Foucault, "A Preface to Transgression," p. 36; see also p. 38. I am grateful to Dianna Taylor for pointing out the importance of this essay for a consideration of Foucault's relationship to Kant and also for helpful and interesting discussions about Foucault's reading of Kant.
51. Ibid., p. 40.
52. On this point, see also Norris, "What Is Enlightenment?" p. 184.
53. Foucault, *The Order of Things*, p. 250.
54. Ibid., p. xix.

55. Ibid., p. xxii.

56. Han, *Foucault's Critical Project*, p. 36.

57. Ibid., p. 37.

58. Foucault, *The Order of Things*, pp. 386, 387.

59. Foucault, *Introduction à l'anthropologie de Kant*, p. 127.

60. Ibid., p. 123.

61. Ibid., p. 128.

62. Veyne, "The Final Foucault and His Ethics," p. 228.

63. Foucault, "Interview with Michel Foucault," p. 276.

64. Foucault, "Truth and Power," p. 117.

65. Alcoff, "Feminist Politics and Foucault," p. 71.

66. Here I agree with Hoy, who makes the same point in "Power, Repression, Progress."

67. For a version of this argument, see McCarthy, "The Critique of Impure Reason," in McCarthy, *Ideals and Illusions*.

68. Habermas, *The Philosophical Discourse of Modernity*, p. 296.

69. Foucault, "What Is Enlightenment?" p. 315.

70. Ibid., p. 313.

71. Schmidt and Wartenberg, "Foucault's Enlightenment," p. 290.

72. In his introductory lectures on logic, Kant writes: "The field of philosophy ... may be reduced to the following questions: 1. What can I know? 2. What ought I to do? 3. What may I hope? 4. What is Man? The first question is answered by Metaphysics, the second by Morals, the third by Religion, and the fourth by Anthropology. In reality, however, all these might be reckoned under anthropology, since the first three questions refer to the last" (*Introduction to Logic*, p. 15). Other commentators have also noted the similarity between Foucault's philosophical projects and Kant's three questions, though they have interestingly neglected to mention Kant's fourth question—what is man?—which is, I think, the most important for understanding Foucault's relationship to Kant. See, for example, Bernauer, "Michel Foucault's Ecstatic Thinking," pp. 46–47; Norris, "What Is Enlightenment?" p. 169.

73. McCarthy, "The Critique of Impure Reason," in McCarthy, *Ideals and Illusions*, pp. 43–44.

74. Ibid., p. 43.

75. Ibid., p. 44.

76. Ibid., p. 48.

77. Foucault, *The Use of Pleasure*, pp. 10–11.

78. Foucault, "What Is Enlightenment?" pp. 316–17.

79. I am grateful to Nancy Fraser for suggesting this point to me.

80. Thus I would agree with Dreyfus and Rabinow when they describe Foucault and Habermas as "the two thinkers who could legitimately be called the heirs to [the eighteenth-century debate over the Enlightenment], because they embody two opposed but equally serious and persuasive ways of reinterpreting the philosophic life through understanding the relation between reason and the historical moment" ("What Is Maturity?" p. 109). However, I think they overdraw the contrast between the two thinkers when they go on to claim that Foucault's and Habermas's understandings of society, critical reason, and modernity are incompatible.

3. The Impurity of Practical Reason

1. Foucault, "About the Beginning of the Hermeneutics of the Self," p. 201.
2. Ibid.
3. Foucault points out that "given the absurdity of wars, slaughters and despotism, it seemed then to be up to the individual subject to give meaning to his existential choices" (ibid., p. 202). For an excellent discussion of Foucault's relationship to Sartrean existentialism, see Flynn, *A Poststructuralist Mapping of History*.
4. Foucault, "About the Beginning of the Hermeneutics of the Self," p. 202.
5. Ibid., pp. 223–24, n. 4.
6. Ibid., p. 203.
7. Ibid.
8. Ibid., p. 204.
9. An exception is Lois McNay, who interprets Foucault's late work as an attempt to "redefine the concept of autonomy so as to reconcile the critical interrogation of the socio-cultural and emotional determinant of an individual's situation with a capacity for critical independence or self-governance" (*Foucault and Feminism*, p. 104). As will become clear, I agree with McNay that Foucault's late work redefines the concept of autonomy, though we develop this idea in very different ways.
10. Fraser, *Unruly Practices*, p. 48.
11. McCarthy, *Ideals and Illusions*, p. 59.
12. Ibid., p. 70. For a related criticism of Foucault on autonomy, see Grimshaw, "Practices of Freedom."
13. See McCarthy, *Ideals and Illusions*, p. 59.
14. Allen, "The Anti-subjective Hypothesis."
15. Fraser, "Foucault on Modern Power," p. 32.
16. Foucault, "The Ethics of Concern for the Self as a Practice of Freedom," p. 299.
17. See "About the Beginning of the Hermeneutics of the Self," p. 204. See also Foucault, "Technologies of the Self," pp. 18, 19.
18. Foucault, "The Ethics of Concern for the Self as a Practice of Freedom," p. 283.
19. I discuss Foucault's attempt to distinguish power from domination in more detail and argue for the importance of keeping these two notions distinct in Allen, *The Power of Feminist Theory*, pp. 43–47.
20. Foucault, *Society Must Be Defended*, p. 168.
21. Ibid., p. 14. Foucault comments briefly on Arendt's view of power in "Politics and Ethics," pp. 378–80. I discuss the similarities and differences between Foucault's and Arendt's conceptions of power in detail in Allen, *The Power of Feminist Theory*, pp. 88–98, and "Power, Subjectivity, and Agency."
22. Foucault, *Society Must Be Defended*, p. 18.
23. Foucault, *An Introduction*, p. 90.
24. Foucault, *Discipline and Punish*, p. 194.
25. See Foucault, *An Introduction*, p. 12.
26. Foucault himself refers to it as "the strategical model" in *An Introduction*, p. 102. Arnold Davidson rightly points out that "the articulation of this strategic model—with its notions of force, struggle, war, tactics, strategy, et cetera—is one of the major achievements of Foucault's thought during this time [the middle of the 1970s]" (Foucault, *Society Must Be Defended*, p. xviii).

27. Foucault, *An Introduction*, pp. 92–93. A more specific use of the term "strategy" is also evident in this definition. Strategy in this sense refers to macrolevel power relations that are anchored in institutional and/or political structures; such relations are distinguished from tactics, which Foucault understands as microlevel force relations between individuals. See Foucault, *An Introduction*, pp. 99–100. I do not focus on this understanding of strategy because both strategies (in this narrower sense) and tactics are strategic in the broader sense of the term, and it is that broader sense that concerns me here. I discuss the relation between the microlevel and macrolevel in Foucault's account of power in Allen, *The Power of Feminist Theory*, chapter 2.

28. Foucault, "The Ethics of Concern for the Self as a Practice of Freedom," p. 298.

29. Foucault, *Society Must Be Defended*, p. 13.

30. Ibid., p. 27.

31. Foucault makes a related point in his 1974–1975 lecture course when he claims that whereas the repressive, negative conception of power may have been applicable to premodern, feudal societies, it is based on an "outdated historical model" that no longer makes sense of "the real functioning of power at the present time" (*Abnormal*, p. 51).

32. Foucault, *Society Must Be Defended*, p. 35.

33. Ibid., p. 36.

34. Ibid., p. 37.

35. Ibid.

36. Ibid.

37. Foucault, *Discipline and Punish*, p. 222.

38. Foucault, *An Introduction*, p. 89.

39. Foucault, "Afterword: The Subject and Power," p. 209.

40. Foucault, *Society Must Be Defended*, p. 27.

41. See Foucault, *An Introduction*, p. 94.

42. Foucault, *Society Must Be Defended*, p. 29.

43. Foucault, *An Introduction*, p. 94.

44. This is a point that Nancy Hartsock's influential feminist critique of Foucault completely misses. See Hartsock, "Foucault on Power." For a response, see Allen, *The Power of Feminist Theory*, chapter 2.

45. See Foucault, *Society Must Be Defended*, p. 30.

46. Foucault, *An Introduction*, p. 94.

47. For a helpful discussion of this difficult and often misinterpreted point in Foucault, see McLaren, *Feminism, Foucault, and Embodied Subjectivity*, pp. 37–38.

48. Foucault, *Society Must Be Defended*, pp. 28, 29.

49. Ibid., p. 43.

50. Ibid., p. 45.

51. Foucault, *An Introduction*, p. 60.

52. Foucault, *Society Must Be Defended*, pp. 29–30. The misunderstandings of Foucault's account of subjection may be due in part to an earlier translation of this crucial passage that did not preserve the subtleties of Foucault's position as well as Macey's translation does. Compare Foucault, "Two Lectures," p. 98.

53. See, for example, Foucault, *Discipline and Punish*, and *Society Must Be Defended*, lectures 1–10.

54. See Foucault, *Society Must Be Defended*, lecture 11, and *An Introduction*, part 5.

55. Foucault, *Society Must Be Defended*, p. 242.
56. Foucault, "Governmentality," pp. 202, 201. This essay is an excerpt from Foucault's 1977–1978 lecture course, recently published as *Security, Territory, and Population*.
57. Ibid., p. 207. On this point, Foucault's work dovetails interestingly with Arendt's account of the rise of "the social"—a sphere that is unique to modernity and emerges when economic concerns are brought into the public political realm. For an interpretation and critique of Arendt's concept of the social, see Pitkin, *The Attack of the Blob*.
58. Ibid., pp. 216–17.
59. Ibid., p. 219.
60. Foucault, "'Omnes and Singulatim,'" p. 307.
61. See ibid., pp. 308–11, for Foucault's discussion of all the transformations.
62. Ibid., p. 310.
63. Foucault, "Afterword: The Subject and Power," pp. 214–15.
64. Ibid., p. 215.
65. Foucault, "'Omnes et Singulatim,'" p. 317.
66. Ibid., p. 321.
67. Ibid., p. 322.
68. Ibid., p. 325.
69. Ibid.
70. Foucault, "Afterword: The Subject and Power," p. 212. The feminist movement and the antipsychiatry movement are two examples of such struggles.
71. Ibid.
72. This point gives us good reason to be suspicious of forms of identity politics that argue for the valorization of oppressed and marginalized identities. Such struggles "for" the individual who is tied to a marked identity leave unchallenged the logic of subjection itself and, as a result, run the risk of unwittingly reinforcing the power relations that mark certain modes of identity as socially abject in the first place.
73. Foucault, "What Is Critique?" p. 386. As Schmidt and Wartenberg note, the phrase "reflective indocility" inverts Foucault's account in *Discipline and Punish* of how "disciplinary institutions produce 'docile bodies' which thoughtlessly take up the positions for which they were designed" ("Foucault's Enlightenment," p. 310, n. 34).
74. Foucault, "Afterword: The Subject and Power," p. 216.
75. Foucault, "Qu'est-ce que la critique?" p. 39.
76. Foucault, "What Is Enlightenment?" p. 317.
77. Foucault, "Afterword: The Subject and Power," p. 216.
78. Norris is no doubt right to emphasize that the terms "subject" and "self" are not interchangeable for Foucault. The term "subject" usually refers to the transcendental-phenomenological subject, the subject understood as the source of knowledge and meaning. The term "self," by contrast, refers to a subject that is constituted by discourse and power and that engages in technologies of the self. Norris is wrong, however, to suggest that Foucault's notion of the self implicitly appeals to the very qualities and characteristics that he typically associates with the subject (in the narrow sense). Although Foucault does appeal to notions such as reflection, autonomy, and agency in his account of the self, he does not appeal to the knowledge- and

meaning-constitutive function of subjectivity, and it is this that Foucault consistently identifies as the hallmark of the transcendental-phenomenological subject. Moreover, as I discuss below, Foucault radically reformulates notions such as reflection and autonomy. Norris's criticism seems to trade on a conflation of the transcendental-phenomenological conception of the subject with the concept of subjectivity per se. See Norris, "What Is Enlightenment?" pp. 182–83.

79. Foucault, "The Ethics of Concern for the Self as a Practice of Freedom," p. 290.
80. Foucault, "Afterword: The Subject and Power," p. 221.
81. Foucault, "The Ethics of Concern for the Self as a Practice of Freedom," p. 300.
82. Foucault, "On the Genealogy of Ethics," p. 256.
83. Veyne, "The Final Foucault and His Ethics," p. 231.
84. See Foucault, "On the Genealogy of Ethics," p. 254.
85. Ibid., p. 260.
86. Foucault, *The Use of Pleasure*, p. 26.
87. Ibid., p. 32.
88. Foucault, "On the Genealogy of Ethics," p. 263.
89. Ibid., p. 264.
90. Foucault, *The Use of Pleasure*, p. 27.
91. Ibid.
92. Foucault, "On the Genealogy of Ethics," p. 265.
93. Ibid., p. 271.
94. Ibid., p. 274.
95. Ibid., pp. 277–78.
96. On this point, see Foucault's discussion of Leuret in "About the Beginning of the Hermeneutics of the Self," pp. 200–201.
97. Foucault, "Sex, Power, and the Politics of Identity," p. 167; emphasis in original.
98. Foucault, "Polemics, Politics, and Problematizations," p. 388. See also the introduction to *The Use of Pleasure*, especially pp. 8–9. For a critical discussion of this conception of thought as reflective problematization, see Han, *Foucault's Critical Project*, pp. 164–65.
99. Foucault, "What Is Enlightenment?" p. 313.
100. Ibid., p. 314.
101. On this point, see Hacking, "Self-improvement."
102. Foucault, "The Return of Morality," pp. 253–54.
103. Kant, *Grounding for the Metaphysics of Morals*, p. 49.
104. Foucault, "What Is Critique?" p. 388.
105. Foucault, "What Is Enlightenment?" p. 309.
106. To be sure, one might object both to my usage of the term "autonomy" here and to my attempt to connect Foucault's account of autonomy to Kant's. With respect to the former point, one might argue that the term "autonomy" is too overloaded with metaphysical assumptions that Foucault would certainly reject to be appropriate here. Why not instead use some other, less metaphysically loaded, term, such as "experimental freedom"? In response, I would say, first, that this is a term that Foucault himself sometimes uses in his late work, and part of my aim here is to try to understand that usage. Second, as I indicated already in chapter 1, I am using the term in a nonmetaphysically loaded sense, simply to refer to the capacities for critical reflection and deliberate self-transformation. As I see it, faith in these capacities is a common thread that runs

through the work of Foucault and Habermas, and using the term "autonomy" in the sense that I use it here highlights that commonality. With respect to the second point, I have no doubt that the Foucaultian conception of autonomy that I am delineating here would be virtually unrecognizable to most contemporary Kantians (just as the Foucaultian account of subjectivity delineated in chapter 2 would be). As I see it, this is beside the point. My aim here, as it was in the previous chapter, is to resituate Foucault's work within the Kantian Enlightenment tradition, in part as a way of better understanding his work as a whole, and in part as a way of highlighting the assumptions that he shares with Habermas. My point, in other words, is not that Foucault has a Kantian theory of autonomy. My point is that his reflections on autonomy are grounded in his deliberate continuation-through-transformation of the Kantian Enlightenment tradition, as he understands it. In that sense, he is much closer to Habermas than has typically been supposed. I am grateful to Colin Koopman for pressing both of these objections.

107. McCarthy, *Ideals and Illusions*, p. 48.
108. Foucault, "Afterword: The Subject and Power," p. 210.
109. Ibid.
110. Foucault, "What Is Critique?" p. 393.
111. Ibid.
112. Ibid., pp. 397–98.
113. Ibid., p. 398.
114. Foucault, "What Is Enlightenment?" p. 317.
115. Foucault, "Afterword: The Subject and Power," p. 221.
116. Ibid., p. 222.
117. For an excellent and extended articulation of this point, see McWhorter, *Bodies and Pleasures*.
118. Grimshaw, "Practices of Freedom," p. 66.
119. Ibid., p. 67.
120. McCarthy, *Ideals and Illusions*, p. 73.
121. McNay, *Foucault and Feminism*, p. 165.
122. I argue this case in more detail in Allen, "Foucault, Feminism, and the Self."
123. Foucault, "On the Genealogy of Ethics," p. 257.
124. Ibid., p. 258.
125. Ibid.
126. Foucault, "Politics and Ethics," p. 379.
127. Quoted in Kelly, *Critique and Power*, p. 1.

4. Dependency, Subordination, and Recognition

1. Butler, *The Psychic Life of Power*, p. 1.
2. Ibid., p. 2; emphasis in original.
3. For two classic feminist critical appropriations of Foucault in this vein, see Bartky, *Femininity and Domination*, and Bordo, *Unbearable Weight*.
4. Butler, *The Psychic Life of Power*, p. 2.
5. Ibid. For a discussion of Foucault's relationship to Freudian psychoanalysis, see Whitebook, "Freud, Foucault, and 'the Dialogue with Unreason.'" For an interesting comparison of Foucault and Lacan, see Rajchman, *Truth and Eros*.

6. See Butler, *Bodies That Matter.* I discuss Butler's use of the notion of citationality and its implications for agency in Allen, *The Power of Feminist Theory,* chapter 4.

7. Benhabib et al., *Feminist Contentions,* p. 161.

8. Bartky, *"Sympathy and Solidarity" and Other Essays,* p. 13.

9. See Bartky, *Femininity and Domination.*

10. Bartky, *"Sympathy and Solidarity" and Other Essays,* p. 14.

11. Butler, *The Psychic Life of Power,* p. 3.

12. Ibid., p. 6.

13. Although Butler does not do so, it would be much less confusing to distinguish these two senses of power by referring to them as "domination" and "empowerment," respectively.

14. Butler, *The Psychic Life of Power,* p. 14; emphasis in original.

15. Ibid., p. 15.

16. Ibid., p. 17; emphasis in original.

17. Ibid., pp. 18–19.

18. Butler acknowledges that this account of reflexivity is paradoxical, inasmuch as there can be no subject who accomplishes this reflexive turn until the turning has already taken place. She attempts to resolve this paradox by arguing that "this logical circularity in which the subject appears at once to be presupposed and not yet formed, on the one hand, or formed and hence not presupposed, on the other, is ameliorated when one understands that in both Freud and Nietzsche this relationship of reflexivity is always and only figured, and that this figure makes no ontological claim" (Butler, *The Psychic Life of Power,* p. 69). Although I have my doubts that Butler's appeal to the figurative actually resolves this paradox, addressing this issue is beyond the scope of this chapter.

19. Ibid., p. 33.

20. See Hegel, *The Phenomenology of Spirit,* pp. 119–38.

21. For an excellent discussion of the French reception of Hegel, see Butler, *Subjects of Desire.*

22. Butler, *The Psychic Life of Power,* p. 61.

23. Nietzsche, *On the Genealogy of Morals,* p. 97; emphasis in original.

24. Butler, *The Psychic Life of Power,* p. 67.

25. Ibid., pp. 102, 79; emphasis in original.

26. Ibid., p. 79.

27. Ibid., p. 62.

28. Ibid.

29. On this point, Butler argues against Lacanian psychoanalysis, which, as she sees it, locates resistance in an extradiscursive psychic domain. See ibid., p. 98. Butler cites Foucault's critique of psychoanalysis in Foucault, *An Introduction,* pp. 95–96.

30. Butler, *The Psychic Life of Power,* p. 100.

31. Ibid., p. 102; emphasis in original.

32. Ibid., p. 108.

33. Ibid., p. 130.

34. Ibid.; emphasis in original.

35. Ibid., p. 131.

36. Freud, "The Ego and the Id," p. 28.

37. Butler, *The Psychic Life of Power,* p. 133.

38. Ibid., p. 180.
39. Ibid., p. 135; emphasis in original.
40. Ibid.; emphasis in original.
41. Butler's strong claims about the constitutive melancholy of heterosexist cultures may seem initially implausible. However, as Stephen White argues, "Butler freely admits that her claims about melancholy are somewhat 'hyperbolic.' In this sense, her characterization of a melancholic society is intended to have an effect analogous to Foucault's characterization of a 'disciplinary' one; that is, its primary intention is to jolt us in specific ways and reorient our attention. In this case the jolt is to involve how we think about gender and political life, more specifically the patterns according to which identity, sexual desire, repudiation, and aggression circulate" (*Sustaining Affirmation*, p. 101).
42. White, *Sustaining Affirmation*, p. 100.
43. The locus classicus for this position in feminist theory is Butler, *Gender Trouble*. Butler draws heavily on Anne Fausto-Sterling's work questioning the scientific basis for the belief in sexual dimorphism. For a helpful overview of Fausto-Sterling's work, see *Myths of Gender*.
44. Zerilli, "Doing Without Knowing," p. 452.
45. Zerilli reaches the same conclusion by a somewhat different route. See ibid.
46. Butler, *The Psychic Life of Power*, p. 7; emphasis in original.
47. Ibid., p. 8. Although Butler does not discuss any empirical literature, the evidence provided by infant researchers and developmental psychologists does support this claim. For an excellent discussion that connects this empirical literature with philosophical conceptions of the self, see Meehan, "Into the Sunlight."
48. Ibid., p. 9.
49. Ibid.
50. Ibid., pp. 7, 8, 9.
51. For a more detailed discussion and critique of these familial and kinship structures, see Butler, *Antigone's Claim*.
52. Butler, *The Psychic Life of Power*, pp. 100, 104.
53. Ibid., pp. 130, 149; emphasis in original.
54. It is interesting to compare Butler with Foucault on this point. Where Butler advocates a critical desubjectivation, Foucault, as I discussed in chapter 3 above, endorses instead a desubjection (*déassujettisement*). The aim of this, for Foucault, is not a refusal or rejection of subjectivity but instead the promotion of "new forms of subjectivity through the refusal of this kind of individuality which has been imposed on us for several centuries" ("Afterword: The Subject and Power," p. 216). In other words, unlike Foucault, Butler does not seem to distinguish subjection from subjectivation, which has the effect of making her account of subjection more pessimistic than his. I am grateful to Jana Sawicki for suggesting this point to me.
55. In a recent essay, Butler admits that resistance requires "suspending the narcissistic gratifications that conforming to the norm supplies" ("Bodies and Power Revisited," p. 191).
56. On Butler, see, for example, Weir, *Sacrificial Logics*, p. 113, and Fraser in Benhabib et al., *Feminist Contentions*, p. 69. On Foucault, see Fraser, "Foucault on Modern Power."
57. Fraser in Benhabib et al., *Feminist Contentions*, p. 69.

58. As I discuss below, Butler, in her more recent work, makes this claim explicitly, if tentatively and somewhat ambivalently.

59. As Alcoff notes, there is a curious convergence here between Butler's account of subjection and "classical liberal or modernist accounts of the self" in which "an a priori oppositional condition is assumed to exist between self and (broadly) other" ("Philosophy Matters," p. 863). To be sure, Alcoff would not deny that, inasmuch as Butler conceives the self as constituted by social relations, there is a sense in which she views the self as social. In that sense, her view is entirely distinct from the atomistic view of the subject that one finds in liberal or modernist accounts. Instead, Alcoff's critique points to the fact that Butler's account of sociality, in which social relations are understood in fundamentally oppositional and conflictual terms, strikes a familiar chord. It is worth noting that Butler's account of sociality has as much affinity with Hobbes's "war of each against all" as it does with Foucault's power/knowledge regimes.

60. Butler, "Bodies and Power Revisited," pp. 191–92.

61. Ibid., p. 192.

62. Ibid., p. 193.

63. On this point, see, for example, Benjamin, "The Shadow of the Other Subject," p. 98.

64. Butler, "Violence, Mourning, Politics," p. 31.

65. Butler, *Giving an Account of Oneself*, p. 82; emphasis in original.

66. Butler, "Violence, Mourning, Politics," p. 31.

67. Butler, *Giving an Account of Oneself*, p. 15.

68. Ibid., p. 135.

69. Butler, "Violence, Mourning, Politics," p. 22.

70. Ibid., pp. 27, 28.

71. Ibid., p. 24.

72. Ibid., p. 45. See also Butler, *Giving an Account of Oneself*, chapter 1.

73. Ibid., p. 44.

74. Ibid., p. 27.

75. Ibid., p. 28.

76. Similarly, in *Giving an Account of Oneself*, Butler indicates a desire "to revise recognition as an ethical project," a move that requires us to see recognition as "in principle, unsatisfiable," because the subject is not and cannot be fully transparent even to itself, let alone to an other (p. 43).

77. Butler, "Longing for Recognition," p. 133.

78. Ibid., p. 134.

79. Ibid.

80. Ibid., p. 135.

81. Ibid., p. 144.

82. Ibid., p. 145.

83. Ibid., p. 147.

84. Ibid.

85. Benjamin, *Like Subjects, Love Objects*, p. 24.

86. Ibid., p. 47.

87. Benjamin, "The Shadow of the Other Subject," p. 96.

88. Ibid., p. 97.

89. Nor, incidentally, does Benjamin ground her notion of recognition in the assumed self-transparency of the subject; as such, her work would not be subject to the critique of Hegelian models of recognition that Butler endorses in *Giving an Account of Oneself* (see, especially, chapters 1 and 2).

90. See Benjamin, *The Bonds of Love.*

91. Benjamin, *Like Subjects, Love Objects*, pp. 47–48.

92. In this sense the book *Giving an Account of Oneself* represents a significant shift in Butler's thought inasmuch as it constitutes an initial attempt to think the intersubjective and the intrapsychic dimensions of subjectivity together. However, even in this book, these dimensions are not fully integrated; instead, Butler claims both that "recognition is a form of power" (p. 123) and that we are nevertheless dependent upon sustaining forms of relationality without giving us a coherent way of combining these two insights. Benjamin's idea that recognition and destruction are both permanent and ongoing possibilities of dynamically unfolding human relationships offers a useful way of integrating these two perspectives that Butler would do well to consider.

93. Benjamin, "The Shadow of the Other Subject," p. 85.

94. Butler, *The Psychic Life of Power*, p. 179.

95. Benjamin, *The Bonds of Love*, pp. 19–20.

96. See Butler, "Longing for Recognition," p. 147.

97. Butler, "Competing Universalities," p. 159.

98. As such, Benjamin's account could also be understood as "an encounter with alterity that is irreducible to sameness" (Butler, *Giving an Account of Oneself*, p. 27).

99. Benjamin, *The Bonds of Love*, p. 171.

100. Arendt, *The Human Condition*, p. 8.

101. Butler, "Competing Universalities," p. 151.

5. Empowering the Lifeworld?

1. Habermas, "Knowledge and Human Interests," p. 314; emphasis in original.

2. Habermas, "Moral Development and Ego Identity," pp. 70–73.

3. For Habermas's acknowledgment of this central role, see *Between Facts and Norms*, pp. 445–46.

4. Habermas, "Morality and Ethical Life," p. 207.

5. See Cooke, "Habermas, Autonomy, and the Identity of the Self."

6. Ibid., p. 276.

7. See ibid.

8. Ibid., p. 277.

9. Ibid., p. 279. For a similar account of autonomy as rational accountability, see McCarthy in Hoy and McCarthy, *Critical Theory*, pp. 42–47.

10. Habermas, "Some Further Clarifications of the Concept of Communicative Rationality," p. 310.

11. Ibid.; emphasis in original.

12. This line of criticism should not be taken to deny the very interesting and fruitful convergences between Habermasian and feminist accounts of autonomy, particularly those of relational autonomy. For positive, though not uncritical, feminist appraisals of Habermas's conception of autonomy, see Cooke, "Habermas, Feminism,

and the Question of Autonomy," Meehan, "Autonomy, Recognition, and Respect," and Weir, "Toward a Model of Self-identity."

13. See, for example, Honneth, *The Critique of Power*, chapter 9.

14. Fraser, "What's Critical About Critical Theory?" p. 121. Habermas, in his more recent work, particularly *Between Facts and Norms*, addresses this problem by distinguishing between social power, which he understands in largely Weberian terms, as "a measure for the possibilities an actor has in social relationships to assert his own will and interests, even against the opposition of others" (*Between Facts and Norms*, p. 175), and administrative power, which he understands in the systems-theoretical sense that he articulated in *Lifeworld and System: A Critique of Functionalist Reason*, volume 2 of *The Theory of Communicative Action* (on which Fraser's critique is based). However, it is not clear that this modification in his understanding of power meets the full force of Fraser's objection, as his account of social power, despite being rooted in the lifeworld, is better suited to diagnosing the influence that interest groups, media outlets, and political parties can have on the political process than it is to analyzing gender subordination.

15. McNay, "Having It Both Ways," p. 17.

16. Fraser, "What's Critical About Critical Theory?" p. 138.

17. Habermas, *The Philosophical Discourse of Modernity*, p. 286.

18. Ibid., p. 287.

19. Habermas, "A Reply," p. 254.

20. Ibid., pp. 252, 258.

21. Ibid., p. 247.

22. In light of this admittedly narrow focus, I shall leave discussion of Habermas's account of power in *Between Facts and Norms* aside, as this account centers on the relationships between social power understood largely on the model of large corporations, media outlets, political parties, and interest groups and their capacity to have an impact on public political debate, the communicative power generated through the public exercise of popular sovereignty, and the administrative power wielded by the state (for Habermas's account of this relationship, see *Between Facts and Norms*, chapter 4). As interesting and rich as this account of power may be, it does not bear directly on the issue that is my primary concern here, namely, the role that power plays in the lifeworld context of socialization processes, and how the account of this in Habermas might need to be rethought in light of the analyses of subjection offered by Foucault and Butler, discussed above.

23. Habermas, *Lifeworld and System*, p. 367.

24. Ibid., pp. 372–73.

25. Habermas, "A Reply," p. 258.

26. McCarthy, "Die politische Philosophie und das Problem der Rasse," p. 645.

27. Habermas, *Lifeworld and System*, p. 388.

28. See, for example, Bohman, "Participating in Enlightenment." Habermas himself praises Bohman's work for demonstrating how the formation of ideology can be analyzed using the theory of communicative action; see Habermas, "A Reply," p. 292, n. 73.

29. Habermas, "Reflections on Communicative Pathology," p. 147.

30. Ibid.

31. Ibid., pp. 154–55; emphasis in original. Habermas argues that "there is no violation of truth that is symptomatic of systematically distorted communication" (ibid., p. 154).

32. Ibid., p. 147.

33. Ibid., p. 156.

34. Ibid., pp. 161–62.

35. Ibid., p. 164.

36. Ibid.

37. For classic feminist analyses of normative femininity and its role in maintaining women's subordination, see Bartky, *Femininity and Domination*, and *"Sympathy and Solidarity" and Other Essays*, especially chapter 1.

38. On this point, see Butler, *Undoing Gender*.

39. Habermas clearly takes Foucault's work to be emblematic of this abstract negation strategy. As I have argued in chapter 2, I think this claim rests on a misreading of Foucault's work.

40. Habermas, *The Philosophical Discourse of Modernity*, p. 310; emphasis in original.

41. Ibid.

42. Habermas, "Discourse Ethics," p. 58; see also Habermas, *Reason and the Rationalization of Society*, pp. 273ff. For more recent refinements of the distinction between communicative and strategic interaction, see Habermas, "Some Further Clarifications of the Concept of Communicative Rationality."

43. Ibid.; emphasis in original.

44. Ibid.; emphasis in original.

45. See Habermas, *The Philosophical Discourse of Modernity*, p. 342.

46. Habermas, *Reason and the Rationalization of Society*, p. 70.

47. Habermas, *The Philosophical Discourse of Modernity*, p. 314.

48. For clarification of the relation between system and lifeworld, see Habermas, "A Reply," pp. 250–64.

49. Habermas, "Individuation Through Socialization."

50. Ibid., p. 153.

51. Ibid., p. 168.

52. Ibid., p. 170.

53. Ibid., p. 177.

54. See Mead, *Mind, Self, and Society*.

55. Dews, "Communicative Paradigms and the Question of Subjectivity," p. 102.

56. Habermas, "Individuation Through Socialization," p. 177.

57. Ibid., p. 180.

58. Ibid., p. 182.

59. For interesting critiques of this move, see Dews, "Communicative Paradigms and the Question of Subjectivity," and Meehan, "Habermas and the Summum Bonum."

60. Habermas, "Individuation Through Socialization," p. 152; emphasis added.

61. Habermas, "Moral Development and Ego Identity," p. 86.

62. Ibid., p. 74; emphasis in original.

63. Habermas, "Individuation Through Socialization," p. 188.

64. Ibid., p. 186. There is a crucial difference, however, between identity claims that aim at intersubjective *recognition* and validity claims that aim at intersubjective *agreement*. Habermas is not suggesting that my sense of myself is dependent on whether

or not others agree with me, but that it is dependent upon whether or not they recognize me as an identical subject and a moral agent. Moreover, Habermas claims that this sort of intersubjective recognition has to be presupposed before the redemption of validity claims can happen (ibid., p. 190). In other words, "among the universal and unavoidable presuppositions of action oriented to reaching understanding is the presupposition that the speaker qua actor lays claim to recognition both as an autonomous will and as an individuated being" (ibid., p. 191).

65. Ibid., p. 192.

66. Ibid.

67. For the comparison of Foucault to Luhmann, see Habermas, *The Philosophical Discourse of Modernity*, p. 354.

68. See Habermas, *Lifeworld and System*, pp. 180, 183.

69. On this point, see, for example, Foucault's methodological claim that one must conduct an ascending rather than a descending analysis of power in Foucault, "Two Lectures," p. 99.

70. Garfinkel, "Studies of the Routine Grounds of Everyday Activities." For discussion of the connection between Garfinkel's ethnomethodology and Habermasian critical theory, see McCarthy in Hoy and McCarthy, *Critical Theory*, chapter 3.

71. Habermas, *The Philosophical Discourse of Modernity*, pp. 242, 249.

72. Ibid., p. 312; emphasis added.

73. Habermas, "A Reply," p. 251.

74. Habermas, *The Philosophical Discourse of Modernity*, p. 293.

75. Ibid., p. 338; emphasis in original.

76. Habermas, quoting Parsons, in *Lifeworld and System*, p. 207.

77. Habermas, "Moral Development and Ego Identity," p. 74.

78. Habermas, "Moral Consciousness and Communicative Action," pp. 153–54; emphasis in original.

79. Johanna Meehan criticizes Habermas's account on precisely these grounds. She argues that Habermas pays insufficient attention to the "psychic cost inherent in socialization," to the fact that "all processes of socialization, no matter how benign or rational, require a psychic subjugation that is almost inevitably blind and furious" (Meehan, "Habermas and the Summum Bonum, p. 13).

80. Habermas, "Moral Consciousness and Communicative Action," p. 154.

81. Ibid.; emphasis in original.

82. Ibid., p. 155; emphasis in original.

83. Ibid.; emphasis in original.

84. Ibid., p. 159; emphasis in original.

85. Ibid., p. 161.

86. Ibid., p. 162.

87. Ibid., p. 139; emphasis in original.

88. Ibid., p. 140.

89. Ibid., p. 147.

90. Ibid., pp. 140–41.

91. Ibid., p. 148.

92. Ibid., p. 152.

93. Ibid., p. 163.

94. This is not to say that the child is wholly dependent on the parent or that the child is unable to exercise any power in the relationship. Habermas isn't talking about young infants here, but about young children (ages 5 to 12).

95. Habermas, "Moral Consciousness and Communicative Action," p. 147

96. Ibid.

97. Ibid., p. 153.

98. Habermas, *Lifeworld and System*, p. 39; emphasis in original.

99. Ibid.; emphasis in original.

100. Ibid.; emphasis in original. Habermas reiterates this point in "Moral Consciousness and Communicative Action," p. 155.

101. Ibid., p. 45.

102. Rehg, *Insight and Solidarity*, pp. 23–24. See Habermas, *Reason and the Rationalization of Society*, pp. 298–305.

103. Habermas, "Remarks on Discourse Ethics," p. 42; emphasis in original.

104. Habermas, *The Future of Human Nature*, p. 62.

105. Butler, *The Psychic Life of Power*, p. 63.

106. Ibid., pp. 66–67.

107. Ibid., p. 64.

108. And, as I also discussed in the previous chapter, Butler herself has qualified her adherence to this Nietzschean account of the formation of the morally accountable subject in her recent book, *Giving an Account of Oneself* (see, especially, pp. 15, 135).

109. Habermas, "Lawrence Kohlberg and Neo-Aristotelianism," p. 131.

110. Butler in Benhabib et al., *Feminist Contentions*, p. 39.

111. See Habermas, *The Future of Human Nature*, p. 62.

112. For an insightful discussion of the Foucault-Habermas debate that situates the debate within the context of Habermas's reading of Nietzsche, see Biebricher, "Habermas, Foucault, and Nietzsche."

113. Habermas, *The Philosophical Discourse of Modernity*, p. 123.

114. Ibid., p. 125; emphasis in original.

115. Meehan, "Habermas and the Summum Bonum," pp. 14–15.

116. McCarthy in Hoy and McCarthy, *Critical Theory*, p. 77.

6. Contextualizing Critical Theory

1. McCarthy, "Die politische Philosophie und das Problem der Rasse," p. 645.

2. Ibid., p. 652. For the charge that Foucault's work offers a totalizing critique of modernity that ultimately undermines its own foundations, see Habermas, *The Philosophical Discourse of Modernity*, chapters 9 and 10, and McCarthy, *Ideals and Illusions*, introduction and chapter 2. For my response to this charge, see chapter 2 above.

3. Ibid., p. 653.

4. Ibid., p. 654.

5. For a similar line of argument with a somewhat different focus, see Whitebook, *Perverson and Utopia*, pp. 12–13.

6. I am grateful to Ciaran Cronin for raising this point.

7. Fraser, "Foucault on Modern Power."

8. McCarthy, *The Critical Theory of Jürgen Habermas*, p. 91.

9. Habermas, *Knowledge and Human Interests*. For helpful discussion, see McCarthy, *The Critical Theory of Jürgen Habermas*, chapter 2.

10. Habermas, *Knowledge and Human Interests*, p. 194.

11. Habermas, "Knowledge and Human Interests," p. 313.

12. McCarthy, *The Critical Theory of Jürgen Habermas*, pp. 92–93.
13. Habermas, "A Postscript to *Knowledge and Human Interests*," p. 176, quoted in McCarthy, *The Critical Theory of Jürgen Habermas*, p. 93; emphasis in original.
14. McCarthy, *The Critical Theory of Jürgen Habermas*, p. 93.
15. Ibid.
16. Habermas, "A Postscript to *Knowledge and Human Interests*," p. 182.
17. Ibid., p. 183.
18. Ibid., pp. 183–84.
19. Ibid., p. 184.
20. Ibid.
21. McCarthy, *The Critical Theory of Jürgen Habermas*, p. 101.
22. Ibid., p. 102.
23. Habermas, *Reason and the Rationalization of Society*, p. 108; emphasis in original. Interestingly, in this context, Habermas mentions Foucault's critique of modernity as an instance of a kind of Hegelian critique of this tendency toward Kantian formalism.
24. Habermas, "Moral Development and Ego Identity," p. 75.
25. Ibid., p. 78.
26. For an excellent critical discussion of this point, see Whitebook, *Perversion and Utopia*.
27. Habermas, "Moral Development and Ego Identity," p. 91.
28. Ibid.
29. Ibid., p. 93.
30. Ibid.
31. Ibid., p. 94.
32. Whitebook, *Perversion and Utopia*, p. 87.
33. Ibid.
34. For discussion of this point, see ibid., p. 181, and Dews, "Communicative Paradigms and the Question of Subjectivity."
35. Ibid., p. 89.
36. See Benjamin, *Like Subjects, Love Objects*, and *The Shadow of the Other*.
37. Benjamin, *The Shadow of the Other*, p. 93.
38. Whitebook, *Perversion and Utopia*, p. 89.
39. See, for example, Habermas, "Moral Consciousness and Communicative Action." For some of Habermas's reservations about Kohlberg, see Habermas, "Lawrence Kohlberg and Neo-Aristotelianism."
40. Habermas, "Moral Consciousness and Communicative Action," p. 183.
41. Ibid., p. 171; emphasis in original.
42. Ibid., p. 187.
43. Ibid.
44. Ibid., pp. 187–88; emphasis in original.
45. For this distinction, see Habermas, *Justification and Application*.
46. Habermas, *The Philosophical Discourse of Modernity*, p. 297.
47. Ibid., pp. 297–98.
48. Ibid., pp. 300–301.
49. Ibid., p. 301.
50. Ibid., p. 322. Indeed, Rorty criticizes Habermas along these lines, arguing that "by insisting that communicative rationality incorporates the notion of universal va-

lidity Habermas accomplishes precisely the resurrection [of the purism of pure reason] he hopes to avoid" ("The Ambiguity of 'Rationality,'" p. 43).

51. Ibid.

52. McCarthy, *Ideals and Illusions*, p. 2; emphasis in original.

53. Habermas, *The Philosophical Discourse of Modernity*, p. 322.

54. Ibid., p. 323; emphasis in original.

55. For a concise statement and defense of these idealizations, see Habermas, "Discourse Ethics," pp. 82–98.

56. On this point, see Habermas, "What is Universal Pragmatics?"

57. Habermas, *The Philosophical Discourse of Modernity*, p. 325; emphasis in original.

58. Ibid., pp. 323–24.

59. Habermas, *Theory and Practice*, p. 40, quoted in McCarthy, *Ideals and Illusions*, p. 151.

60. Habermas, *The Philosophical Discourse of Modernity*, p. 116; emphasis in original.

61. For this argument with respect to Foucault, see ibid., pp. 276–81.

62. Ibid., p. 127; emphasis in original.

63. Habermas, "Reconstruction and Interpretation in the Social Sciences," p. 32.

64. An example of this might be the claim, based on Carol Gilligan's feminist ethics of care, that Kohlberg's work, which was based on research conducted solely on boys, offers a stereotypically masculine account of moral development. By relying on this account, Habermas relies on a potentially ideological conception of moral development, one that is grounded in and serves to reinforce the view that men (or at least those who are masculine) have a better developed capacity for rationality and sense of justice. If this is how we understand Gilligan's challenge to Kohlberg, then Habermas's response to this challenge, which basically says that Gilligan confuses ethical with moral issues and difficulties of application with those of justification, misses the point entirely. For Gilligan's critique of Kohlberg, see Gilligan, *In a Different Voice*. For Habermas's response, see Habermas, "Moral Consciousness and Communicative Action," pp. 175–82.

65. Habermas, *The Philosophical Discourse of Modernity*, p. 96.

66. Cooke, *Re-presenting the Good Society*, p. 2; emphasis in original.

67. Ibid., p. 3.

68. Ibid., p. 4.

69. Ibid.

70. See ibid., pp. 14–15.

71. Ibid., p. 15.

72. Ibid., p. 16.

73. Ibid., pp. 14, 15.

74. Ibid., p. 23; emphasis in original.

75. Ibid; emphasis in original.

76. Ibid., p. 34.

77. Of course, one might object to Cooke's criticisms of Rorty, first, on the grounds that his combination of frank ethnocentrism and cosmopolitan liberalism allows him to avoid the charge of the restriction in scope, and second, by pointing out that Rorty drops the idea of truth as a goal of inquiry in favor of a focus on social practices of justification, and that his account of such practices is compatible with viewing disputes across contexts as rational but without relying on a strong notion of context transcendence. If these responses are convincing, then

it might seem that Cooke overplays the differences between her version of contextualism and Rorty's. Although I think it is quite possible that a close examination of this issue would reveal that the position of contextualist Habermasians such as Cooke (and McCarthy, as we shall see below) is much closer to that of Rorty than they would care to admit, a full discussion of this issue will have to wait for another occasion. I am grateful to Colin Koopman for helpful discussion of these issues.

78. Cooke, *Re-presenting the Good Society*, p. 4.

79. Ibid., p. 44.

80. Ibid., p. 47.

81. Ibid.

82. Ibid., pp. 47–48.

83. See Habermas, *Postmetaphysical Thinking*.

84. Cooke, *Re-presenting the Good Society*, pp. 49–50.

85. Ibid., pp. 50–51.

86. Ibid., p. 5.

87. Ibid., p. 51.

88. Ibid.

89. Ibid., p. 52. Indeed, Habermas seems to acknowledge as much when he admits that argumentation as such is a more demanding form of communicative action that emerges only at the collective level with the advent of modernity and at the individual level with the achievement of a postconventional ego identity. For discussion of this point, see Cooke, *Language and Reason*, pp. 31–34.

90. Ibid.

91. Ibid., p. 55.

92. Ibid.

93. Ibid.

94. Ibid., p. 57. Habermas acknowledges this point in "A Genealogical Analysis of the Cognitive Content of Morality," p. 45.

95. Ibid., p. 58.

96. Ibid.

97. Moreover, there are two further problems with Habermas's account of modernity that Cooke does not discuss. First, as we saw in chapter 2, Habermas's critique of one of the main rivals to his account of modernity—that of Foucault—is based in a misunderstanding of Foucault's stance vis-à-vis modernity and the Enlightenment. With respect to Foucault at least it would thus be inaccurate to claim that Habermas "successfully exposes the confusions and contradictions" of this rival account. Second, even if one granted Habermas the substance of his critique, much of that critique rests on the truth or at least the plausibility of Habermas's formal pragmatics (see especially Habermas, *The Philosophical Discourse of Modernity*, pp. 276–86). Thus, if we have independent reasons to doubt the plausibility of that account—or at least of its claim to universality—then we have further reason to wonder about the success of Habermas's critique of Foucault.

98. Cooke, *Re-presenting the Good Society*, p. 105.

99. Ibid., p. 109.

100. For this criticism of Habermas, see Laclau, "Identity and Hegemony," pp. 81–82.

101. Cooke, *Re-presenting the Good Society*, p. 114.

102. Ibid., p. 115.

103. Ibid., p. 176.
104. Ibid., p. 129.
105. Ibid., p. 132.
106. Ibid., p. 147.
107. Ibid.
108. Ibid.
109. Ibid., p. 148.
110. Ibid., p. 149.
111. On this point, see ibid., p. 20.
112. McCarthy, *Ideals and Illusions*, p. 1.
113. Ibid., p. 3.
114. Ibid., p. 145.
115. Ibid., p. 150; emphasis added.
116. Ibid., pp. 150–51.
117. Ibid., pp. 181–82.
118. For a similar critique, see Benhabib, *Situating the Self.*
119. McCarthy, *Ideals and Illusions*, p. 182.
120. Ibid., p. 185.
121. Ibid., p. 186.
122. Ibid.
123. Ibid., p. 188. On the politics of need interpretation, see Fraser, *Unruly Practices*, chapters 7 and 8.
124. McCarthy, *Ideals and Illusions*, p. 194.
125. Ibid.; emphasis in original.
126. Ibid.
127. Ibid.
128. Ibid., p. 5.
129. Ibid., p. 6.
130. Hoy and McCarthy, *Critical Theory*, p. 14.
131. Ibid., p. 15.
132. Ibid., p. 21.
133. For an interesting critique of McCarthy that suggests that the insights of ethnomethodology push in a more radically contextualist direction than McCarthy realizes, see Rehg, "Adjusting the Pragmatic Turn."
134. Hoy and McCarthy, *Critical Theory*, p. 72.
135. Ibid.
136. Ibid., pp. 75–76.
137. Ibid., p. 77.
138. Ibid., p. 47.
139. Ibid.; emphasis in original.
140. Ibid., p. 40.
141. Ibid., pp. 74, 75. These formulations are similar to Cooke's use of the term "context-transcend*ing* validity," which also emphasizes the dynamic, temporal aspect of such claims. See Cooke, *Re-presenting the Good Society*, p. 20, and note 111 above.
142. Ibid., p. 81; emphasis in original.
143. Ibid., p. 8.
144. Ibid., p. 36.

145. Habermas, "From Kant's 'Ideas' of Pure Reason to the 'Idealizing' Presuppositions of Communicative Action," p. 12. For a similar line of argument, see Rorty, "The Ambiguity of 'Rationality,'" p. 50.

146. Foucault, "Space, Knowledge, Power," p. 358.

147. One might argue that, in Habermas's recent work (particularly in his writings on religion and his reflections on contemporary political events post-9/11), he himself has moved further in the direction of the kind of pragmatic, contextualist formulation of critical theory that I am advocating here. (For an overview of Habermas's views on religion, see Habermas, *Religion and Rationality*; for his reflections on contemporary politics, see Habermas, *The Postnational Constellation*.) As I see it, this remains an open question. However, even if this is the case, it is all to the good and would only serve to strengthen the overall argument of this book: that the critical-theoretical approaches of Foucault and Habermas are much closer than has previously been realized and that we can and should draw simultaneously on both thinkers in our efforts to understand the relationship between power and autonomy in the constitution of the self. I am grateful to Eduardo Mendieta for raising this point with me.

7. Engendering Critical Theory

1. Benhabib, "Sexual Difference and Collective Identities," p. 337.
2. Ibid., pp. 337, 338.
3. Benhabib et al., *Feminist Contentions*, p. 20.
4. Ibid., p. 36.
5. Ibid., p. 46.
6. Butler, *The Psychic Life of Power*, p. 3.
7. See Benhabib, *Critique, Norm, and Utopia*, pp. ix–xi.
8. See Taylor, *Sources of the Self*, and MacIntyre, *After Virtue*.
9. Benhabib, *Critique, Norm, and Utopia*, p. 242.
10. Ibid., p. 263.
11. Ibid.
12. See ibid., pp. 263–70.
13. Ibid., p. 267; emphasis in original.
14. Ibid., p. 269.
15. Ibid., p. 274.
16. Ibid., p. 276.
17. Ibid.
18. Ibid., p. 279.
19. Ibid., p. 298.
20. Ibid., p. 306.
21. See Benhabib, *Situating the Self*, pp. 29–33.
22. Benhabib, *Critique, Norm, and Utopia*, p. 306.
23. Benhabib, *Situating the Self*, p. 3.
24. Ibid., p. 4.
25. Ibid., p. 5.
26. Ibid., p. 6.
27. Ibid., p. 8.
28. Ibid., p. 30.

29. Ibid.; emphasis in original.

30. Ibid., pp. 61–62.

31. Ibid., p. 38.

32. Ibid.; emphasis in original.

33. Ibid., p. 74.

34. Benhabib, *Critique, Norm, and Utopia*, p. 252.

35. Ibid., p. 253.

36. Benhabib, *Situating the Self*, pp. 109–10.

37. Ibid., p. 110.

38. Ibid., p. 8.

39. Ibid.

40. Ibid., pp. 188–89.

41. Benhabib, "Sexual Difference and Collective Identities," p. 339.

42. Ibid., p. 340.

43. Ibid.

44. It is far from clear that Benhabib's Habermasian view really does a better job of explaining the possibility of creativity and spontaneity than does Butler's account. Critics of Habermas such as Dieter Henrich have argued that his account of subjectivity does not so much explain as presuppose this possibility. For a discussion of the Habermas-Henrich debate, see Dews, "Modernity, Self-Consciousness, and the Scope of Philosophy." Similarly, Benhabib's claim that we are born into webs of narrative does no more to explain how we come to be capable of constructing our own narratives than does saying that although we are compelled to perform our gender, we are capable of performing it differently. Both views presuppose a fundamental capacity for spontaneity and creativity on the part of the subject. It seems to me, however, that this isn't a particular fault of Benhabib's narrative conception of the self; most views of subjectivity run into this problem.

45. Benhabib, "Sexual Difference and Collective Identities," p. 341.

46. Benhabib, *Situating the Self*, p. 162.

47. Benhabib et al., *Feminist Contentions*, p. 21.

48. Benhabib, *The Reluctant Modernism of Hannah Arendt*, p. 112.

49. Benhabib, *The Claims of Culture*, p. 15.

50. Benhabib, "Sexual Difference and Collective Identities," p. 344.

51. Ibid.

52. Ibid., p. 346.

53. Ibid., pp. 346–47; emphasis in original.

54. Ibid., p. 345.

55. Ibid., p. 347; emphasis in original.

56. Ibid., p. 350.

57. Ibid., p. 348.

58. Ibid., p. 349.

59. Ibid.

60. Benhabib, *The Claims of Culture*, p. 16.

61. Benhabib, *Situating the Self*, pp. 161–62.

62. Benhabib, *The Claims of Culture*, p. 15.

63. Benhabib, *Situating the Self*, p. 198.

64. Benhabib, "Sexual Difference and Collective Identities," p. 343.

65. Ibid.

66. Benhabib et al., *Feminist Contentions*, p. 21.
67. Benhabib, "Sexual Difference and Collective Identities," p. 344.
68. Ibid., p. 348, n. 10, quoting Somers and Gibson, "Reclaiming the Epistemological 'Other,'" p. 73.
69. Ibid., p. 345.
70. Indeed, elsewhere Benhabib acknowledges that "the gender-sex system," defined as "the social-historical, symbolic constitution, and interpretation of the anatomical differences of the sexes," "is the grid through which the self develops an *embodied* identity, a certain mode of being in one's body and of living the body" (*Situating the Self*, p. 152; emphasis in the original).
71. See Benhabib, *Situating the Self*.
72. Benhabib et al., *Feminist Contentions*, pp. 110–11. To my knowledge, Benhabib does not actually discuss this empirical literature in detail.
73. See ibid.
74. Golombok and Fivush, *Gender Development*, p. 27.
75. Ibid., pp. 22–23.
76. See ibid., p. 25.
77. Ibid., p. 26. See Stern and Karraker, "Sex Stereotyping of Infants."
78. Ibid., p. 25.
79. That Benhabib considers the ability to construct a narrative to be a necessary condition for being a self is implied by her suggestion that it is not possible to be a self at all without the ability to generate coherent and meaningful narratives. See Benhabib, "Sexual Difference and Collective Identities," p. 347.
80. On this point, see Fivush and Schwarzmueller, "Children Remember Childhood," and Nelson, "The Psychological and Social Origins of Autobiographical Memory."
81. Fivush and Schwarzmueller, "Children Remember Childhood," p. 457.
82. Fivush, "The Stories We Tell," p. 484.
83. Fivush and Schwarzmueller, "Children Remember Childhood," p. 457.
84. Fivush, "The Stories We Tell," p. 486.
85. Buckner and Fivush, "Gender and Self in Children's Autobiographical Narratives," pp. 421–22. Buckner and Fivush point out that these differences cannot be explained by gender difference in language skills.
86. Benhabib et al., *Feminist Contentions*, p. 109.
87. Ibid., pp. 109–10; emphasis in original.
88. Benhabib, *Situating the Self*, pp. 217–18.
89. Benhabib et al., *Feminist Contentions*, p. 110.
90. Benhabib, *Critique, Norm, and Utopia*, p. 298.

Concluding Reflections

1. Foucault, "What Is Enlightenment?" p. 317.
2. An acknowledgment of this problem may well be why Butler herself has started to develop a broader conception of the social—and, as a result, a less negative conception of the ethical—in her recent book, *Giving an Account of Oneself*.
3. Foucault, "Politics and Ethics," p. 379.
4. Butler, "Longing for Recognition," p. 133.
5. Lynch, "Is Power All There Is?" p. 65.
6. Foucault, *An Introduction*, p. 93, quoted in Lynch, "Is Power All There Is?" p. 67.

7. Foucault, "Afterword: The Subject and Power," pp. 222–23.
8. Ibid., p. 218.
9. Brumberg, *The Body Project*, p. xviii.
10. Ibid., p. 195.
11. Ibid., p. 196.
12. Heath, "Ideology, Irrationality, and Collectively Self-defeating Behavior."
13. Mansbridge, "The Role of Discourse in the Feminist Movement," p. 1.
14. Ibid.
15. Lara, *Moral Textures*, p. 5.
16. Ibid., p. 77.
17. Foucault, "What Is Enlightenment?" p. 316.

Bibliography

Alcoff, Linda Martín. "Feminist Politics and Foucault: The Limits to a Collaboration." In *Crises in Continental Philosophy*, ed. Arlene Dallery and Charles Scott. Albany: SUNY Press, 1990.

——. "Philosophy Matters: A Review of Recent Work in Feminist Philosophy." *Signs: Journal of Women in Culture and Society* 25 (2000): 841–82.

Allen, Amy. "The Anti-subjective Hypothesis: Michel Foucault and the Death of the Subject." *Philosophical Forum* 31:2 (Summer 2000): 113–30.

——. "Foucault, Feminism, and the Self: The Politics of Personal Transformation." In *Feminism and the Final Foucault*, ed. Dianna Taylor and Karen Vintges. Champaign: University of Illinois Press, 2004.

——. *The Power of Feminist Theory: Domination, Resistance, Solidarity*. Boulder, CO: Westview Press, 1999.

——. "Power, Subjectivity, and Agency: Between Arendt and Foucault." *International Journal of Philosophical Studies* 10:2 (May 2002): 131–49.

——. "Reconstruction or Deconstruction? A Reply to Johanna Meehan." *Philosophy and Social Criticism* 26:3 (May 2000): 53–60.

Anderson, Amanda. *The Way We Argue Now: A Study in the Cultures of Theory*. Princeton, NJ: Princeton University Press, 2006.

Arendt, Hannah. *The Human Condition*. Chicago: University of Chicago Press, 1958.

——. "What is Freedom?" In *Between Past and Future: Eight Exercises in Political Thought*. New York: Penguin Books, 1993.

Bartky, Sandra. *Femininity and Domination: Studies in the Phenomenology of Oppression*. New York: Routledge, 1990.

——. *"Sympathy and Solidarity" and Other Essays*. Lanham, MD: Rowman and Little-field, 2002.

Benhabib, Seyla. *The Claims of Culture: Equality and Diversity in the Global Era*. Princeton, NJ: Princeton University Press, 2002.

——. *Critique, Norm, and Utopia: A Study of the Foundations of Critical Theory*. New York: Columbia University Press, 1986.

——. *The Reluctant Modernism of Hannah Arendt*. London: Sage, 1996.

——. "Sexual Difference and Collective Identities: The New Global Constellation." *Signs: Journal of Women in Culture and Society* 24:2 (1999): 335–61.

——. *Situating the Self: Gender, Community, and Postmodernism in Contemporary Ethics*. New York: Routledge, 1992.

Benhabib, Seyla, Judith Butler, Drucilla Cornell, and Nancy Fraser. *Feminist Contentions: A Philosophical Exchange*. New York: Routledge, 1995.

Benjamin, Jessica. *The Bonds of Love: Psychoanalysis, Feminism, and the Problem of Domination*. New York: Pantheon, 1988.

——. *Like Subjects, Love Objects: Essays on Recognition and Sexual Difference*. New Haven, CT: Yale University Press, 1995.

——. *The Shadow of the Other: Intersubjectivity and Gender in Psychoanalysis*. New York: Routledge, 1998.

——. "The Shadow of the Other Subject: Intersubjectivity and Feminist Theory." In Benjamin, *The Shadow of the Other*.

Bernauer, James. "Michel Foucault's Ecstatic Thinking." In *The Final Foucault*, ed. James Bernauer and David Rasmussen. Cambridge, MA: MIT Press, 1988.

Biebricher, Thomas. "Habermas, Foucault, and Nietzsche: A Double Misunderstanding." *Foucault Studies* 3 (November 2005): 1–26.

Bohman, James. "Participating in Enlightenment: Habermas's Cognitivist Interpretation of Democracy." In *Knowledge and Politics: Case Studies in the Relationship Between Epistemology and Political Philosophy*, ed. Marcelo Dascal and Ora Gruengard. Boulder, CO: Westview Press, 1989.

Bordo, Susan. *Unbearable Weight: Feminism, Western Culture, and the Body*. Tenth anniversary ed. Berkeley and Los Angeles: University of California Press, 2003.

Brown, Wendy. *States of Injury: Power and Freedom in Late Modernity*. Princeton, NJ: Princeton University Press, 1995.

Brumberg, Joan Jacobs. *The Body Project: An Intimate History of American Girls*. New York: Vintage, 1997.

Buckner, Janine and Robyn Fivush. "Gender and Self in Children's Autobiographical Narratives." *Applied Cognitive Psychology* 12 (1998): 407–22.

Butler, Judith. *Antigone's Claim: Kinship Between Life and Death*. New York: Columbia University Press, 2000.

——. "Bodies and Power Revisited." In *Feminism and the Final Foucault*, ed. Dianna Taylor and Karen Vintges. Champaign: University of Illinois Press, 2004.

——. *Bodies That Matter: On the Discursive Limits of "Sex."* New York: Routledge, 1993.

——. "Competing Universalities." In *Contingency, Hegemony, Universality: Contemporary Dialogues on the Left*, ed. Judith Butler, Ernesto Laclau, and Slavoj Zizek. London: Verso, 2000.

——. *Gender Trouble: Feminism and the Subversion of Identity*. New York: Routledge, 1990.

——. *Giving an Account of Oneself*. New York: Fordham University Press, 2005.

——. "Longing for Recognition." In Butler, *Undoing Gender*.

——. *The Psychic Life of Power: Theories in Subjection*. Stanford, CA: Stanford University Press, 1997.

——. *Subjects of Desire: Hegelian Reflections in Twentieth Century France*. New York: Columbia University Press, 1987.

——. *Undoing Gender*. New York: Routledge, 2004.

——. "Violence, Mourning, Politics." In *Precarious Life: The Powers of Mourning and Violence*. London: Verso, 2004.

Cooke, Maeve. "Habermas, Autonomy, and the Identity of the Self." *Philosophy and Social Criticism* 18:3–4 (1992): 268–91.

——. "Habermas, Feminism, and the Question of Autonomy." In *Habermas: A Critical Reader*, ed. Peter Dews. Oxford: Blackwell, 1999.

——. *Language and Reason: A Study of Habermas's Pragmatics*. Cambridge, MA: MIT Press, 1994.

——. *Re-presenting the Good Society: Philosophical Issues in Critical Social Theory*. Cambridge, MA: MIT Press, 2006.

Dews, Peter. "Communicative Paradigms and the Question of Subjectivity: Habermas, Mead, and Lacan." In *Habermas: A Critical Reader*, ed. Peter Dews. Oxford: Blackwell, 1999.

——. "Modernity, Self-Consciousness, and the Scope of Philosophy: Jürgen Habermas and Dieter Henrich in Debate." In *The Limits of Disenchantment: Essays on Contemporary European Philosophy*. New York: Verso, 1995.

——. "The Return of Subjectivity in the Late Foucault." *Radical Philosophy* 51 (Spring 1989): 37–41.

Dreyfus, Hubert and Paul Rabinow. "What is Maturity? Habermas and Foucault on 'What is Enlightenment?'" In *Foucault: A Critical Reader*, ed. David Hoy. London: Blackwell, 1986.

Fausto-Sterling, Anne. *Myths of Gender: Biological Theories About Women and Men*. 2d ed. New York: Basic Books, 1992.

Fivush, Robyn. "The Stories We Tell: How Language Shapes Autobiography." *Applied Cognitive Psychology* 12 (1998): 483–87.

Fivush, Robyn and April Schwarzmueller. "Children Remember Childhood: Implications for Childhood Amnesia." *Applied Cognitive Psychology* 12 (1998): 455–73.

Flynn, Thomas. *A Poststructuralist Mapping of History*. Vol. 2 of *Sartre, Foucault, and Historical Reason*. Chicago: University of Chicago Press, 2005.

Foucault, Michel. *Abnormal: Lectures at the Collège de France, 1974–1975*. Ed. Valerio Marchetti and Antonella Salomoni. Trans. Graham Burchell. New York: Picador, 2003.

——. "About the Beginnings of the Hermeneutics of the Self: Two Lectures at Dartmouth." *Political Theory* 21:2 (1993): 198–227.

——. "Afterword: The Subject and Power." In *Michel Foucault: Beyond Structuralism and Hermeneutics*, 2d ed., ed. Hubert Dreyfus and Paul Rabinow. Chicago: University of Chicago Press, 1983.

——. *The Archaeology of Knowledge and the Discourse on Language*. Trans. A. M. Sheridan-Smith. New York: Pantheon, 1972.

——. "The Art of Telling the Truth." In Kelly, *Critique and Power*.

——. *Discipline and Punish: The Birth of the Prison*. Trans. Alan Sheridan. New York: Pantheon, 1978.

——. *Dits et écrits*. 6 vols. Paris: Vrin, 1994.

——. "The Ethics of Concern for the Self as a Practice of Freedom." In *Ethics, Subjectivity, and Truth*. Vol. 1 of *The Essential Works of Michel Foucault*, ed. Paul Rabinow. New York: The New Press, 1997.

——. "Governmentality." In *Power*. Vol. 3 of *The Essential Works of Michel Foucault*, ed. James Faubion. New York: The New Press, 2000.

——. *Histoire de la folie à l'âge classique*. Paris: Éditions Gallimard, 1972.

——. "Interview with Michel Foucault." In *Power*. Vol. 3 of *The Essential Works of Michel Foucault*, ed. James Faubion. New York: The New Press, 2000.

——. *An Introduction*. Vol. 1 of *The History of Sexuality*. Trans. Robert Hurley. New York: Vintage, 1976.

——. *Introduction à l'anthropologie de Kant, thèse complémentaire*. Photocopy of typescript available in Centre Michel Foucault, IMEC.

——. *Madness and Civilization: A History of Insanity in the Age of Reason*. Trans. Richard Howard. New York: Vintage, 1965.

——. "'Omnes et Singulatim': Toward a Critique of Political Reason." In *Power*. Vol. 3 of *The Essential Works of Michel Foucault*, ed. James Faubion. New York: The New Press, 2000.

——. "On the Genealogy of Ethics: An Overview of Work in Progress." In *Ethics, Subjectivity, and Truth*. Vol. 1 of *The Essential Works of Michel Foucault*, ed. Paul Rabinow. New York: The New Press, 1997.

——. *The Order of Things: An Archaeology of the Human Sciences*. Trans. A. M. Sheridan-Smith. New York: Pantheon, 1970.

——. "Polemics, Politics, and Problematizations: An Interview." In *The Foucault Reader*, ed. Paul Rabinow. New York: Pantheon, 1984.

——. "Politics and Ethics: An Interview." In *The Foucault Reader*, ed. Paul Rabinow. New York: Pantheon, 1984.

——. "A Preface to Transgression." In *Language, Counter-Memory, Practice: Selected Essays and Interviews by Michel Foucault*, ed. D. F. Bouchard. Ithaca, NY: Cornell University Press, 1977.

——. "Que'est-ce que la critique?/Critique et Aufklärung." *Bulletin de la société française de philosophie* 84:2 (1990): 35–63.

——. "The Return of Morality." In *Michel Foucault: Politics, Philosophy, Culture*, ed. Lawrence Kritzman. New York: Routledge, 1988.

——. *Security, Territory, Population: Lectures at the Collège de France, 1977–78*. Ed. Arnold Davidson. Trans. Graham Burchell. New York: Palgrave Macmillan, 2007.

——. "Sex, Power, and the Politics of Identity." In *Ethics, Subjectivity, and Truth*. Vol. 1 of *The Essential Works of Michel Foucault*, ed. Paul Rabinow. New York: The New Press, 1997.

——. *Society Must Be Defended: Lectures at the Collège de France, 1975–1976*. Ed. Mauro Bertani and Alessandro Fontana. Trans. David Macey. New York: Picador, 2003.

——. "Space, Knowledge, Power." In *Power*. Vol. 3 of *The Essential Works of Michel Foucault*, ed. James Faubion. New York: The New Press, 2000.

——. "Technologies of the Self." In *Technologies of the Self: A Seminar with Michel Foucault*, ed. Luther H. Martin, Huck Gutman, and Patrick H. Hutton. Amherst: University of Massachusetts Press, 1988.

——. "Truth and Power." In *Power/Knowledge: Selected Interviews and Other Writings, 1972–1977*, ed. Colin Gordon. New York: Pantheon, 1980.

——. "Two Lectures." In *Power/Knowledge: Selected Interviews and Other Writings, 1972–1977,* ed. Colin Gordon. New York: Pantheon, 1980.

——. *The Use of Pleasure.* Vol. 2 of *The History of Sexuality.* Trans. Robert Hurley. New York: Vintage, 1985.

——. "What Is Critique?" In *What Is Enlightenment? Eighteenth-Century Answers and Twentieth-Century Questions,* ed. James Schmidt. Berkeley: University of California Press, 1996.

——. "What Is Enlightenment?" In *Ethics, Subjectivity, and Truth.* Vol. 1 of *The Essential Works of Michel Foucault,* ed. Paul Rabinow. New York: The New Press, 1997.

Fraser, Nancy. "Foucault on Modern Power: Empirical Insights and Normative Confusions." In Fraser, *Unruly Practices.*

——. *Unruly Practices: Power, Discourse and Gender in Contemporary Social Theory.* Minneapolis: University of Minnesota Press, 1989.

——. "What's Critical About Critical Theory? The Case of Habermas and Gender." In Fraser, *Unruly Practices.*

Freud, Sigmund. "The Ego and the Id." In *The Standard Edition of the Complete Psychological Works of Sigmund Freud,* ed. and trans. James Strachey. London: Hogarth Press, 1961.

Garfinkel, Harold. "Studies of the Routine Grounds of Everyday Activities." *Social Problems* 11:3 (1964): 225–50.

Gilligan, Carol. *In a Different Voice.* Cambridge, MA: Harvard University Press, 1982.

Golombok, Susan and Robyn Fivush. *Gender Development.* Cambridge: Cambridge University Press, 1994.

Grimshaw, Jean. "Practices of Freedom." In *Up Against Foucault: Explorations of Some Tensions Between Foucault and Feminism,* ed. Caroline Ramazanoglu. New York: Routledge, 1993.

Habermas, Jürgen. *Between Facts and Norms: Contributions to a Discourse Theory of Law and Democracy.* Trans. William Rehg. Cambridge, MA: MIT Press, 1996.

——. "Discourse Ethics: Notes on a Program of Philosophical Justification." In *Moral Consciousness and Communicative Action,* trans. Christian Lenhardt and Shierry Weber Nicholsen. Cambridge, MA: MIT Press, 1990.

——. "From Kant's 'Ideas' of Pure Reason to the 'Idealizing' Presuppositions of Communicative Action: Reflections on the Detranscendentalized 'Use of Reason.'" In *Pluralism and the Pragmatic Turn: The Transformation of Critical Theory,* ed. William Rehg and James Bohman. Cambridge, MA: MIT Press, 2001.

——. *The Future of Human Nature.* Cambridge: Polity Press, 2003.

——. "A Genealogical Analysis of the Cognitive Content of Morality." In *The Inclusion of the Other: Studies in Political Theory,* trans. Ciaran Cronin and Pablo de Greiff. Cambridge, MA: MIT Press, 1998.

——. "Individuation Through Socialization: On George Herbert Mead's Theory of Subjectivity." In Habermas, *Postmetaphysical Thinking.*

——. *Justification and Application: Remarks on Discourse Ethics.* Trans. Ciaran Cronin. Cambridge, MA: MIT Press, 1990.

——. *Knowledge and Human Interests.* Trans. Jeremy Shapiro. Boston: Beacon Press, 1971.

——. "Knowledge and Human Interests: A General Perspective." In Habermas, *Knowledge and Human Interests.*

——. "Lawrence Kohlberg and Neo-Aristotelianism." In Habermas, *Justification and Application.*

——. *Lifeworld and System: A Critique of Functionalist Reason*. Vol. 2 of *The Theory of Communicative Action*, trans. Thomas McCarthy. Boston: Beacon Press, 1987.

——. *Moral Consciousness and Communicative Action*. Trans. Christian Lenhardt and Shierry Weber Nicholsen. Cambridge, MA: MIT Press, 1990.

——. "Moral Consciousness and Communicative Action." In Habermas, *Moral Consciousness and Communicative Action*.

——. "Moral Development and Ego Identity." In *Communication and the Evolution of Society*, trans. Thomas McCarthy. Boston: Beacon Press, 1979.

——. "Morality and Ethical Life: Does Hegel's Critique of Kant Apply to Discourse Ethics?" In Habermas, *Moral Consciousness and Communicative Action*.

——. *The Philosophical Discourse of Modernity: Twelve Lectures*. Trans. Frederick G. Lawrence. Cambridge, MA: MIT Press, 1987.

——. *Postmetaphysical Thinking: Philosophical Essays*. Trans. William Mark Hohengarten. Cambridge, MA: MIT Press, 1992.

——. *The Postnational Constellation: Political Essays*. Ed. and Trans. Max Pensky. Cambridge, MA: MIT Press, 2001.

——. "A Postscript to *Knowledge and Human Interests*." *Philosophy of the Social Sciences* 3 (1973): 157–89.

——. *Reason and the Rationalization of Society*. Vol. 1 of *The Theory of Communicative Action*, trans. Thomas McCarthy. Boston: Beacon Press, 1984.

——. "Reconstruction and Interpretation in the Social Sciences." In Habermas, *Moral Consciousness and Communicative Action*.

——. "Reflections on Communicative Pathology. In *On the Pragmatics of Social Interaction*, trans. Barbara Fultner. Cambridge, MA: MIT Press, 2001.

——. *Religion and Rationality: Essays on Reason, God, and Modernity*. Ed. Eduardo Mendieta. Cambridge, MA: MIT Press, 2002.

——. "Remarks on Discourse Ethics." In Habermas, *Justification and Application*.

——. "A Reply." In *Communicative Action: Essays on Habermas's* The Theory of Communicative Action, ed. Axel Honneth and Hans Joas. Cambridge, MA: MIT Press, 1991.

——. "Some Further Clarifications on the Concept of Communicative Rationality." In *On the Pragmatics of Communication*, ed. Maeve Cooke. Cambridge, MA: MIT Press, 1998.

——. "Taking Aim at the Heart of the Present." In Kelly, *Critique and Power*.

——. *Theory and Practice*. Trans. John Viertel. Boston: Beacon Press, 1973.

——. "What is Universal Pragmatics?" In *Communication and the Evolution of Society*, trans. Thomas McCarthy. Boston: Beacon Press, 1979.

Hacking, Ian. "Self-improvement." In *Foucault: A Critical Reader*, ed. David Hoy. London: Blackwell, 1986.

Han, Béatrice. *Foucault's Critical Project: Between the Transcendental and the Historical*, trans. Edward Pile. Stanford, CA: Stanford University Press, 2002.

Hartsock, Nancy. "Foucault on Power: A Theory for Women?" In *Feminism/Postmodernism*, ed. Linda Nicholson. New York: Routledge, 1990.

Heath, Joseph. "Ideology, Irrationality, and Collectively Self-defeating Behavior." *Constellations* 7:3 (2000): 363–71.

Hegel, G. W. F. *The Phenomenology of Spirit*. Trans. A. V. Miller. Oxford: Oxford University Press, 1977.

Honneth, Axel. *The Critique of Power: Reflective Stages in a Critical Social Theory*. Trans. Kenneth Baynes. Cambridge: MIT Press, 1991.

Hoy, David. "Foucault: Modern or Postmodern?" In *After Foucault: Humanistic Knowledge, Postmodern Challenges,* ed. Jonathan Arac. New Brunswick, NJ: Rutgers University Press, 1988.

——. "Power, Repression, Progress: Foucault, Lukes, and the Frankfurt School." In *Foucault: A Critical Reader,* ed. David Hoy. London: Blackwell, 1986.

Hoy, David and Thomas McCarthy. *Critical Theory.* Cambridge: Blackwell, 1994.

Kant, Immanuel. *Anthropology from a Pragmatic Point of View.* Trans. M. J. Gregor. The Hague: Martinus Nijhoff, 1974.

——. *Grounding for the Metaphysics of Morals.* Trans. James W. Ellington. Indianapolis: Hackett, 1981.

——. *Introduction to Logic.* Trans. T. Kingsmill Abbott. Westport, CT: Greenwood Press, 1963.

——. "What Is Enlightenment?" In *Kant: Selections,* ed. Lewis White Beck. Englewood Cliffs, NJ: Prentice-Hall, 1988.

Kelly, Michael, ed. *Critique and Power: Recasting the Foucault/Habermas Debate.* Cambridge, MA: MIT Press, 1994.

Laclau, Ernesto. "Identity and Hegemony." In *Contingency, Hegemony, Universality: Contemporary Dialogues on the Left,* ed. Judith Butler, Ernesto Laclau, and Slavoj Zizek. London: Verso, 2000.

Lara, María Pía. *Moral Textures: Feminist Narratives in the Public Sphere.* Cambridge: Polity Press, 1998.

Lynch, Richard. "Is Power All There Is? Michel Foucault and the 'Omnipresence' of Power Relations." *Philosophy Today* 42:1 (Spring 1998): 65–70.

Mansbridge, Jane. "The Role of Discourse in the Feminist Movement." Paper delivered at the annual meeting of the American Political Science Association, Washington, DC, September 2–5, 1993.

McCarthy, Thomas. *The Critical Theory of Jürgen Habermas.* Cambridge, MA: MIT Press, 1978.

——. *Ideals and Illusions: On Reconstruction and Deconstruction in Contemporary Critical Theory.* Cambridge, MA: MIT Press, 1991.

——. "Die politische Philosophie und das Problem der Rasse." In *Die Öffentlichkeit der Vernunft und die Vernunft der Öffentlichkeit: Festschrift für Jürgen Habermas,* ed. Lutz Wingert and Klaus Günther. Frankfurt: Suhrkamp Verlag, 2001.

McIntyre, Alasdair. *After Virtue.* 2d ed. Notre Dame, IN: University of Notre Dame Press, 1984.

McLaren, Margaret. *Feminism, Foucault, and Embodied Subjectivity.* Albany: SUNY Press, 2002.

McNay, Lois. *Foucault and Feminism: Power, Gender, and the Self.* Cambridge: Polity Press, 1992.

——. "Having It Both Ways: The Incompatibility of Narrative Identity and Communicative Ethics in Feminist Thought." *Theory, Culture, and Society* 20:6 (2003): 1–20.

McWhorter, Ladelle. *Bodies and Pleasures: Foucault and the Politics of Sexual Normalization.* Bloomington, IN: Indiana University Press, 1999.

Mead, George Herbert. *Mind, Self, and Society.* Chicago: University of Chicago Press. 1962.

Meehan, Johanna. "Autonomy, Recognition, and Respect: Habermas, Benjamin, and Honneth." In *Feminists Read Habermas: Gendering the Subject of Discourse.* New York: Routledge, 1995.

——. "Feminism and Habermas's Discourse Ethics." *Philosophy and Social Criticism* 26:3 (May 2000): 39–52.

——. "Habermas and the Summum Bonum." Unpublished manuscript (on file with the author).

——. "Into the Sunlight: A Pragmatic Account of the Self." In *Pluralism and the Pragmatic Turn: The Transformation of Critical Theory*, ed. William Rehg and James Bohman. Cambridge, MA: MIT Press, 2001.

Nelson, Katherine. "The Psychological and Social Origins of Autobiographical Memory." *Psychological Science* 4:1 (1993): 7–14.

Nietzsche, Friedrich. *On the Genealogy of Morals.* Trans. Walter Kaufmann and R.J. Hollingdale. New York: Vintage, 1989.

Norris, Christopher. "What Is Enlightenment? Kant According to Foucault." In *The Cambridge Companion to Foucault*, ed. Gary Gutting. Cambridge: Cambridge University Press, 1994.

Pitkin, Hanna Fenichel. *The Attack of the Blob: Hannah Arendt's Concept of the Social.* Chicago: University of Chicago Press, 1998.

Rajchman, John. *Truth and Eros: Foucault, Lacan, and the Question of Ethics.* New York: Routledge, 1991.

Rehg, William. "Adjusting the Pragmatic Turn: Ethnomethodology and Critical Argumentation Theory." In *Pluralism and the Pragmatic Turn: The Transformation of Critical Theory*, ed. William Rehg and James Bohman. Cambridge, MA: MIT Press, 2001.

——. *Insight and Solidarity: The Discourse Ethics of Jürgen Habermas.* Berkeley: University of California Press, 1994.

Rorty, Richard. "The Ambiguity of 'Rationality.'" In *Pluralism and the Pragmatic Turn: The Transformation of Critical Theory*, ed. William Rehg and James Bohman. Cambridge, MA: MIT Press, 2001.

Schmidt, James and Thomas Wartenberg. "Foucault's Enlightenment: Critique, Revolution, and the Fashioning of the Self." In Kelly, *Critique and Power.*

Somers, Margaret R. and Gloria D. Gibson. "Reclaiming the Epistemological 'Other': Narrative and the Social Construction of Identity." In *Social Theory and the Politics of Identity*, ed. Craig Calhoun. Cambridge, MA: Blackwell, 1994.

Stern, M. and K.H. Karraker. "Sex Stereotyping of Infants: A Review of Gender Labeling Studies." *Sex Roles* 20 (1989): 501–22.

Taylor, Charles. *Sources of the Self: The Making of Modern Identity.* Cambridge, MA: Harvard University Press, 1989.

Veyne, Paul. "The Final Foucault and His Ethics." In *Foucault and His Interlocutors*, ed. Arnold Davidson. Chicago: University of Chicago Press, 1997.

Weir, Allison. *Sacrificial Logics: Feminist Theory and the Critique of Identity.* New York: Routledge, 1996.

——. "Toward a Model of Self-identity: Habermas and Kristeva." In *Feminists Read Habermas: Gendering the Subject of Discourse*, ed. Johanna Meehan. New York: Routledge, 1995.

Wellmer, Albrecht. *The Persistence of Modernity: Essays on Aesthetics, Ethics, and Postmodernism.* Cambridge, MA: MIT Press, 1991.

White, Stephen K. *Sustaining Affirmation: The Strengths of Weak Ontology in Political Theory.* Princeton, NJ: Princeton University Press, 2000.

Whitebook, Joel. "Freud, Foucault, and 'the Dialogue with Unreason.'" *Philosophy and Social Criticism* 25:6 (1999): 29–66.

——. *Perversion and Utopia: A Study in Psychoanalysis and Critical Theory*. Cambridge, MA: MIT Press, 1995.

Zerilli, Linda. "Doing Without Knowing: Feminism's Politics of the Ordinary." *Political Theory* 26 (1998): 435–58.

——. *Feminism and the Abyss of Freedom*. Chicago: University of Chicago Press, 2005.